Sins of the Abused

Marco Bernardino, Sr.
&
Helen Wisocki

ISBN: 978-0-9846392-7-4

Library of Congress Control Number: 2011931234

Cover design by All Things That Matter Press

Published in 2011 by All Things That Matter Press

This book is dedicated to all who have lived through any type of abuse and addiction. May your cries be heard and comforted.

And for my beloved children . . . you should have never had to suffer for my past. May you find forgiveness in my recovery. I wish you happiness and good health in life.

Acknowledgments

I'd like to acknowledge the compassionate therapists and groups that help those of us in pain from the horrors of clergy abuse and addictions. Special thanks to Steve, who opened my mind to understanding my true self, and bringing order and enlightenment to my chaotic life.

CHAPTER ONE
~GROOMING THE BEAST~

The pungent aroma of simmering tomato gravy wafted through the house on Sunday morning. Breathing in the delicious bouquet, I paused before jumping out of bed. I raced around my bedroom, putting on my best trousers and a clean white shirt, readying myself for church services.

"Can't be late for Mass today, Mom," I said, bursting into the kitchen.

"Father McCool has been wonderful to you. Sit down for breakfast," Mom said, scooping gravy onto a piece of bread and adding a fresh-made meatball.

Joining my three-year-old brother, who was already shoveling cereal into his mouth, I folded the bread around the meatball and took a bite. "Mmmm. This is my favorite breakfast ever," I mumbled with a mouthful of food. "Father said he's counting on me today."

"Father is such a kind man," Mom said. "He treats you well and is friendly to the rest of us. It's an honor to have him coming for dinner tonight. I hope you were polite with him last night when he took you to the basketball game."

"Yes, Mom. I was polite. And Father said this summer he'd take me to see the Yankees play. I *can't wait*. It's sure great when he comes to watch me play baseball. Wish you and Dad could come see me play," I said, getting up from the table and putting my dish in the sink. "Hey, Mom. Listen to this song Father and I sang with the fans at the game last night. One, two, three, four, five, Sixers. Ten, nine, eight, Seventy Sixers! Isn't that neat, Mom? Did you hear me?"

"What's that, honey?" she said, scooping cereal and milk into my one-year-old sister's mouth.

"It was a cheer, Mom. For the Sixers."

"Mmmhmm."

As I paced across the kitchen floor, Mom looked up at the clock. It was eight thirty and Mass was at nine. She rushed to the stove and added the meatballs from the black cast iron frying pan to the pot of gravy, turning the burner to low.

"Okay, everyone in the car," Mom said, picking up my sister and grabbing my brother by the hand.

Once we were all piled inside her new 1971 black Chevy Impala, she sped down the street for the one-mile trip to St. Michael's Catholic Church. I bolted from the car with a wave. "Bye, Mom. I'll see ya after church."

She drove off while I ran around the side door of the recently modernized church in my new home town of Gibbstown, New Jersey. I threw open the heavy wooden door and rushed inside where Father McCool was preparing for the service.

"I'm here, Father," I said, catching my breath.

"Slap me five," Father McCool greeted me, holding up his hand. I smacked his palm, and he patted my head. "Let's get ready for Mass," he said.

I started setting up, gathering all the accessories we needed. "Have some communion wafers," Father urged, handing me a handful of the unconsecrated hosts with a small glass of wine. "Only a sip. We don't want you too drunk for the liturgy," he said with a laugh.

I stuffed the wafers in my mouth and guzzled down the wine, rolling my eyes and knocking into things, pretending to be drunk. Father McCool chuckled as he started to get dressed. He was a young priest and not like the strict fear-of-God-type priests I was used to before I was enrolled in St. Michael's fourth-grade class.

Once Mass was underway, Father placed his hands on my head and prayed, "Dear Lord, bless Marco today as we celebrate this sacrament together." During the ceremony of washing his hands, Father grinned and splashed a little holy water on me.

After the service was over and everything cleaned up, I walked outside to wait for my ride. A half hour later, Father walked outside and saw me sitting on the curb. "Do you want to come to the rectory and call your mom?"

"Yes, Father. She must've forgotten about me."

We walked across the street to the rectory, and Father handed me the phone in the vestibule. I called home. "Mom, did you forget to pick me up? Mass is over now."

"Oh, my! What time is it? I can't believe it's this late. I'll be right there," Mom said.

"Can I have the phone, Marco?" Father said, reaching out. After I handed it to him, he said into the receiver, "Would you like me to bring him home after we have lunch? It's no problem."

Father smiled, nodding, as he listened, then said, "You're very welcome. I look forward to seeing you tonight for dinner." After another pause he said, before hanging up, and with a wink in my direction, "I'm honored for the invitation."

He led the way to the rectory kitchen, and I followed, taking in the opulent antique furniture and handsomely decorated walls.

"Wow!" I exclaimed when he opened the door to the huge pantry. "Your cupboards are packed with food."

"How about a tuna fish sandwich?" Father said, taking down a can of tuna.

"Sure. That'd be great."

Father made the sandwiches and served them with potato chips and pickles. Afterwards, he treated me to a Tastycake apple pie.

"Would you like to see some of my home movies, Marco," Father asked when we were through eating.

"I probably should go home."

"It'll only take a moment. Besides, I spoke with your mother, and she said it would be okay."

"Alright. Then I guess I can stay."

We started to walk upstairs. As we got to the second floor, Father McCool's Pastor came from his bedroom. "Hello, Father," he said with a smile.

"Hello, Pastor. Have you met Marco? He's one of our finest altar boys. I'm going to show him some of my famous home movies."

"Hello, Marco. It's nice to meet you. Have fun and keep up the good work. May God bless you," Pastor said.

"It's nice to meet you, too," I said, offering my hand.

The Pastor held my hand gently. He looked at me and said, "Good lad." He continued toward the staircase, and we continued on to Father McCool's bedroom. He closed the door behind us.

"I don't want to bother the other priest who's taking a nap next door," he said as he went to the closet and pulled out a movie projector. "Sit right there on the bed. I'll get it set up."

Once Father had the projector ready, he sat next to me while we watched his home movies of boys from other parishes who were around my age playing and joking around. In one of the scenes, a kid pretended to say some magic words, and all of a sudden he magically disappeared and then reappeared a few seconds later.

"Wow! How'd he do that?" I said with amazement.

"Let me show you," Father said with a laugh. "Now stand over by the bookcase, Marco." He turned on his movie camera and aimed it at me. "Stand perfectly still and remember the exact position you're in. This will be fun."

He filmed me for about ten seconds before I looked away, feeling self conscious. Father turned off the camera. "Now step out of the picture," he said. I stepped off to the side of the shot. He took footage of the empty area for another ten seconds or so. "Now go back to the spot you were in," Father said, pointing back to the original place. "Stand in the exact position."

I did as I was told, stepping back into the picture. "Now smile and laugh at me," Father suggested. Again, I did what he asked, grinning at him. "You have magically disappeared and reappeared."

"That's neat!" When can I see it?" I said, as he continued to focus the camera on me.

"When I get the film developed you can come over and see it. Do something goofy for the camera," Father said.

"Um. Can we stop filming," I asked, looking at the floor.

"Hey, Marco. Do you want to see the pictures I have of Yankee Stadium?"

"Sure. I love baseball. I can't wait to go with you to see the Yankees play."

"I'm really looking forward to that, too," Father said, patting the bed.

I joined him on the bed, and Father showed me photos of New York City and Yankee Stadium. It was a couple of hours before Father drove me home.

"I'll see you later tonight," he said as he drove off.

"Great! See you then!"

I rushed into the house. Mom was vacuuming. "Mom! I had the best time. Father showed me home movies in his bedroom and pictures of Yankee Stadium. It was neat! Did you hear me, Mom? Father showed me how to make a person disappear. Mom?"

"Mmmhmm. That's nice," she said, not looking up from the vacuum cleaner.

"I can't wait for him to come for dinner tonight. What time's dinner, Mom? Mom?"

"What's that, honey?"

"What time is dinner?"

"Whenever your father decides to come home from the club," she snapped. "He thinks that because he's president of the men's club, he has to be there all day. Can you take the little ones out back? I have to finish cleaning and start dinner before Father gets here."

"Sure, Mom," I said, taking my little brother and sister by their hands. I led them out back to the sandbox to play. Once they were settled in with their shovels, pails and toys, I looked around and noticed my baseball bat next to the tire swing that hung from a big oak tree. Swinging the bat as hard as I could, I smacked the tire and pretended to be hitting homeruns.

My neighbor friend, who was a tomboy, saw me out back and came over with her baseball glove. We played catch for a while and spent some time in the sandbox building sandcastles with my brother and sister. Before it was time for dinner, she went home and I took the little ones inside to clean up.

The door bell rang at five o'clock sharp. I ran to open the door. Father McCool stood there beaming down at me. His wavy red hair was well groomed and parted to the side. He was wearing blue jeans, sneakers, and a red flannel shirt with a white t-shirt underneath. The plain clothes on his tall and thin frame caught me by surprise as I stood there quiet, not knowing how to act or what to say. After a few seconds, I finally spoke.

"Hi Father."

"Hello again, Marco," Father said, as he patted me on the head. "Where are your parents?"

"Mom's in the kitchen cooking dinner and Dad hasn't come home from the club yet."

"Did I hear the door bell," Mom asked, sticking her head out from the kitchen door. "Oh. Hello, Father. I'm glad you could come for dinner. It will be ready shortly, and we can eat as soon as everyone arrives. We usually eat Sunday dinner at my in-law's house, but I thought it would be nice to have you over for a traditional Italian meal."

"It smells delicious. I can hardly wait," Father said, walking into the kitchen.

It was five-thirty when my father stumbled into the house. He had been playing cards and drinking all afternoon at St. Michael's men's club. "Let me fix you a drink, Father," was the first thing he said when walking into the kitchen.

"Thought you'd never ask," Father McCool said with a toothy grin.

"What can I get you?"

"I'll take a scotch and water," Father said, sampling a fried stuffed olive appetizer from a bowl on the table.

"Can I make it, Dad?" I said.

"Sure. Follow Father's instructions."

I went to the liquor shelf and grabbed the bottle of scotch. Using tongs, I filled the glass with ice and began to pour. When I stopped pouring, Father McCool said, "Keep going son, I want to get my money's worth."

My parents laughed, and I kept pouring until I was told to stop. There was only enough room for a splash of water.

After everyone had their drinks, my mother went into the fridge and pulled out the antipasto that my father had made earlier in the day. On the platter were rolled up Italian cold cuts, with homemade dried sausage and sharp provolone cheese. It was sprinkled with pickled vegetables and various types of olives. As my mother put the plate down next to the fried stuffed olives, Nanny and Poppy walked into the house.

They were my mother's parents, and I had lived with them until the age of four. They were married during World War II in England where my mom was born. Poppy was elected into the Legends of Horse Racing for his contribution as a successful agent for the jockeys. He not only was a jockey but had been a professional boxer, too.

Poppy had a reputation as a comedic character, frequently doing commercials for the Garden State Park and Atlantic City Race Tracks. He was known for his dapper attire and his trademark Stetson hat that sported a feather in the band. The industry knew him well during the golden years of horse racing, and he frequently conversed with well-known sports figures and entertainers. Whatever sporting event or show was in town, Poppy got the best seats in the house.

While I lived with my grandparents, Poppy took me to the backstretch of the racetrack at the crack of dawn every morning. As the sun came up on the horizon, the early mist rose in the haze while the warm-up riders trotted around the track. How I loved the smell of horse manure!

I'd hang out with the jockeys who'd put me up on the racehorses while going for their warm ups. Poppy and I always had a doughnut and hot chocolate in the cafeteria afterwards.

Everyone treated me like a celebrity because I was the grandchild of Schnozz—nicknamed because of his resemblance to Jimmy Durante. After Poppy was through with his business, he'd take me back home to Nanny and return for the day's race card.

Nanny always smelled of lavender and baby powder. She recited childhood nursery rhymes while pulling me and her pet poodle, Coco, in my red wagon. We'd ride around the block together; Nanny on her bicycle with a wicker basket and me on my tricycle. Naptime was at the same time each day, followed with a snack on a TV dinner stand while we watched the soap *Dark Shadows* together. She'd fill a small swimming pool for me in the summer months.

Once all the dishes were cleared from Nanny's dinner table I'd look forward to desert ... pound cake with Cool Whip ... and usually strawberries. I had it with milk. Poppy had Sanka Coffee. Nanny had her British tea.

On Sunday mornings, Poppy and I dropped Nanny off at the Presbyterian Church. We'd then go out to breakfast together. After church, we'd all go off to the movie theatre. Life had structure until I was pulled from their home after my mom came back into the picture. I loved it when my grandparents came to visit us at our new home.

"Hey Champ!" Poppy said with a smile from ear to ear, placing a fresh loaf of Italian bread that he'd picked up from the bakery on the table. "Put 'em up!" he said, holding up his hands for me to punch. "Jab with the left. Then punch with the right. That's my boy," he said, shaking his hands and grimacing, pretending my punches hurt.

Nanny greeted me with a kiss on the forehead. "Hello, sweetie. How's my little guy doing?"

"I'm not little," I whined. "I'm big." I stretched my slight frame to look taller.

"You'll always be my little boy no matter how big you get," Nanny said with a laugh, pulling me in for a hug.

There was a knock on the door as my dad's parents, Mum Mum and Pop Pop came into the house carrying a baked pork roast with roasted potatoes and broccoli rabe. Mum Mum worked as a seamstress at a local factory. She adored children and was very outgoing.

Pop Pop was slightly heavy and tall, with thick hands and gray wavy hair. He worked as an electrician at the local oil refinery and loved to garden in his massive vegetable field that was outlined with a variety of fruit trees. He had a small stable with three horses, a pig pen, rabbit pen, pigeon coop, chickens and geese. We had fresh meat when he would slaughter the chickens and rabbits. He loved to bake and cook. Unlike Mum Mum, he kept to himself.

Pop Pop placed the roasted pork in the oven to keep warm and Mum Mum put the vegetables on the stove. She passed me by without a word and ran to my brother and sister who were playing with their toys on the living room floor.

"Hello, my little precious ones," Mum Mum said, hugging my brother and picking up my sister for a kiss.

Pop Pop went to the fridge and pulled out a cold beer. He sat at the kitchen table and picked up slices of prosciutto and provolone from the antipasto tray. "This prosciutto is excellent—tasty and tender. You cured this meat just right, Son," he said, washing it down with a gulp of beer.

"Thanks, Dad. Wait till you try the sausage."

Pop Pop tasted the sausage. "Delicious," he said, smacking his lips. "Somebody taught you well."

"Hi Mum Mum and Pop Pop," I said, coming up close for them to notice me.

"Oh, hi Marco. How are you?" Mum Mum said.

"I'm fine. Father McCool is eating dinner with us today."

"I know. I heard. That's nice he took the time to spend Sunday dinner with us."

"Dinner is ready," Dad announced.

Everyone squeezed into the tiny kitchen and sat around the table. I sat next to Father McCool. My little brother and sister had already eaten and were playing around the table, climbing onto my grandparents' laps. Father said grace and Poppy followed with his version, "The Father, Son, and Holy Ghost. Whoever eats the fastest gets the most." I laughed, but the rest of the family seemed to be embarrassed. Father politely chuckled.

We started out with wedding soup, to which I quickly added a handful of homemade egg and cheese croutons. I buttered a piece of the crusty Italian bread and dunked it in the broth. When we finished the soup, the table was cleared. Mom carried in two big platters of fresh linguini and tomato gravy sprinkled with aged pecorino Romano followed with two big bowls of homemade meatballs. I grabbed the pitcher of extra gravy and poured it over my platter of linguini and meatballs. I grated enough cheese over my linguini that you couldn't see the pasta.

When everyone had finished their pasta course the table was cleared again and the meat course was served. At this point I was already stuffed. Nonetheless a plate of pork roast with golden roasted rosemary potatoes and broccoli rabe sautéed with garlic and olive oil was put in front of me. I did my best to finish what I could.

After the meat course, the table was cleared once again and a large bowl of fresh salad mixed with extra virgin olive oil and red wine vinegar was put on the table. Even though I was gorged and felt like I couldn't fit anything more down my throat, I still was forced to eat a little bit of salad.

"Let me help you clear the table," Father McCool insisted when Mom stood up and started collecting plates.

"Why, thank you, Father," Mom said, surprised at the offer. "But that's not necessary."

"I insist," Father said with a grin, leaning over the table to gather the serving bowls.

"Now don't go spoiling her," Dad said with a roar. Everyone laughed and Dad led them all out to the tight quarters of the living room for after dinner drinks.

Poppy sat next to me, patted my leg and asked, "How's your baseball coming along."

"Good."

"Always keep your eye on the ball."

I rolled my eyes. "I know. You told me a thousand times, Poppy."

From the kitchen, I could hear Father McCool telling my mother, "Marco is such a nice boy. You should be very proud of him."

"Yes, he's a good boy," Mom said.

"I noticed that he doesn't have many friends, being fairly new to the neighborhood and all. I'd be happy to help him get acclimated with the other boys through our parish's youth group. We have a trip planned next weekend to go to Clementon Lake Park, and I'd be pleased to take him."

"That sounds wonderful. Marco's lucky to have you in his life. It's been a little tough on him making friends. This is his second move in the last few years. That can be hard on a nine-year-old boy. My parents raised him until he was four, and then we moved to Delaware. I had to work and leave him with neighbors every day while his dad was gone for months at a time, traveling around the world for work."

"It's really no problem. Marco's a pleasure to have around."

"You are very kind, Father. And thank you for your help with the dishes," Mom said, setting the cake and coffee cups on the kitchen table. "Desert is ready," she called out.

The family came back to the kitchen and sat down. Father McCool turned to me and said, "Marco, you've done such a good job learning how to serve in church with me. Would you like to start serving morning Mass?" He then whispered in my ear, "You get to be excused from your morning classes."

I smiled, shaking my head up and down. Father then turned to Poppy and said, "I see you like baseball."

"Only when my team is winning," Poppy growled, trying to tune in the station for a better reception on the pocket transistor radio he was carrying. Poppy was a gambler and always bet on the games.

"I'm a Yankees fan," Father McCool said. "I have a friend who gets me good tickets, and I promised Marco that I'd take him to see a few games."

"Old Yogi Berra would always come to me for some tips on the races." Poppy said.

Father McCool's eyes lit up. For the rest of the evening Poppy told him his stories about knowing famous Yankees while working at Belmont Park Race Track in New York.

Mum Mum and Pop Pop were the first to leave. They both went to my brother and sister for a kiss good-bye. They waved to me on their way out the door.

Nanny and Poppy followed. Poppy kneeled down to my level and gave me a hug. "Going to miss you, Marco. Maybe we can pick you up to spend a weekend with us real soon."

"I'd like that," I said, returning his embrace.

Nanny leaned over to give me a kiss on the forehead. "Yes, we must pick you up for a weekend as soon as possible. Love you, honey."

Father McCool was the last to leave. "Thank you for the hospitality," he said to my parents, then turned to me. "I'll let you know which day I'll need you to serve Mass."

"Can't wait, Father. Good night."

CHAPTER TWO
~BECOMING BEST FRIENDS~

The following Thursday Father McCool came into my morning reading class, and everyone's eyes lit up. "May I speak with you, Sister Charlotte?" he said.

They kept their voices low, but they both looked at me, waving for me to come over. Nervous, I left my seat and walked up to them with all eyes focused on me.

Sister whispered, "Father needs you to help him serve morning Mass."

My concerned look turned into a smile, and I followed Father out of the classroom. "Now how was that for an exit?" Father said. "I told you I'd get you out of your morning class, didn't I?"

"I was a little bit nervous. I thought maybe I'd done something wrong."

Father laughed and patted my head. "Nah. I can get you out of your classes anytime. Now let's go say Mass together."

When the service was over, I helped clean up and turned to leave to go back to class. Father stopped me and said, "Marco, I developed the film that we shot last week of you disappearing. Would you like to come see it?"

"Shouldn't I get back to class?"

He winked. "You'll be fine. Sister Charlotte knows you're with me."

"I guess," I said with a hesitant shrug. "If you think it's okay."

"Sure. There's no hurry to get you back to class," Father said, rustling up my hair.

We walked across the street to the rectory. As before, we walked up to his bedroom and shut the door behind us. Father McCool set up his projector and showed the film of me disappearing.

"That's the neatest thing! Can we do it again?" I said.

He grabbed the camera and turned it toward me. I enthusiastically acted as a magician snapping my fingers, pretending to disappear. Smiling and goofing for the camera, I became more comfortable with Father filming me like he did the other boys I watched on his home movies. After about an hour of playing around and watching movies, Father escorted me back to class.

The following Saturday, Father McCool picked me up for the trip to Clementon Lake Park with the parish's youth group. The other children rode in the school bus, but I got to ride with Father. On the way, we were cut off by a speeding vehicle.

"Hey, jackass!" Father yelled out the window. "Where'd you get your license? Two for one at your local five and dime store?" He turned to me and smiled. "That driver's a real jackass, isn't he?"

"He sure is a jackass," I said, laughing.

Ahead of the group, we arrived at the amusement park as it was opening, got out and looked around. The school bus pulled in, and Father and I walked up to the rest of the group.

"Hey," Father called out to two other altar boys. "Do you two guys want to come on the rides with Marco and me?"

"Sure!" they called out, running toward us.

I stood by quietly; a little annoyed that Father asked them to join us. Our group walked toward the rides and stood in line.

"I brought my movie camera along. I'll get some great footage of you boys," Father said, turning the camera on us. The other two boys ran around making silly faces at the camera. "Go with them, Marco," Father urged.

Not yet feeling comfortable, I put my thumbs in my ears and wiggled my fingers at Father. As the day went on, I got to know the boys better and had fun on the rides and playing the arcade games.

"You boys should come by the rectory one day to see the movies," Father said.

"That would be great!"

"Sure!"

"When will you have them ready, Father?" I said.

"I'll get all of you boys together after I get them developed."

When it was time to go home, everyone loaded onto the bus. Father and I left in his car. "I have to stop by the rectory," Father told me before we got there.

I hopped out of the car, ran into the rectory, and bolted up the stairs to Father McCool's bedroom. Jumping on his bed, I said, "Can you show me some more movies?"

"Not today, Marco. I have to get ready for a marriage counseling session."

I wrinkled my forehead, still jumping. "What's that?"

"It's to show and tell two people who are getting married how to live with each other."

"What do you mean?"

"Well, when two people are ready for marriage, they are ready for certain special things."

"What things?"

"Things like love making."

I stopped jumping. "What's love making?"

"It's when two married people show their love for each other and become one through intercourse."

Confused and embarrassed, I just said, "Oh."

Father walked out of the bedroom into his personal study. I went to the drawer where he kept his pictures and pulled out the photo album. Taking it back to his bed, I sat at the end of the bed flipping through the album. A few minutes later, Father walked back in. "It's time to go," he said.

We walked down the stairs and got into his car. "I had a great time, Father," I said as he pulled up in front of my house. "Thank you for the best day ever."

"I had a good time today, too. You're welcome. We've got more fun things coming up this summer. See ya," Father said with a wave.

***

It was a couple of weeks into the summer when Father took me to Yankee Stadium to see the Yankees play the detested Boston Red Sox. Father McCool picked me up early that morning to tour New York City before the game. We visited the Empire State Building and Central Park. Our last stop before the game was Times Square. "Wait here, Marco, while I run into this store for a minute," Father said.

I was scared standing alone on a New York City street in front of a store that said it was for adults only. A few minutes later Father came out of the store holding a brown paper bag. "What's in the bag," I asked.

"It's a secret. I can't say right now."

"Come on. Please? Show me *now*."

"Not now," he said as he threw the bag in the trunk of his car.

We arrived at Yankee Stadium a couple of hours before the game to tour the stadium. In the parking lot, before we went in, Father changed from his flannel shirt to his priestly collar. When the game started, we took our seats on the third base side. The Yankee's nemesis, Carlton Fisk, came up to bat first. Father yelled, "You suck!"

The fans around us reeled with laughter. "You sure are passionate for your team, Father," the fan next to us said.

"Well, he does suck," Father said with a chuckle.

"Would you like a beer, Father," another fan behind us asked.

Father grinned, turning to face the questioning man, with a thumbs up gesture. "I never turn down a beer."

Again, the people around us roared with laughter as a beer peddler was called over and a beer was purchased by the stranger. Father bought me hotdogs, soda, peanuts and crackerjacks as the game went on. People sent beers over to Father McCool, which he graciously accepted.

"Let me show you how to keep score on the program's score card," Father said, leaning into my shoulder.

"There's a lot of history in this park," a man sitting next to me said, and he proceeded to tell me all that he knew.

"That was the best game ever," I said to Father after the Yankees won three to one that night.

"This is only the beginning. We'll be coming back here as much as possible this summer. I'm going to turn you into a real Yankees fan."

"I *am* a huge fan, Father," I said with a wide grin. "But I can't wait to come back again. I think my favorite players are third baseman Greg Nettles and the catcher, Thurman Munson."

"Good choices," Father said, with a pat on my head.

After that glorious day, Father McCool became like family. Often times he would stop by my house to say hello to my mother and me. He spent most holidays with us when my dad would host his many blowout parties. Soon Father and I became inseparable.

"Father McCool is my best friend," I told my mother one day.

"He's someone for you to trust and admire, Marco," Mom said. "We love having him in our home."

CHAPTER THREE
~EDUCATION IN SEX~

"Marco, I'll be right back," Father McCool said, leaving the room and closing the door behind him. It was during the first month of fifth grade when he left me alone in the personal study off his bedroom.

Beside me on a table was a sex education book. Waiting a minute or two staring at the cover, my curiosity finally got the better of me. Hmmm. What is this? I wondered, picking up the book. Flipping through the pages, I felt butterflies in my stomach like I did when a girl talked to me. It was a rush like I had never felt before. The women in the pictures had looks of pleasure on their faces. I quickly put the book down when I heard Father coming back.

A few days later, Father left me in the study again, and once more I zipped through the book, enjoying the feeling of activity in my stomach. But I slammed it shut when I heard Father walking in.

It was the third time that he left me in the room with the book when Father caught me with it in my hands.

"U-um, I-I was j-just wondering what this was," I said, closing the book and slowly putting it down.

"It's okay, Marco. These are normal human functions. Have your parents ever explained the act of love making to you?"

"No," I said, shaking my head, eyes wide with excitement.

"Well, you're ten years old now and becoming a man. Sex is a normal function."

"Is it a sin, Father?"

"If a man and woman had sex before they were married, it'd be a sin," he explained. "But if two people of the same sex do it, it's all right."

My eyes got bigger. "What does it feel like?"

"It's fun and relaxing. But it's something that you need to keep between you and me. No one must know about this or we wouldn't be able to hang out with each other anymore."

"I wouldn't want that to happen," I said, feeling like my heart dropped to my stomach. "I'm happy when I'm with you, and we have good times together."

"And I feel the same, Marco. That's why you can't tell a single soul. You have to promise me that you won't tell anyone that we talked about this."

"I promise," I said, shaking my head up and down. "At home it's lonely, but with you it's fun. I won't tell anyone."

"That's my boy, Marco."

With each visit, I became more curious about sex. "How does a man and woman have sex," I asked one day.

Father sat next to me on the bed and turned to the page of a man and a woman in the missionary position. "The woman arouses the man by stimulating his penis until it gets hard. When the man is stimulated, he penetrates in and out of the woman through her vagina until he has an orgasm."

"What's an orgasm?"

"It's such a special feeling that words cannot explain. I could show you how this is done if you'd like."

I looked down. "I don't know."

"Do you want to see the surprise in the brown bag that I bought in New York?" My eyes shot wide open as I snapped my face back to him. "Yes, Father. I sure do!"

Out of the bag came a *Playboy* magazine. "Let me show you some of the pictures in this book," Father said, folding the book open to the centerfold.

"Wow!" I said, my stomach turning summersaults.

"She's beautiful isn't she? One day you'll be having sex with someone like her. In the meantime, I could teach you how to have sex."

"Um. I don't know," I said, looking away and walking toward the door.

"That's fine, Marco. This is a big step toward becoming a young man. You might not be mature enough yet for something like this."

"I am so!"

"Okay, we'll see," Father said before he took me home.

The next time I came to Father's room, there was a *Penthouse, Hustler,* and a full blown-out XXX penetration magazine. One of the publications showed demonstrations on how to self-masturbate and how to masturbate each other.

As I was sitting on the bed, going through a magazine, Father said, "This is a normal function in life, Marco. It's something special that I want to share with you," he said, taking the book from my hands and placing it down next to me. He knelt in front of me and pulled my pants down to my knees. I gulped when he reached out and touched my hardened penis.

"Marco, relax," Father said, soft and assuring. "This is normal."

I closed my eyes and couldn't move. He picked up the book and put it back in my hands. I pushed it away, but he put it back in my hands and said, "Let me show you how the woman pleases the man." He put his mouth on my penis.

While I concentrated on the pictures in the magazine, Father McCool performed oral sex on me until I ejaculated. He then stood and pulled out his penis.

"Now, Marco, you do the same to me."

"No. Stop," I said, as he pushed his enlarged penis toward my mouth.

"It's okay, Marco. It's okay. Keep looking at the magazine," he said while masturbating in front of me.

I couldn't move and sat as still as I could. Sensing my fear, Father got up and went to the bathroom, shutting the door behind him.

Immediately, I jumped off the bed and pulled up my pants. I went to his desk and took out the photo album of our trips to Yankee Stadium, trying to imagine being at the ballgame and having fun. More loud sounds were coming from the bathroom, but I tried to shut them out.

Father came out of the bathroom a few minutes later, naked. I couldn't look at him.

"Now you know that you can't tell anyone about this, don't you Marco? It'd ruin everything that we have. You know that. Right?" he said as he put on a fresh pair of pants and a button-down shirt.

My head stayed buried in the photo album. When he was dressed, he walked to the door and I followed. He drove me home, reminding me, "Don't say anything about this to anyone, Marco. Can I count on you?"

Nodding my head, the word was hardly audible. "Yes."

From then on, there was no explaining the draw I had to Father McCool. When he invited me to his room, I went. He'd make a scotch and water and hand it to me.

"Have a sip, Marco," he said. "This will help you relax. The magazines will show you how to do new and different things. You're becoming a man, Marco. This is a normal function."

The fun and games started to dissipate, while the sexual engagements became more frequent. Sometimes we'd have oral sex in his bedroom while other priests were in their own rooms down the hall. Other times, Father McCool would pull his car over to the side of the road and take me into the woods where he'd spread out a blanket on the ground. There were times he'd make his advances on me in my own home when he'd stop by, knowing my parents weren't there.

Father invited the two altar boys who hung out with us on the field trip to his room to watch the movies we had taken that day. They excitedly agreed.

While the movie played, Father said, "Marco, do you want to show the boys the magazines I have? I have to go downstairs for a minute."

"Sure," I said, going to the drawer of Father's desk and pulling out the stack of magazines.

"Wow," the guys said in unison, ogling the pictures.

Father came back with Scotch and poured us all our own drinks. "Take a sip," he instructed. We all did as we were told and started giggling. "It's time you boys learn about the birds and the bees. But this has to be our secret. We don't want anyone spoiling our fun. Right, Marco?"

I nodded my head and burst out laughing. By now, I was addicted to porn, constantly sexually aroused, and masturbating on a regular basis at home with my father's *Playboy* collection that I'd found hidden in the basement.

"Show the boys how it's done, Marco," Father said, taking out his camera.

"It's okay," I said to the others. "You'll like it. It's normal." I performed oral sex on one of the boys, and Father instructed him to perform oral sex on the other one while he filmed us. We were all sworn to secrecy, and we kept that secret for three years.

CHAPTER FOUR
~REALIZATION~

A short time before my thirteenth birthday, I was in religion class. One of my altar boy friends whispered in my ear, "Hey. Did you hear that the pharmacist who developed Father McCool's pictures of us told the Church about it?"

"Uh. Yeah. Father told me to tell everyone that we took naked pictures of each other when he wasn't in the room to prank him when he developed the film."

"Oh. Okay. That sounds good."

When my dad heard the gossip, he said, "What goes on between you and that priest? You sure spend a lot of time with him."

"He takes me to ball games. W-we, ahm ... talk and ... stuff," I said, head down and shifting my weight from side to side.

He got right in my face, screaming, "What's with these pictures I'm hearing about? I'll kill that bastard and tell the world he's been fucking with you."

"It was a prank on Father when he developed the pictures," I said, as my face turned brilliant red.

He turned and walked away, shaking his head.

He knows, I thought. How could I let this happen? Everyone's going to think I'm a ... a *perverted freak*.

I felt embarrassed and overwhelmed. The foulness of my actions now repulsed me. Father McCool wasn't cool anymore. He had convinced me that having sex with him and the other boys was a normal function of human sexuality. My father didn't think so and was ready to shout it to the world. What will my mother think? My body had been violated by a trusted adult, I then realized, and my mind had been programmed with ... filth.

Right during this time, I was feeling an attraction to a girl in my class. This realization, this dawning on me of what Father had done to me, turned me into ... I was at a loss. How do I approach her? What if she knows what I've done?

It was time, I knew, to separate myself from Father McCool. There were no more amusement parks, ball games, and good times. The innocent moments that he used to lure me into his sick world were all but gone. It hit me, hard. They had all been an illusion he created to hide his plan to dupe me and corrupt my trusting spirit. The only time Father McCool would come around or pick me up now was to have sex. I no longer wanted him in my life. I wanted to have a relationship with a girl, not him. I began to ignore Father McCool. Whenever he would call, I wouldn't answer. When he would come around, I would leave the house. I stopped serving Mass, and if he approached me at school I ignored him. It wasn't long before he was moved from our parish to another community — to prey on new victims, I figured.

As I look back, I can see the damage he'd inflicted on my psyche was already done. I continued to eat, breath, and live for porn and sex, masturbating several times a day. Viewing or even thinking about pornographic material hyped me with adrenaline, sometimes causing me to vomit.

I started self-medicating at fourteen years old by binge drinking and using marijuana. There was plenty of alcohol in our house and marijuana was easily obtainable from a guy at school.

Even though my dad had stopped traveling and now worked nearby from his company's corporate office, he didn't pay attention to what I was doing. He was also busy assisting with his grandfather's neighborhood deli. On Friday evenings after work he'd rush off with his friends, getting drunk at St. Michael's men's club. There was constant fighting between him and my mother over the little time he spent with us.

Mom didn't pay much attention either. She was busy running the household, waking in the early morning hours to exercise, preparing breakfast for us kids, and making sure we were sent off to school with a freshly made lunch. The rest of her day was spent cleaning the house and running errands. She'd make sure we would finish our homework before she started making dinner. After cleaning up, Mom would head off to her night job, working as a cosmetologist at the local mall.

In addition to self medicating, I searched intensely for an outlet to convert me to a manlier image. Baseball was a "man's" sport. I worked tirelessly on techniques to improve my swing and throwing release.

I swung a bat, hitting balls through the old tire swing hanging from the big oak tree in our backyard, until I couldn't pick up my arms. I'd throw a ball against a brick wall for hours, fielding it as it ricocheted off the wall. I soon improved my level of play, encouraged that I had potential to compete at a higher level. But then a wave of doubt would overtake me. Who am I kidding? I'll never be good enough. I'm a shameful creature.

When fall came around, my interest turned to football. Now this was indeed a "manly" sport. I started out below average. I practiced relentlessly to improve, spending hours of punting and throwing the football in an empty field. I took up weight lifting and running. Most of my spare time was spent training for tryouts.

In my last year of Pop Warner football, I eventually became one of the best players on the team. I played the positions of halfback on offense, middle linebacker on defense, kickoff and punt receiver, and punter. But when it came to advancing to the next level, I felt I wasn't good enough. I had no confidence to compete with the other players, sure that they all knew what I was, too.

To be a varsity wrestler in my high school meant that you were something special. I labored day and night to make the squad, finally lettering in my junior year. I was sixteen years old, and it was in the spring after wrestling season when my guidance counselor called me to his office during chemistry class. I was nervous and thought I'd done something wrong, never having had to see him before. I didn't even know our school had a guidance counselor.

When I arrived at his office, a cute senior girl was sitting in one of the two chairs in front of his desk. I became immediately shy and uncomfortable being in her presence, forgetting about possibly being in trouble.

"Take a seat," the counselor instructed. Our personal folders were in front of him. To expedite his future career enhancement speech, he was talking with two students at a time. "What are your future goals when you graduate," he asked us.

"Well," the attractive girl said, "I would like to--"

"Can I see you for a moment?" the secretary said, sticking her head in the door.

"Excuse me," the counselor said, standing up and walking out of the room.

The girl and I leaned over his desk, reaching for our personal folders. When I opened my folder, she said, "Why is your folder stamped adopted?"

"What?" I said, not noticing.

"Look. Right there." She pointed to the big red letters, tapping each one, as she spelled aloud, "A. D. O. P. T. E. D."

"Uh. Um. It must be some kind of mistake," I said, putting the folder back on the desk.

When the guidance counselor came back into the room, I didn't question it. I was afraid of what his answer would be. He finished his career speech, and we both went back to our classes.

That night, I told Mom and Dad, "I saw my guidance counselor today. My personal folder was stamped that I was adopted. I was wondering why."

"We don't know why either," Mom said.

"Schools are always messing up those things," Dad said.

"Oh. Okay. I thought it had to be a mistake. Maybe we should say something."

"Yes, we'll get it straightened out," Mom said.

But that weekend Mom said, "Marco, come and sit down with us. We have something we want to tell you."

I couldn't imagine what they'd have to say. They seemed serious. But I dutifully sat down at the kitchen table.

"I'm not your real father," Dad said.

"What?"

He squirmed a bit in his chair, then cleared his throat and said, "I'm not your real father." He forced a smile that was to be taken as genuine and jutted his chin. "But I adopted you."

My mind started to race. I felt boiling blood rushing to my reddened face as I clenched my teeth and balled my fists. "Is that why I have no Godfather and why there are no baby pictures of me? I always wondered why my cousin who's a year older than me is in your wedding pictures, but I'm not."

"We got married at Poppy's house when you were only four years old," Mom said.

"That's what that commotion was. I remember a lot of people filling the house when you finally came back, and I got shipped off to a neighbor's house. The next thing I knew, you dragged me away from the only home I knew and moved me to that secluded place in Delaware. I hated that place. Neither of you were *ever* home."

I slammed a fist onto the tabletop and bolted out of my seat, enraged. "Things are starting to make sense to me. We were a half hour away from your hometown here in Gibbstown, Dad, and we never once visited. You were *ashamed* of me. Now I know why there's no connection between me and your family and why people were surprised that you had a son my age. You had to fill in the gap. When we moved here, you could play out your lie and convince people I was your biological son. All of it has been a huge *lie*." I stormed out of the kitchen to my bedroom and slammed the door. Sitting on my bed, I wanted to punch something. Instead, I ran from my room and retreated to the basement where I lifted weights until my arms felt like they'd break off if I did anymore.

After that incident, my parents, in what was to me an amazing and enraging manner, acted as if nothing had ever happened. They just continued on with their lives. My relationship with them was never the same.

CHAPTER FIVE
~SCHOOL STRUGGLES~

My senior year of high school was supposed to be my breakthrough year in wrestling, but I didn't make the cut for the varsity squad. I lost to someone I'd thought was a much lesser opponent.

The pain and dishonor of failure was of such intensity I decided to transfer mid-way through my senior year to another school near Poppy and Nanny. Once I got the okay to move in with them, I packed my belongings as fast as I could. It was the safest place to soothe the magnitude of the disgrace. I made their varsity squad but wasn't able to advance past Regionals in the tournament.

College wasn't much different. In the fall of 1982, I attended the University of Tennessee in Chattanooga. It was a college rich in sports tradition, surrounded by Look Out Mountain in the Appalachians, and bordered by the scenic Tennessee River. During my freshman year, both the wrestling and basketball teams were ranked in the Division I top-twenty polls. The tennis team was the reigning Division II national champions. It was the opening year of the college's new coliseum, "The Round House," which seated 12,000 spectators. I could see it from my dorm window.

I was honored to meet Gerald Wilkins, a member of our basketball team and future NBA star of the New York Knicks. I also met Sherry Goggins, a cheerleader who later became an American National Fitness Champion, Miss Fitness USA, and a popular model. Watching Gerald play and Sherry cheer during a close game against the University of North Carolina Tarheels (UNC), was a highlight in my first year. A sophomore from UNC scored twenty-seven points, leading his teammates to the seven-point victory. He turned out to be future superstar Michael Jordan.

Things seemed to be going well with the excitement on campus, as I kept busy training for wrestling, maintaining a modest 2.8 grade-point average, and socializing with the other athletes.

Upbeat and feeling better about myself, I came home to our close-knit neighborhood in Gibbstown, New Jersey, for the holiday break. The house was packed with drunken party guests when I walked in, with more than a hundred people at our house on Christmas Eve. Everyone knew that Father McCool and I had been like each other's shadows from fifth to eighth grade.

News in the neighborhood had spread. After Father McCool had been booted out of our parish, he was sent to a parish in Brigantine, New Jersey. There, everyone had been aghast to learn, he'd done the same thing to a boy he'd done to me and the other altar boys at our parish. He'd been caught, convicted and sent to prison. No one from my parish had, or would apparently, come forward to admit to the atrocities. Once Father McCool was gone—the subject was closed. My entire family knew what had happened to me, but nothing was ever said or done about it.

In my town, high school wrestling was like a religion, and the team won every conference title for over thirty years. Shortly after I arrived, an alumnus of our high school wrestling team showed up. The guy was an obnoxious loud mouth like my stepfather. He got everyone's attention and grabbed a buddy, putting a wrestling move on him.

"Hey, everyone!" he called out. "What is this?"

"Half Nelson," the crowd answered.

He then grabbed his buddy and did another move on him and said, "What's this one?"

"Full Nelson," was the reply.

While in the Full Nelson position with his buddy's back to him, he then started to move his hips back and forth in a sodomizing motion.

"What's this?" he called out. And then he screamed, "Father Nelson!"

The house erupted in laughter, including everyone in my family. I wanted to run and hide. They all knew.

I went back to college with reduced confidence, feeling worse than ever. I was winning my matches, and even beat out a popular four-time Tennessee State wrestling champion to make varsity my sophomore year. I was a solid member of the college's nationally-ranked wrestling team. But, I was convinced, I was the lesser man in the competition.

The same lack of faith carried over to my academics. I was certain I wasn't smart enough for college. In addition, the partying intensified as I was introduced to new drugs. Drinking and marijuana became a daily habit along with new numbing drugs such as opiates, acid, and methamphetamines. I dropped out after my sophomore year, returning home as a failure.

I was a nobody, depressed and alone. There was no one to talk with about what was going on internally with me. And anyway, I didn't deserve anyone's respect.

I turned to weight lifting and bodybuilding as a means to improve my self-esteem and confidence. As with everything else, I tried to be perfect. I worked my ass off lifting weights nearly four hours a day. Sometimes I'd lift to the point where I'd vomit after a set.

I kept to an extremely strict diet. I ate six to seven meals a day of the cleanest, leanest, and freshest foods. Nightly, I'd sedate myself with marijuana. I eliminated all the other drugs and alcohol. Soon, I was noticed by a local gym owner. They wanted to sponsor me in competition. I was determined to do this.

My first competition was the New Jersey Classic Championships at the Tropicana Casino in Atlantic City, New Jersey. I was in peak condition. Vascular veins overlapped the striated dense muscular definition I had all over my body. People looked in amazement at my sculptured physique. Some even winced at the outlandish way my body transformed as I flexed for them. My confidence was at an all-time high, the memories of abuse suppressed for the moment.

There was a field of fifteen competitors at the middleweight class that day. But the top two competitors were well known and had placed high in previous national competitions. I placed third, although most observers said the choices for the top two finishers were political, and I should have either won the show or definitely at least placed second. Only the first and second winners qualified to move forward to the nationals.

I should've been proud to finish in the top three in a national qualifying competition at a first-class venue. The place was packed and cheering me on. But my mind didn't work like that. I worried about what a loser I was. I had no right being on the stage with the rest of the competitors.

Immediately following the competition, my gym sponsor said, "Hey, Marco. Don't look so down. There's an agent for a sports network in California interested in representing you. He's traveling to the East Coast in a few months to see you compete in the next national qualifier. Take some time off. Let your body recuperate from all that intense training before we get you ready for the Mideastern Regionals."

Negative thoughts raced through my mind. I couldn't comprehend his suggestion of my competing again after my failure to qualify for Nationals. I was ashamed and unworthy. There was no way I would put myself out there again and lose. But I walked away from my sponsor saying, "You're right. I could use a break."

CHAPTER SIX
~MEETING MY WIFE~

A few days after the competition, I went out with a friend from work for a few beers. After I dropped out of college, Poppy had gotten me a job working as a valet at the Garden State Race Track in Cherry Hill, New Jersey, and I felt like taking a much needed break. We smoked a joint in the parking lot and walked into a local pub. There was an attractive blond who worked at the track sitting at the bar. She was looking hot, wearing a short skirt and tight top. She kept looking my way and smiling.

"Go talk to her," my buddy said, giving me a nudge.

"She's cute," I said, nodding. I wrinkled my nose and clucked my tongue. "But she wouldn't want to talk to me."

"Go on," he urged, jabbing me in the shoulder. "She's coming on to you."

I looked down and shook my head. Lifting the beer mug to my mouth, I downed a big swig. When I put it back down, I felt someone standing behind me.

"Um," a velvety voice said. "My girlfriend, Louise, thinks that you're the best looking guy she's ever seen and wants to meet you." She giggled and ran back to her friend sitting at the bar only ten feet away.

I finished my beer with one long gulp. The joint I had smoked helped me have the courage to go over to the petite, vivacious, blond bombshell.

"Hi, Louise," I said, struggling to think of what to say next. "I'm Marco."

There was no problem carrying on a conversation with her, and ... we hit it off. She was a party girl, smoked pot regularly, and liked going out for a few beers at night. I enjoyed doing the same, although my motivation was hardly so frivolous and casual.

We worked at the track during the same hours of the day, getting out late at night. I parked cars, and she worked as a pari-mutual, taking bets at the track.

Our relationship flourished. What a comfort it was to be loved. I eventually gave up training—at least the concentrated regimen of a professional—and married her on May 15, 1988. Her family loved me, and I loved them. Three years later, we had a son named Julian, and the following year we had a daughter named Angel.

Julian was all boy—stout and ornery. He had his mother's pale skin and stick-straight, dirty-blond hair. Angel was more like me—darker skin and black wavy hair. Both were blessed with brilliant blue eyes—and they learned at a young age how to use that feature to their advantage. And boy, did Julian love to test the limits—constantly teasing his little sister just to hear her cry. Angel was a girly girl, sweet, and gentle.

My new wife and I worked the night racing card at the racetrack, which ended at midnight. We worked six days a week and double shifts on Saturdays. This left us with little quality time with each other and our two young children.

I made good money parking cars for a living. Louise made a decent salary, along with receiving tips from her regular patrons. We were also members of a union and secured favorable benefits. In an average week, I'd pull in a hefty amount of cash gratuities plus my salary, making respectable money for the mid-eighties through the early nineties.

My grandfather's connections hooked me up to a cliental of heavy gamblers who tipped well to have their cars pulled up as soon as they walked out of the grandstand. To make the money I needed to support my family, I had to maintain a hustling pace every night.

After work, Louise would head home and relieve the babysitter, who would already have the kids in bed. I'd stop at a late-night fast food place and a junk food convenience store for our nightly munchies attack, which we'd spread across our bed while surfing the cable channels. We'd pop a couple cans of beer while smoking a joint, finally crashing around three in the morning.

My wife and I didn't get out of bed until ten or eleven o'clock in the morning. When the kids were still too young for school, they'd rush to our bed when they awoke, pulling back the comforter and climbing in, badgering us to get up and play with them. We'd try to keep them at bay with videotapes of *Barney and Friends* to watch and boxes of dry cereal to snack on to stay in bed as long as possible.

By the time we'd get up and have a cup of coffee to snap us out of the fog from the prior night's high, we had a few hours with the kids before we had to get ready for work. I would slip out of the house for an hour a day to catch a quick workout at the local gym.

We lived in a spacious Spanish-style house with a generous amount of land. It was a fair distance from the surrounding suburban neighborhoods. There were no sidewalks connecting our community, and the kids didn't have many friends close by to play with. We weren't from the area and didn't meet many of our neighbors because of our work schedule.

Resting a huge camcorder on my shoulder, I'd film the kids at play in the yard, on their swing set or in the sand box. Zooming in on my wife's butt, I'd say in jest, "What's that?"

During the summer season on our only day off each week, we customarily went to the Atlantic City beach. We'd pick up clams and crabs to have a seafood feast when we got home. I'd pull the live crabs from the bushel with a pair of tongs, chasing the screaming kids around the house while the crab pinched its claws. This was a special remembrance that I held onto from my marriage.

A portrait of Louise's family could be used in a picture dictionary as the definition of the 'perfect family'. Even though her parents were divorced and her mother had remarried a nice guy, it was an amicable arrangement. They celebrated every significant occasion and holiday together. Birthdays were remembered with cards and gifts from every family member.

They were affectionate, loving, and interested in what I had to say. I wasn't used to this. My stepfather's family didn't show this kind of attention, and I felt awkward. I usually stayed quiet at their family functions, trying to be invisible, lacking the confidence for being sociable. I'd smoke a joint before attending to loosen me up a bit. I wanted to be a part of a family like theirs, their interest in me warmed my heart, but I didn't feel worthy. They treated me like gold, but with the self-medicating, I couldn't truly appreciate it at the time.

I relished the domesticated routine. I worked out in the morning, messed around with the kids during the day, and worked the track at night. We'd come home, smoke a doobie and chill. This worked for me, but eventually my wife grew wearisome of the habitual schedule.

Our love making, about the time when Louise's dissatisfaction with our—to her—'boring' diurnal regimen, had become mechanical, too. After each session, I would become cold and distant, feeling aberrant. I'd wonder if I was doing something wrong. "Can't we cuddle a little," Louise would ask. "Do you have to get up and walk out of the room? Why can't you show me any affection after sex? What's wrong with you?"

After a while she started complaining about having to work, work, work with no play. Ultimately, she got to the point where almost daily she'd say, "I want to go out dancing with my friends." She kept nagging me about it. "It'll only be a couple of nights a week," she promised.

"I don't really get into the nightclub scene anymore," I told her. "I can't see any harm in your going out, though."

And I tried, I really did. I wanted her to have some fun. And it was only to be a couple nights a week, so she deserved the break. But it soon became obvious she had no intention of keeping her promises of how often and how long. I would rush home after work to relieve the babysitter, and then wait ... for Louise to come back ... *the next morning*. "Where were you all night," I'd say, "and what were you doing until the wee hours of the morning?"

She'd roll her eyes and huff, sometimes screaming, "What? You don't trust me?"

"I want to trust you," I'd say in an accusatory tone. "But you're out every night, *all* night, now. It was supposed to be a few hours a couple of nights a week. I try my best to maintain the household duties and take care of the kids. Are you looking for someone better than me?"

"That wouldn't be hard," she'd say with a laugh. One morning, several months into the mounting tension building between us over this issue, she said, with scorn and disdain, "You're nothing but a piece of shit."

I was crushed. I fought feverishly to preserve the ideal husband/father image and keep my sanity in check, but something dark inside of me was fighting to be released. I was being torn apart by the battle for my soul between the implanted evilness and the beaten down innate goodness that still wanted to prevail.

CHAPTER SEVEN
~IMPROVING MYSELF~

I went back to college six years after dropping out, in another attempt to bolster my self-esteem. But this time I was determined to maintain an impeccable 4.0. I studied day and night, trying to attain the perfect grade-point average. I wound up graduating with an Associate's Degree at the local community college on the president's list with a respectable 3.86 average.

I transferred the next semester to a four-year university to work toward my bachelor's degree. Interested in accounting, I thought it a good idea to get experience in the field. For a while, I'd go to school early in the morning, work as a staff accountant from late morning to late afternoon, and park cars at night. I wanted to be the "perfect man," hard working and intelligent. Like in athletics, the perfectionist personality took over in my pursuit for higher education and career.

I put my marriage on hold and ignored Louise's nightly antics and demeaning rampages. It was more important for me to be a good father to my children. I figured if I worked hard to better myself that things would change for the better in the marriage.

I had worked as a staff accountant for one year. But there was an urge to feel important and run the show, proving to myself that I'd overcome the shame and guilt. But along came an offer for a high-paying position as controller for a cellular phone company, and I took the job. Attaining this authoritative status with its increased financial benefits enabled my addictions and sins with theretofore unimaginable, unrestrained wildness.

Anxiety from school and my career were at the highest level. My wife contributed little to the marriage and less to the normal household responsibilities. I was falling as far out of love with her as she was with me. And the memories ... those horrid memories of my corrupted childhood past.

With the demands of going to school, working two jobs, and the stress of having a marital partner whose favorite pastime was clubbing with her girlfriends, I was unable to maintain my night job at the racetrack. I couldn't finish off my bachelor's degree even though it was only a little over a semester away.

When I'd come home from work, Louise and I passed each other through the front doorway of our house as she left for work at the racetrack. I was greeted by a wrecked house. My children were unsupervised all day, as my wife slept off her nightly hangover from the prior night's clubbing. Julian was six years old and Angel was five during this dysfunctional marital time.

I savored my one-on-one time with my children. I still smoked weed nightly, for all the same reasons: a necessary alleviation from current stress and haunting bad memories. When first home from work, I'd lock myself in the bathroom and take a couple hits of pot from a pipe. Then I'd come out, straighten up the house, and order a smorgasbord of munchies to be delivered. Spreading a tablecloth across our bed, the kids and I would have "picnic night" while watching a rented video. When we finished stuffing ourselves, I cleaned up the mess as the kids got ready for bed. We'd fall asleep together in each other's arms, my daughter on one side of me and my son on the other.

Most mornings, when I awoke for work, my wife still wasn't home. Again, we'd pass each other coming through the front door. I began thinking maybe there was a little more going on than dancing and drinking with her girlfriends.

After I had worked at the cellular company for a few months, my original employer approached me, promising more money. I accepted at the time. But when one of the owners of the cellular phone company offered an even larger salary to come on board with his parent company, a sixty-branch financial exchange, I reneged on my agreement with my former employer and took the new position.

The job was very demanding. Seventy-two-hour workweeks were the norm. Millions of dollars were reconciled and exchanged. The list of services to rectify and manage were endless: check cashing, direct deposits, pay-day loans, income taxes, transportation tokens and passes, bill payments, money orders, western union, stamps, cigarettes, cellular phones and pager sales, candy, and condoms. You name the service, and we provided it.

I had to do everything, from arbitrating millions of dollars daily to designing improved and more efficient systems. I was the first one in at five-thirty in the morning to download the data from sixty stores, process the day's cash deliveries and deposits, distribute the clerk's faxes, and even make the coffee. I wanted to be considered a necessity in running the operations. I became obsessed with trying to be the consummate employee. It was a futile plan. I was never able to attain peace within myself.

While at this job I was introduced to cocaine, the most amazing drug. It was the day after tax season, and the owner of the company chartered a bus trip to Atlantic City. While waiting for the bus at the office, he laid out two lines of the drug. He snorted up one of them through a rolled up hundred dollar bill and then handed the bill to me. I took it and inhaled the powder. A rushing sensation came over my entire body. When I handed the c-note back, he said to keep it and gave me a little brown envelope with more coke in it.

I felt, strange as it might seem, comfortable with myself. Furthermore, I became sexually excited instantly, where before I had hidden it in shame. The excitement reminded me of the same sensation porn gave me the first time when I was ten. It seemed new, fresh, and exhilarating.

On the way to Atlantic City, the video screen on the bus showed a porn film. The bus then stopped at a strip club in Philadelphia. What excitement! I was promptly addicted to both the drug and the sexual openness and comfort it gave me. Without the stimulant, even normal lovemaking seemed wrong and shameful. With cocaine, I didn't care who or what anyone thought. I had an anything-goes attitude. Coke had released something obscure and evil that I was struggling to keep inside.

After I was introduced to cocaine, I brought it into our marriage. Sometimes my boss rewarded my work with an eight ball from his stash at the office. I remember the first night I brought it home. What a surprise I got when my wife grabbed it from my hands and used one of her credit cards to shave off and lay out two lines of the soft, brilliant white powder like an experienced user.

I started putting the pieces together. I knew what she was doing all night long while I was home with the kids. Once the cocaine use started, it blew the doors off any hope of pulling our marriage together. With the drug, who needed a relationship? I had no idea how bad it could get.

All feelings for Louise dissipated. I kept my mind open for ways out of the marriage. The only issue that tormented me was what to do with the children.

CHAPTER EIGHT
~MORE MARITAL WOES~

During this matrimonial hardship, I met a woman straight out of an impossible dream. Mary was beautiful, shapely, down to earth, and had a good solid head on her shoulders. We met at work, where I was the controller and she was a sales representative for the cellular subsidiary company of the financial exchange.

At company outings, she would go out of her way to make sure she was sitting or standing by me. With each event, we became increasingly more affectionate. While the dysfunctional episodes at home with my wife became increasingly intolerable, my time spent with my co-worker was filled with attention and support. I started to have an affair with her and, we eventually fell in love.

It was a love like I had never experienced before. Mary was my guardian angel. When I stood by her side and looked into her beautiful green eyes, my inner turmoil subsided. I felt truly loved and at peace. She didn't do drugs, nor did she drink consistently. She gave me a backbone to stop using drugs during this time.

In my marriage, my wife preferred not to work and craved partying and the materialistic things in life. But this new woman was career driven and came from a humble upbringing. She satisfied every aspect of my life. Mary was more concerned with my needs than her own.

Contrarily, my marriage was all about satisfying my wife's needs and wants. Louise had been my first attraction, and I had tried to use her to fill the void of loneliness. At the time we had met and first married, I was desperate for attention.

My newly acquired lover supplied both the companionship and interest in me I craved. I separated from my wife and two children. My wife was initially hurt by the breakup. She begged me to come back, saying that she would change her ways. That promise was short lived. I learned she, soon after our separation, started having a more open relationship with the man she had already been messing around with early on at the clubs.

The relationship with Mary flourished. There was no longer a need for the drugs to stimulate my life. It wasn't long before she was pregnant with our daughter. I lived with my pregnant mistress for a short time in a small apartment in Northeast Philadelphia, near my corporate office. It was a serene existence and stable life. I loved having a responsible woman that cared for me and the child she was carrying. The only thing that still plagued me was missing my two older children, wishing they could share in this secure environment. My nights were restless, worrying about their welfare.

With the self-condemning thoughts of having abandoned my wife and children adding to my already disgusting past, I needed to leave reality. I started to slip back into using cocaine. The drug use and resulting return of guilt feelings became overwhelming. Mary's strength wasn't enough to keep me from the drugs.

Even knowing my wife had been unfaithful, and was in no way what a mother and wife should be, I felt I had to go back to her and our two children. I left my pregnant girlfriend, who had given me a level of happiness I'd never known before in a relationship. I moved back in with Louise, and Mary had our baby girl, Jennifer, without me by her side. Yet another line item to compound the shame and guilt I had on my ever-growing list of disgraces.

In an attempt to revamp our relationship, Louise switched her shift at the racetrack to the day card, which enabled her to be home at night with the children and me.

Shortly after I settled in with my wife and two older kids again, I stopped in to a popular strip club in Philadelphia to pick up some coke. I hired a topless stripper to perform a lap dance. As she was grinding up against my privates cooing obscenities to me, I got a phone call from my wife. "Your mom called," she said. "She's been diagnosed with leukemia."

"Yeah. All right," I answered, not giving it a second thought. After a few hours at the club, I bought more coke and took it home with porn that I picked up on the way.

When I walked in, my wife was angry. "Where have you been?" she growled. "Hey, look what I brought home," I said, pulling out the goods.

"What are you going to do about your mother?" she said, flipping through the porn magazine I had dropped in front of her.

"The diagnosis was probably nothing," I said, taking her hand, leading her to the bedroom. "Come on. Let's party.

***

A couple of weeks later, my mother went into septic shock and passed away. I wasn't with her in her final days. The excruciation it caused me, knowing this, the debasing mortification I felt ... was insufferable.

Following my mother's death, my wife and I used cocaine and watched porn every chance we could. We'd rush the kids off to bed even though they'd want to spend more time with us. I'd sing to them, "You are my sunshine, my only sunshine," and "twinkle, twinkle, little star." We'd recite the ABC's, before saying 'God bless' ... naming everyone in the family. On nights when we had no plans to do drugs, they got the slow version, but when we planned an evening of drugging, I sounded like an auctioneer, going through the songs at high speed. I'd have to pry their tightly gripped little arms from my neck as they tried to prevent me from leaving them.

I'd go to the adult bookstore to buy all kinds of porn movies, magazines, lingerie, card games, lubricants, and toys on our sex nights. I wanted her to have sex with multiple partners, humiliating me while I watched. I demanded that she say things about the other guys that she got off on. The rush and excitement I experienced was at a level that could not be measured.

Our drug use escalated to crack and pills. We were running into financial problems, having difficulty paying the normal household bills. At times we had no food in the house. We were in a sea of credit card debt and IRS arrears, owing numerous friends hundreds of dollars. The electricity was even turned off in the middle of the night for not paying the bill as we smoked crack together, viewing porn magazines by the glow of a flashlight. Nothing kept us from buying the drug.

My perversions and financial stress stockpiled in my consciousness and compounded with each drug episode. I was on the verge of total collapse—in every way imaginable. Human morality was nonexistent in my life. I cared for one thing and one thing only—the high and rush from the drugs and the distorted sexual escapades that took place. I didn't even *know* how much trouble we were in, numbed by the massive amounts of drugs and alcohol. It was a grim moment not only in our marriage but also in our lives, and something had to be done.

I decided I had to leave Louise for good to stop the dangerous course our lives were taking. I determined to go back to Mary, the mother of my second daughter. I walked out and left.

Louise's father, mother, and stepfather assisted in caring for our children from the moment I left. She was never self-sufficient and couldn't care for them alone. Eventually, she sold the house and moved into an apartment with Rich, the guy she had had the affair with. She took our two kids, who were seven and eight years old at the time, with her. Louise had initially called off the relationship when I moved in with Mary, hoping I would return. But when she realized I wasn't coming back, she brought Rich back into her life again.

About a year into their re-established relationship, I overheard my daughter talking to her brother about Rich. She said he wasn't able to see his own daughter because of a restraining order. When I questioned her mother about the matter, she blew it off, saying his ex-wife was crazy and made up a bunch of stories. She said they lived in Florida anyway, and he wasn't able to see her to fight the legality of the issue. I wish I would've pursued it more.

CHAPTER NINE
~LIVING WITH MY MISTRESS~

Life back with Mary was glorious in this new beginning. I felt such intense love for her that I wanted to shout it to the world. My devils were calmed with her by my side, and we led a somewhat normal life for a while. Things got even better when Louise agreed to my taking the kids to Mary's house on weekends. But, oh ... the guilt I suffered for leaving my first two children for another family. And the financial hole I was in also took its toll on my sanity.

Once I'd settled in with Mary and our daughter, I'd ease the stress with small amounts of cocaine, going out for a few hours after work. I usually covered it up by telling her I was working late or going out for a few drinks with the guys. I would most often head to the strip club or local adult bookstore to get my kicks. The sabbaticals got longer. I started coming home in the early morning hours, lying about where I had been.

Mary would relentlessly call my cell phone trying to get through. I didn't care about anyone, anything, or who I was hurting. The only thing on my mind was satisfying the urge created almost thirty years before.

Within a few months, I began seeing one of the clerks from work. It didn't bother me that she was in a relationship, living with her fiancé and their daughter. I was hooked on the thrill that she'd join in on my perverted sexual desires, not worrying that I was destroying a family. I met her after work at hotel rooms with porn and acted out my sexual fantasies on her. She was younger than me and wanted to try new things. I took advantage of that.

I couldn't get enough. My cocaine use intensified. I'd go into the work safe and borrow money. I soon had amassed an IOU note for two thousand dollars ... this wanton expenditure *on top* of going through each paycheck. Following months of slithering in and out of these drug binges and erotic escapades, I had slipped back into the same disgraceful place where I had been before.

One night, I had a bad reaction to a batch of cocaine and was hospitalized with a kidney infection. Mary let the owner of my company know what had happened and told him I would not be coming back. She took care of me, continually offering support while I straightened out. I stopped seeing my sexual escapade partner from work.

About a month later, in the spring of 1999, I was hired as a Senior Project Accountant for a Manhattan-based construction management firm. I had presented the company with a power point presentation of all the past work I had implemented into the operations of the multimillion dollar financial exchange. Because I was being hired for the satellite office that was operating for the Manhattan-based firm, there was no human resource department to follow up on my prior experience. That lack of information worked to my great advantage and, with the strength of my presentation, they were extremely impressed. I was hired on the spot after my second interview. It was a high-paying job at eighty thousand a year, plus they reimbursed me for travel expenses to and from work. I started to feel respectable again; my relationship with Mary recovered and was back to where it was in the beginning. We purchased a three-bedroom townhouse closer to her family, a few miles from our old apartment.

Cash flow problems developed at work. Weekly travel expenses were delayed and then reimbursed in one large lump sum check. The best thing about it was that Mary had no knowledge of the payment I'd receive for travel expenses. I had done well combating demonic temptations and staying the course of normal domestic living, but when I realized I would be getting a check for three thousand dollars, I caved in. I conspired to have my day out—and planned for it in detail—the night before I received the pay.

I notified my cocaine contact that I would need a large amount to be sure he'd have enough for me when I got there. It was like the night before Christmas when I was a kid. And the secrecy was a macabre, delicious intoxication. Mary couldn't know about the money.

I set out the next day to put my plan in motion. I purchased eight hundred dollars of cocaine, twenty-five Valiums, and a half dozen Viagra. From there, I went straight to the adult book store, purchasing large quantities of porn magazines, DVDs, toys, lingerie, and whatever else I could get my hands on. I proceeded to a hotel that showed adult movies and had a strip club attached. I sped like a maniac to get there, sure my heart was going to beat out of my chest.

When I arrived, I hurriedly changed into comfortable loose-fitting sweat pants. I wanted the strippers at the club to feel my penis as they rubbed against it during the lap dances. I snorted a line of coke, and the erotic rush enveloped me. I set up my laptop and inserted a porn movie, while another one was playing on the hotel TV. I laid out half a dozen magazines across the bed and stroked myself up and down. When the cocaine took full effect, I picked up my cell phone and called a sex line, playing out a fantasy with the person on the other line. Midway through the call I hung up, walked to the strip club, and acted out my sick chimeras with the strippers.

Five hundred dollars later, I left the club and walked around the shadowy, dirty hallways of the motel—looking for someone to party with. I found a street prostitute hanging around, and she accepted my invitation. I convinced her to wear the lingerie I purchased earlier and began to speak obscenities to her as if we were in a porn scene. We snorted coke off each other's private parts as we got higher and higher. I'd never been this excited in my life. With a woman of no morals, I could be one hundred percent comfortable saying and doing anything. I repeatedly had her humiliate me verbally as we watched and commented on the porn actors. Sick, scandalous, sexual fantasies overcame me as I asked her to get another guy and let me watch. I was getting delusional while snorting more cocaine. I had orgasm after orgasm. The Viagra kept my penis hard through the whole event. There wasn't a sexual act I wouldn't perform at that moment.

When the other man arrived, we partied together and the two started to get it on. His phallus was immense. The prostitute seemed to be in pain as he drove himself into her with relentless vigor. I commanded her to denigrate me by saying how massive and manlier the other guy was as he pounded himself in and out of her. I'd had such a multitude of orgasms that my body could no longer produce semen.

We started running low on coke. I had fifteen hundred dollars left. The three of us stopped what we were doing and hit the streets of Camden, New Jersey, to buy more drugs. This was a nightmare. I parked at the corner, dropping the prostitute and her companion off to do the buy. The dealer's lookouts surrounded my car. They would've mugged me if my two sex partners hadn't come to my rescue, telling the thugs, "Hey, it's cool. He's with us."

We bought a thousand dollars of crack cocaine and headed back to the hotel room with one more prostitute, who brought even more coke. We performed every imaginable sex act on each other while we watched sex movies. I even talked on the sex line during the acts. This went on for almost another twenty-four hours. I finally passed out from exhaustion.

When I awoke hours later, depression slammed me with the weight and force of a fifty megaton bomb. My heart was pounding. I was dripping sweat. Panic and anxiety gripped me, paralyzing me in the wet, sex-stained bed. The smell in the air was of something evil and satanic. I wondered, What in the hell have I done? Then I knew. I had taken my despicable disease to the greatest heights ever, vaulting the compulsive, stigmatic remorse and self-loathing with an exponential increase. I'd set a new, deadly high precedent in my need for adulterated carnal indulgence.

Fear overtook me as I realized Mary and I were probably through. How could I commit such an atrocity against her? She was everything to me. We had it all, a good relationship, great communication, friendship, and a beautiful daughter. There was intimacy and normalcy with a more traditional sex life between us. I adored and exalted the terrain where she treads.

And how could I hurt my baby girl? She could put me in a trance when she looked up at me with those wild silver eyes. It sickened me to think I was also jeopardizing my life with Jennifer.

No! I trembled with the stark-raving mad thought. This cannot be happening ... this is *not who I am*. I grabbed my aching head, grimacing under the pressure of not knowing ... *what was I missing*? I returned home begging for mercy. After my morose confession, I made a feeble but hopeful attempt for mercy by divulging to her the truth of my sordid childhood experience. Hands wringing, shifting my weight from side to side like a kid who's been bad, deserving, but so dreading a spanking, I stumbled through it.

"I've never been able to tell you this before ... I ... ahm ... haven't told anyone. I ... uh ... was ... uh ... sexually abused by my priest when I was ten." I looked down at the floor. Tears welled in my eyes. I partially covered my face with my hand. "I can't control myself. My past keeps pulling me back." Blinking away the tears, I dared to look into Mary's steely glare. "I love you and Jennifer. I don't know why I do these things to hurt you. I want a normal family life."

Mary sighed, shaking her head. "Oh, Marco. I can't begin to tell you how badly you've hurt me. I'm sorry that you had to go through such an atrocity." She took a deep breath. "But it doesn't take away the pain you've caused our family. I *do* love you. I want a normal family life, too. I'll do what I can to get you ... and us ... the proper help to make this relationship work." I took her in my arms and held tight, whimpering into her shoulder.

Once again, Mary proved what an exemplary woman she was. She forgave me, took me back, and worked diligently to find me some help. She set up a meeting with my stepfather shortly thereafter. I confessed to my having used cocaine and divulged my having been sexually abused. She hoped that my stepfather would rally the family together for support. Her assumption couldn't have been more wrong. There was a cold and uncaring expression on his face. Nothing was a big deal to him. No benefit came from the meeting, and the abuse was never brought up again.

Mary set up an individual therapy session once a week. I didn't care much for the therapist, and I stopped going after a two meetings.

A couple of months later, when our life was back on track, I started to get that familiar desire again. I couldn't control myself. The devil within was ripping and tearing me apart inside, struggling to be released. I tried to fight it. But, no way, it was too powerful. I knew perfectly well where those desires had taken me before, but I didn't care. It didn't matter to me if I lost the woman I loved, my children, or my home. My mind and body were no longer under my control.

Mary had taken charge of our finances after I came close to wiping out the bank account, leaving me with little money. I was only able to get a couple twenty-dollar bags before heading to the local peepshows. Two hours later, she knew something was wrong and came looking for me.

She found me, I confessed to her, and she again gave me yet another chance. This time she tried getting me help at *Cocaine Anonymous*, thinking that was the problem. For about a month she carted me around to different meetings for fear I wouldn't go or maybe slip off on another sabbatical. Something wasn't right at the meetings. This wasn't the place I needed to be. After two months, I stopped attending.

This same vicious cycle went on for two years. I even stayed out without coming home two nights before the due date of our second child, a son. I would be the normal hardworking good-hearted father who loved his girlfriend and children more than anything in the world. Then the sinister element would come over me, controlling my ability to combat and defend against the evil desires that lurked within my subconscious.

With the intense perverted precedent I had set with my last major event, these little episodes of sneaking off for a couple of hours with a twenty-dollar bag were Sunday school in comparison. My desire to be satisfied was not being met; the fire and anxiety within were building and building.

I caused my girlfriend immense pain. She pulled me from strip clubs on New Year's Eve when we'd had our own plans. She'd locate me at hotel rooms and take me home. She followed everywhere I went. She took me to meetings, psychiatric evaluations, hospitals, and couple's therapy. Nothing she tried prevailed over my lurid, perverse addictions.

CHAPTER TEN
~UNCONTROLLABLE ADDICTIONS~

In the year 2000, my company was closing their satellite offices in Philadelphia and Atlantic City and I was let go. I had two months to find another job. I had received a phone call from a recruiter for a position as a controller for a Manhattan-based construction management firm, which I accepted.

It was an excellent job for me, one that I felt like I was born to have. The pay was great. I started out at a hundred four thousand dollars annual salary plus a five hundred dollar monthly auto expense, a ten percent bonus on my base salary after ninety days, and a year-end performance bonus. In addition, Manhattan was a different world. It was like Disneyland to me. I felt like I'd made it big and was again someone important.

When I returned to the cyclical phase of living a healthy, domestic life committed to my family and career, it once more gave me the deceptive impression that my life was going well. The birth of my fourth child, a son named Brandon, a successful career, and the love of the sincere, caring woman I had, provided a life that a lot of people imagine only in fantasies. Alas, as was the case many times before, that was about to change.

I was continuously fighting such an unlimited amount of anxiety and addictive urges that it was like trying to contain infinite energy in a limited space. From the moment I awoke until the moment I went to sleep, I struggled — wobbling, but for some time managing to catch myself, not falling off the tight, straight path.

I slipped. As before, I stayed out all night partying and having sex with an employee from work. When I arrived home my stuff was packed. I was told to leave. Mary had had it this time. I didn't beg as usual. I was still high, and had been invited by the girl from work to come to her place for the weekend anyway, so ... I left. On the July Fourth weekend in 2001, I headed to the Hamptons. We partied for four days there and then went back to her apartment in the city to stay.

Upon sobering up, I missed my family life with Mary. She had always taken in my two older children each weekend and made us a family unit. We would have fun apple picking in the fall, sledding and ice skating in the winter. In the summer we would frequent a local waterslide park and the Philadelphia Zoo. Repeatedly, I called her. She eventually let me come home. Yes, once again.

Daily living with their mother was not as stable and domesticated for Julian and Angel as it was when they spent their weekends with Mary and me. Even though Louise was trying hard and had been doing her best, she still retained residual amounts of bad habits we had developed when together. Eventually her addictions grew once again to problematic proportions. They became intolerable for the rest of her family to handle, and they had her admitted into an intense eight-month live-in rehab facility in a rough area of New Brunswick, New Jersey.

When she got out, she showed signs of improvement, staying sober for a time. But she had fallen in love with a guy named Rocco while in rehab and brought him into the children's lives. Turned out he had a rap sheet as thick as a cosmopolitan phone book. He was soon back in trouble with the law and sentenced to five years in prison for robbery.

After he was sent to jail, Louise became incoherently intoxicated almost every day. Some family members feared she had been involved in the robberies, too. Then she was arrested while driving under the influence of alcohol.

The family threatened to report her to the Division of Youth and Family Services if she didn't agree to give up custody of the kids. Julian, who was twelve at the time, went to live with his Aunt Donna and Uncle Lawrence. Angel, who was eleven, went to live with her grandmother.

As was typical, my relationship with Mary recovered and things were going well. I was working in a building in Manhattan at 33rd and Park Avenue when the planes hit the World Trade Center Towers on September 11, 2001. I watched the Towers collapse from my office window. I recall seeing ash-covered faces filled with shock and the somberness of the situation as we evacuated our building.

That tragic event appeared to strengthen my relationship with Mary. The worry and love she expressed on that day cemented in me the realization of just how extraordinary she was. I committed then to getting help with my problems—for fear of losing her. Upon advice from my sister, I went to a doctor to be put on anti-depressants. This was the first step in seeking aid through prescription medication for my problems.

My newfound determination was as short lived as all the other attempts. The monster inside was restaging its ongoing rioting to be freed and go wild. I fought hard to hold it in. It felt like there were good and evil personalities inside of me grappling for possession of my soul. In addition to the narcotic-based anti-depressants, I started using alcohol in combination with them to numb my nerves and bring me down. One pill led to two, then to four, then eventually handfuls at a time. This process of drinking and taking street drugs in combination with the narcotic anti-depressants put me in a nightly comatose state.

Mary was justifiably disgusted. I was good for nothing and only taking up space. The only life we had together entailed me getting wasted and passing out, with her worrying if I would overdose or when my next binge would occur. It was wearing her down mentally and physically. I tried again to straighten out my act and stop with the narcotics and drinking. But the pain from the past was overpowering; I couldn't stop.

The urges would always overcome me. I was merciless under their power. Like a madman possessed by an evil spirit, I had to satisfy the desires and urges. I went back to the hotel with the strip club. I did everything like before and then some. I relentlessly attempted to set a new precedent. I purchased mass quantities of drugs, porn, sex-line services, and prostitutes. The binge only came to a crashing halt when every credit card was maxed out, and our bank account was drained.

But I was still not satisfied. Panic took over. I combed every nook and cranny of the hotel room looking for anything that resembled a rock. I found old broken crack pipes and tried to smoke the residue. Finding other people's old coke and crack bags that were thrown under the bed and behind the night stands, I put them in my mouth trying to get high on the little bit of residue left inside. I was even willing to sell myself for sex. I half-heartedly tried, but fortunately failed. I eventually passed out and woke up sometime later.

I returned home, and ... something wasn't right. Mary wasn't that upset. It was as if she was expecting it. Disgust and hatred was on her face rather than the "I love you and how could you hurt me like this" look. She'd obviously had enough, but still attempted to get me help while she decided what to do with me. She admitted me into an outpatient drug program mainly for people on parole or under lenient incarceration for a couple weeks. I wasn't allowed to sleep in our bed or even attempt to talk reconciliation.

Finally, she made me leave. The memory of my young daughter, Jennifer, crying hysterically as I packed to leave is, and will be, permanently etched in my mind till the day I die. I still get sick to my stomach thinking about her pale and pure facial skin irritated from the stream of tears running down her puffy red cheeks, her light brown hair tangled in knots. Gripping the stair railings with her face sandwiched in between, she screamed, "Don't leave me, Daddy." I was packing my things in the basement as she continued, "Please don't leave. I love you and I don't want you to go." She ran upstairs crying, "Mommy, please help. Don't let him go."

Brandon was a year and a half at this time. He slid his chubby body down the stairs, waddling over to me. Gazing up at me with his tearful brown eyes, he reached for me to pick him up. I stroked his thick brown mop. "It's going to be alright," I said, trying to convince myself. "I love you."

How could I have hurt my beloved babies? The pain was monstrous. I knew that I'd irrevocably lost the woman of my highest hopes, my best friend, soul mate, and lover. But most of all, I lost the everyday life with my children.

There had been occasions, during the time with Mary, when I would leave and go back to my wife. She had many times, I thought in emotional agony, put up with me and taken me back. Not anymore. Now she was gone for good.

CHAPTER ELEVEN
~TEMPTATIONS IN THE CITY~

I packed up my belongings and moved to Manhattan with my brother at 23rd Street and 3rd Avenue. The two adversarial personalities residing within were tearing at me more than ever. The so-called 'good' one was in tremendous pain, yearning for my family life; the evil one was loving being single in Manhattan with a six-figure income.

My job was the only outlet I had to maintain my sanity and make me feel important. The irresponsible junkie in me continued to ebb and flow in and out of my life. It was the overachiever part that enabled me for the time being to continue to retain my high-standing employment status.

I continued to live with my brother for six months. I went out every night drinking and smoking pot, but kept away from the hard stuff.

My morale was at an abysmal depth. I started seeing one of my employees, another married woman who had a young daughter. When I received my yearly bonus from work, I moved into a place in the East Village near Washington Square Park. My immoral escapades began escalating at an extremely rapid and dangerous pace.

I tried to keep things under control, but negative triggers surrounded me. I had six or seven adult stores near my apartment door. There were bars and clubs everywhere. Drug-infested Washington Square Park was within one block. To make matters worse, there was a contact number I could beep and have a backpack of goods delivered to my door. Cocaine, ecstasy, pot, and pills were at my disposal any time of day, every day.

I could work hard, behave normally, and even go to church for three to four weeks at a time. But the compulsions would then overwhelm me with such force that I'd drop everything in life to satisfy them. I'd make the call and get anything and everything I wanted, many times spending a quick thousand. I'd comb the adult shops looking for a female to take home with the five hundred dollars in pornographic material I'd purchase.

Upon finding someone, we'd go to the apartment, and I'd call the oriental escort service, requesting one or maybe two escorts at a time for four or five hours while constantly on a sex line. I'd call the couples line and invite multiple partners. Each event became more abhorrent than the prior one. The day after each episode, my disgust, remorse, and sense of depravity was dreadful. I wanted to die. I would immediately throw out all the porn and head to the local priest to be consoled.

From there, I'd work twelve-hour days, seven days a week, going above and beyond what my position entailed to make up for the three or four days I missed because of the binge. I tried to ease the pain and shame of my actions, going to the gym, seeing my children on weekends, and handing out breakfast to the homeless. I continued in this vicious cycle: repeatedly attempting to bring the good in me to lasting fruition, but after another whole of trying, and always losing, I realized it was futile.

During that year, I had started seeing a psychiatrist to monitor my medication and a psychologist for therapy. My anxiety and depression became progressively worse as the months went on. The variety and quantities of medications prescribed to me during the course of the year reached staggering levels. I was on a combination cocktail of a variety of anti-depressants, anti-psychotics, mood stabilizers, sleep aids, and narcotics which included 60 mg of Valium a day. I was lucky if a month's supply of a hundred eighty Valiums lasted me two weeks—a deadly combination!

I was terminated from my job in October, 2003, after going on another three-day binge. I hadn't contacted the company because I was high on coke, unable to speak coherently. I wasn't fired because of poor performance; it was due to a lack of respect to my employer. I had an excellent performance evaluation and was considered valuable in running the operations for the company's half-a-billion-dollar annual revenue. The CFO called me into his office the day after my last binge and lectured me on my absenteeism, informing me I'd be held responsible for every mistake my project accountants had made during my irresponsible hiatus.

Being brain dead and still in a fog from the massive quantities of cocaine and pills, I became irate with a pompous attitude. I had the cocky audacity to think I was indispensable. I had designed, and improved upon, every system that was in place. I had written a hundred-page accounting procedure and software instructional manual that was the bible of the accounting department. I had current real-time numbers on any given day for every project's work in progress, billings, receivables, and payables. I had designed audit packages that supplied a reconciliation of the project's general ledger. I was known as a person who got the job done and was approached with every type of accounting problem to solve.

Didn't matter. All these accomplishments and hard work I'd put into this company meant nothing compared to the disrespect I showed.

"I've worked hard," I said. "I've accomplished great things for this firm."

"You've shown no respect."

"If you continue to treat me like this, I'm going elsewhere."

My boss leaned forward with a grim face and directed a forefinger at me. "You're fired!"

In shock, and sickened by what had occurred, I turned completely white—like a Looney Toon cartoon character seeing a ghost. Fear and panic overtook me. I blacked out for a second, and ... then went ballistic, having to be escorted from the office by security. I could hardly catch my breath. I was dizzy and struggled to keep from passing out.

Once outside, I called my psychiatrist. He agreed to see me on an emergency basis. I rushed to his office. He sedated me and called my therapist to set up another crisis appointment. After seeing the therapist, the local priest gave me additional counsel. I finally was able, by nightfall, to calm down and sleep that night.

CHAPTER TWELVE
~BREAKDOWN~

When I awoke the next morning, I was worse off than before. In shock, my entire universe crumbled to bits. I was at the beginning point of a breakdown, haunted by the thirty years of holding the abuse inside. The disgrace and humiliation for reprehensible actions and sins held a sturdy fortress within me.

I was in agony over losing Mary and the family I had with her. My mind flashed with scenes of leaving my second family. The mother of my two youngest and I had never married, but our life together as a family had been remarkably peaceful and loving. She had been a strong and stable mother and life partner.

I was in New York having my own breakdown. My career was threatened, sending me into a state of hopelessness and panic. Suicidal thoughts ravaged through my mind. My immediate reaction was to go out, buy a six-pack, smoke a joint, down 120 mg of Valium with a handful of Seroquel and Trazodone, slowly slipping out of what was left of my right mind. From what I can recall, I would repeat this cycle of waking up and sedating myself for the next seven days.

I stopped and tried to recoup from the chaotic mess I had created. I filed for unemployment and started submitting my resume to the various headhunters throughout the city. I went on a few interviews but was unable to function properly.

Something wasn't right. I had difficulty reading and putting simple syllables together. I frequently lost my train of thought. Feelings of fear, anxiety, depression, panic, nervousness, embarrassment constantly occupied my beleaguered body and mind. Numerous plans ran through my mind on how I would end my life. I was in a hopeless position, more desperate than anything I'd thought bearable.

But things just kept getting worse. I began to run out of money. Fortunately, my company had given me a thirteen-week severance package, netting me approximately twenty-one thousand dollars. In addition, I cashed in my 401K for fifteen thousand dollars. My attitude began to improve knowing I had thirty-six thousand dollars, plus unemployment to hold me over until I secured a position. I began interviewing intensely, trying to straighten myself out, but the difficulty with my thinking and verbal skills continued. I was discouraged to the point of being broken in half, devoid of any willpower to continue to strive to achieve goodness.

Then the demon inside me broke loose—released with a furious vengeance. I went through thirty-five thousand dollars in a few weeks, partying with prostitutes, purchasing mass quantities of drugs and porn. I performed every sexual fantasia I could dream up with these harlots of the night. I elevated my debauchery to hellacious new heights, each session outdoing the last. This went on as long as I had the money to fuel the flames of hell I was relishing rotting in. I proceeded to set a new precedent in perversion with each session. When the money was depleted? So was I. I proceeded to set a new precedent in perversion with each session. Wretched and despondent, I put my pride aside and called my stepfather, whom I hadn't spoken to in two years. He wasn't happy, but he accepted me back into his house.

This period was grossly humiliating. Forty years old, and I had to depend on someone else for support. It was like I was a teenage kid again, having to abide by certain rules and regulations, constantly under stress and pressure to get my show in shape. My stepfather had no idea or understanding what I was going through. He thought it was nothing deeper than a typical drug problem.

For the first two months, I tried to go cold turkey off not only the illegal drugs but also the psychiatric medications. I basically laid in a fetal position twenty-four hours a day, a complete mess. I was afraid of everything and anything, having no hope or desire to live. Struggling to act normally when my stepfather was present, I tried to not lose it, fighting with every last bit of life in me.

To appease my stepfather, I looked for a job, although I had no right at that time to enter the work force. Scoring an interview for a controller position with a payroll company, I was stricken with paralyzing fear the night before. With little experience in doing payroll, I knew I wasn't qualified for the position.

During the interview, I kept my words to a minimum. The owner of the company called back later in the day.

"We're very impressed with you, Marco," she said. "We'd like you to come in for a second interview with my partner."

I went in the next day, trying again to keep my words to a minimum. They gave me the job. My former employer at the financial exchange had told them I was amazing. I couldn't fathom it. This was the same owner I'd hurt by taking a two thousand dollar note from his safe. I was responsible for his best clerk quitting, after screwing and acting out my sexual fantasies on her. Not able to function on the job, it lasted only three days, and I was let go.

My stepfather was furious that the job ended so quickly. "You have to toughen up," he lectured. "You're going to work in the deli."

The whole time working at the deli I was in a panic state, mortified to be around people. I admitted myself into the crisis center at the local hospital.

I don't recall much of that experience, but upon reviewing my medical documents, I know I was there for a week. Going back on psychiatric meds, I entered into a short-term, two-week outpatient therapy program with medication monitoring. My bearings came back toward the end of the program.

Then it was on to a long-term, five-days-a-week behavioral health outpatient course. I stayed in that for a year.

My attitude during this stretch was discouraging. I had no fight in me anymore. On autopilot, going through the motions, suicidal thoughts continuously played out in my mind.

The therapists worked on my cognitive skills to suppress my emotions, while the psychiatrists experimented with different combinations of medication cocktails, hoping something would click to snap me from the funk I was in. Nothing worked. They were dealing with the symptoms—not the fundamental disease itself.

Unable to work, I had to go on General Assistance and Food Stamps to pay my stepfather for rent and car insurance. My will to exist on this planet was diminishing with each passing moment. Nothing made sense to me. I had no happiness, no pride, and no love. Life was black and white—my existence one of darkness.

Little things I used to appreciate meant nothing anymore. Simple pleasures like a good song or movie, a fine meal, working out, or a nice crisp sunny morning didn't stimulate any emotion. Depression and anxiety were my mind's constant occupants. Even the priceless brief moments with my four children—whom I adored and loved—became a task, rather than enjoyable. I feared I was going to be in this anguish for the rest of my life.

I let my body go to waste. I couldn't find the strength or motivation to drag myself to the gym. The medications diverted my energy. I habitually gorged myself, packing on the pounds. I wanted life to end. But I couldn't find the nerve to end it. Something deep inside prevented me from committing the act.

My mental state of colossal anxiety declined even more. Alone with my stepfather, I'd pace the entire length of the house all day, pausing to sit for a minute and then back to pacing. While sitting, I'd either rock back and forth or bounce my leg up and down. When alone, I heard muffled voices from a distance, causing me to search the house for a TV left on. I was in a constant panic and paranoid state with no drive or desire. I prayed without ceasing for death.

One night, after taking a half dozen Valiums and smoking a joint, I decided to take a ride. I got an urge for a drink and stopped at what I thought was a secluded bar. It was like I was a magnet for attracting the dark side. A couple sat at the bar partying with a girlfriend of theirs.

They bought me drinks, one after the other.

As we played a game of couple's pool, the couple's girlfriend got extremely friendly with me. By the end of the night, they scored bags of cocaine and crack in the streets of Camden, New Jersey, and we spent a night of wild, twisted sex with each other in a sleazy hotel showing porn movies. My idea, of course.

While high, committing these debased sex acts, a numbing feeling of ecstasy came over me. I wasn't feeling depressed or anxious anymore. My addiction to drugs and carnal perversion was reactivated and on high. Convinced that this was what I needed to survive, I started seeing this girl.

We acted out my erotic fantasies while inhaling cocaine or smoking crack, viewing and using every piece of triple X material the adult bookstore carried. I soon became as obsessed as ever, needing the drugs and sex constantly. The level of licentiousness I craved and took it to was too much for her, and ... she stopped dating me.

I kept up the debauchery, solo, spending nights at dirty motel rooms, getting crack and porn. I still worked at my stepfather's deli where I'd cash in my food stamps, use my general assistance money, and max out all my existing credit cards. When that money ran out, I started taking money from the deli. Now, on top of everything else, I had to carry the remorse and dishonor of having become a thief.

At this point in my life, I was a mental cadaver. I was only a functioning body of mass, breathing air and consuming space. No normal human emotions existed in the brain-deadened state of mind I was in.

It was fortunate for me to be in this state of numbness, only in that during this phase of my life I had to bear the loss of Nanny and Poppy — my true parents, best friends, and childhood saviors. These two were the only ones who had provided me pleasant, innocent, and wholesome memories as a youngster. They alone had given my abusive-possessed soul a break, with nights of tea, pound cake, and Sunday matinees.

Nanny had become demented and broke her hip, needing special attention. Poppy was there for her, as always, through their many challenges. My mind vaguely remembers their deaths. I recall only that they died within a short period of time of each other. Nanny first from complications developed from Alzheimer's disease, and Poppy of a broken heart. Poppy, being the spunky character that he was, had still driven and gambled on the horse races every day, right up to the end, or ... at least until he lost Nanny. That killed not only his spunk; it killed him. He died in his sleep at the well-mellowed age of ninety-five.

On the home front, my stepfather was emotionally killing me. Every look, every comment, was derogatory and demeaning. I did the best I could to keep his humiliating comments at bay, and tried whatever I could do at the deli to prove to him I wasn't the piece of shit he thought I was. Sure, I was stealing from the deli, but I justified it by overextending myself—I kept the deli immaculate. At home, I'd clean the house and do laundry until the skin on my fingers was wrinkled and stung from the cleaning agents.

He'd explode, screaming at me in a fury, "You're a weak fuckin' loser!"

My stepfather was always crude and vulgar, involving sexual acts in discussions. His social skills were mainly motivated by sexual innuendoes. Throughout my childhood, he maintained a collection of *Playboy* magazines, frequently bragging about his extramarital affairs. He tried to maintain the macho image with the "comare," an Italian slang for mistress. Even in front of his children, following our mother's death, when in a drunken state he'd boast of getting blow jobs from various women.

He'd order free samples of KY jelly packets, which amounted to a couple of droplets. You could only get one per household. He'd put different mailing addresses of friends, family, and the deli to receive as many as possible. I was working in the deli one day when the sample came in. Thinking it was nothing but junk mail, I threw it away.

"Did a pack of KY jelly come in?" he said one day.

"I may have thrown it away," I said, shrugging my shoulders.

Getting right in my face, he shrieked, "You what? You're a fuckin' idiot! How can you be that *stupid*."

After taking a few more of his obscenities, I blew up and jumped him. We fell to the floor fighting each other.

"Get the fuck out of my house and never come back," he screamed with—I could swear—steam spouting from his ears.

CHAPTER THIRTEEN
~ROCK BOTTOM~

My mind screamed with mortification. Satanic images scarred my soul. Descriptive pictures of murkiness, death and decay occupied my every waking moment. Physically exhausted and submerged in addiction to drugs and sex, thinking I needed them to exist, I stormed out of the house following the fight. I proceeded to extinguish the flames that possessed my soul the only way I knew how, by inebriating myself with mass quantities of drugs and unloving, gratuitous sex. This led to my consummate immoral escapade, and I had my final breakdown on April 30, 2005.

The following day, my thoughts raced through the prior day's events. Then I relived the night's humiliating, perverted and self-abusive actions. My God! Something's terribly wrong. There seemed to be some disconnect in my nervous system—like an electrical wire had been frayed, preventing the current from reaching its destination. When I realized what was happening to my simple motor skills and thoughts, I started to tremble with trepidation.

I stumbled into things, somehow making my way to the mental behavioral outpatient facility I attended five days a week. My dire state was obvious as soon as I walked in. One of the therapists saw that I was in crisis, and frantically rushed me into her office. "Sit," she commanded, leading me to the couch. Hurriedly, she patted my forehead with a cold compress and a sip of water. "What's wrong?" she said, gently wiping the stream of tears flowing from my eyes with a tissue from the box on her desk.

I was quaking, hysterical. "I'm such a piece of shit. I'll never get out of this hole," I said, shaking my head and looking at the floor. "I'm hooked on drugs, sexual humiliation, porn ... you name it. I'm the lowest form of animal in existence. I'm a quarter million in debt. I owe back child support, the IRS, state taxes, credit cards, auto loans, utilities, welfare, Medicare. And my family! I worked hard for my career, and I ruined it! I'm worthless! I'm never getting my career back. Really blew that one. How could I work this hard and lose it all?" Through a flood of tears, I looked up into the therapist's concerned eyes.

"I'm homeless, on food stamps and Medicare," I wailed, putting my head down into my hands. Suddenly I shot upright. "Look at me. I'm an obese two hundred forty pounds from the effects of all the psychiatric medications I'm taking. I was an athlete and bodybuilder with single-digit body fat!" I sat back down and cried, uncontrolled, miserable. "I lost the woman of my dreams. I have no relationship with my children."

I grabbed my head so hard my knuckles whitened, wincing from the mental anguish. "I love them *so much*. I don't deserve to be alive."

The therapist bolted out of her chair and made a phone call. Before I knew it, I was transported from the outpatient facility to the emergency crisis center at the local hospital. I was admitted for the second time in a year.

Much of my time in this facility is a blur. But I was there for four weeks, until I was transferred to a long-term treatment facility. The list of medications I was on before and during my hospitalization—all used in an attempt to stabilize me—was mind-boggling: Ativan, Depakote, Effexor XR, Lemectle, Remron, Risperdal, Seroquel, Trazodone, Thorazine, Valium, and Zyprexa.

I was discharged from the crisis center and transferred to a Mentally Ill Chemically Addicted (MICA) unit at a nearby psychiatric facility. With the exception of my current therapist, this was my thirteenth facility/treatment for anxiety, depression, and or drug use over the past three years.

At the time of my transfer there was no vacancy in the MICA program. As a result, I was admitted to the "South Wing," which housed many of the mentally ill patients. For nearly two weeks I lived in undiluted hell.

Pure dread and terror enslaved me. I felt paralyzed with every gram of energy siphoned from my body. During the day, I was full of distress and heavily medicated on Valium and Thorazine. I walked around catching myself drooling at times—in a trance like some zombie in a cheap horror flick. I prayed for nightfall so I could be sedated and escape the nightmare.

There was insanity all around me. I was literally run over by orderlies in their attempt to apprehend an out of control patient. Patients were screaming as they were strapped down and left in the 'quiet room'. I had to watch where I walked and sat because of some patients' urges to defecate on the spot. One day, a meek and gentle individual was standing in front of me in the dinner line when another patient sucker punched him, knocking him unconscious—a common occurrence in this place.

My roommate had enormous amounts of anger and hatred. I was always on edge, having trouble sleeping for fear he'd attack me. There were times he would get up in the middle of the night and urinate between our beds.

The crying, the bizarre conversations with no one, the blank dead stares, the smell of human waste and decay can only be described as a near-*death* experience. Words can't explain this tragedy. This is something no one should have to experience. It was like I was watching a bad horror flick. The real me had checked out and was watching from a distance, similar to an out-of-body experience. I had slammed ground zero and was possibly at the point of no return.

When I was transferred to the MICA unit, it felt like I had been moved to a country club. Most of the patients were young kids hooked on heroine and needing guidance. Much of my time there was spent being weaned off the multitudes of medications; most of them way over the FDA recommended dosages. Doctors were shocked when reviewing my prescription chart. Because of the pain and problems of the past thirty years, I was hesitant and scared to be withdrawn from the medication.

For the first thirty days in the MICA unit things were pretty tough. I was basically on autopilot. My mind was not connected to my motor skills. Simple tasks like putting syllables together, reading, trying to guide a fork and spoon to my mouth without missing, even making it to the bathroom on time was as difficult as performing brain surgery.

Once the medications were dramatically reduced, I began to read and speak again. From there, I was able to hit a wiffle ball in the courtyard during recreation period. I progressed to nailing shots into the trashcan with a wadded piece of paper and focusing my eyesight on a list posted on a wall ten feet away. Having the capability of holding my urine in time to make it to the toilet made me feel like "The Man." Performing these tasks could be compared to being the most valuable player, scoring the winning touchdown of the Super Bowl with no time remaining, or hitting the winning home run in game seven of the World Series in the bottom of the ninth with two strikes and one out remaining.

On the down side, with my brain cells awakening from the coma came pain: worry, anxiety, fear, and loneliness. All my past problems came racing back, enveloping my psyche over and over like a skipping record. Even though I was an emotional wreck again, some internal force refused to slip back into the comatose/autopilot state I was living in for the past few years.

On July 8, 2005, sixty-nine days later, I was released back into society. With no money and little more than the clothes on my back, I was elected into an Oxford House, a democratically run, self-supporting, and drug-free home maintained by fellow addicts. Each occupant held a responsible position in running the operations of the residence. In addition to staying clean, strict rules and regulations had to be followed in order to stay there.

The first day I was petrified and nervous, forcing myself to function as normal as possible. It was my first day going cold turkey off all medication. On the outside I may have seemed ordinary, but inside I was being torn apart by a barrage of negative emotions, wanting to be pacified with a fat line of cocaine and satisfied with a compilation of lurid sexual material. The next few months were a horrendous season of my life, which seemed extremely hopeless and not worth living. It was an incomprehensible hole of emptiness. I could've easily slipped back to where I was two and a half months earlier if it weren't for those people and Alcoholics Anonymous. I wrestled to maintain my composure over the next couple of months.

A few days after my discharge from the hospital, I got a job doing concrete work down the New Jersey Shore through the fellowship of AA. It was a tough transition from spending months in a hospital bed to breaking up concrete and digging footers in one hundred degree weather. The insects ate me alive. After work I'd go back to the house for a shower and a bite to eat. Then it was on to what the fellowship of AA calls, "The Herd," for various meetings.

During one of the meetings, I was engrossed in the story of another addict speaking that night. Tim was a funny and popular guy. Everyone in the room busted his chops throughout his speech, which he took very well. He gave it right back to his fellow constituents who had voted him to speak that night.

After the meeting, I stood alone in a corner waiting for one of my Oxford House roommates to give me a ride. Tim approached me with a goofy grin and gleeful manner. He was the first person to get me to crack a glimmer of a smile in a long time.

"Marco, do you have a sponsor?" he said.

Impressed that he remembered my name from the meeting's introductions, I shrugged my shoulders and said, "What's a sponsor?"

"Me, now," he said with a laugh.

This man provided me with the knowledge and foundation needed to build on my sobriety. And he added a little entertainment and humor along the way.

I have boundless gratitude for the people, especially Tim, and resources that were provided to me. I had been mentally dysfunctional and on the verge of suicide, addicted to a concoction of psychiatric medications and illegal drugs. I lost nearly everything and everyone in my life. I was physically on the threshold of a heart attack. Yet, I was fortunate to find the means to have a roof over my head, food in my stomach, an income, and support.

Toward the end of the summer, things were slow with the concrete work and, I wasn't needed anymore. The next day, out of the blue, came a carpenter's job paying more money. With the extra dollars, I bought some decent clothes, got my driver's license back, and interviewed for a position as a professional. But the job-hunting experience didn't go as fast as I hoped.

The economy had started to show signs of vulnerability as gas prices soared to record levels. Personnel with more impressive credentials now occupied the professional level I attained prior to my breakdown. The competition was fierce as I waited in line to be interviewed with people much more seasoned and overqualified for the hunted job described. I was now competing with people with Master Degrees and years of experience. Previously, my work ethic and merit would have landed me the job on the spot.

In September of 2005, I attended a religious retreat with the Matt Talbot group at the Men of Malvern campus in Malvern, Pennsylvania. Matt Talbot was a chronic alcoholic in the eighteen hundreds. He was put into a rehabilitation program, incorporating the Twelve Steps of Alcoholics Anonymous, with the help of a priest. He found sobriety through prayer and self-sacrifice. Reformed addicts continually campaign for his canonization with the Catholic Church. The retreat's purpose was to bring together fellow addicts in a spiritual environment to work on and strengthen their sobriety.

The campus was magnificent and peaceful. The serene landscape and rolling hills put my ever-running mind in first, instead of fifth, gear. There were winding nature trails throughout the tree-lined hillsides and deer frequently crossed my path. Throughout the trails were the Stations of the Cross with various sculptures similar to the Pieta, leading to the Grotto with a rolling stream and a statue of the Virgin Mary set in the valley of the hills. There were terraces and rest stops set high on the side of the hills to sit and relax, overlooking the enchanting view.

At night, the scenery changed from grand to spectacular. Soft lighting lit the pathways and artwork leading to the Grotto. Once reaching the main destination, my breath was spirited away at the sight of hundreds of candles illuminating the area. I knew this was truly a special place, natural and tranquil. It was the first time in years that I was focused on peace and beauty rather than gloom and hopelessness.

CHAPTER FOURTEEN
~THE ADMISSION~

It was a balmy fall evening, with a touch of crispness in the air. The leaves rustled in the light breeze. My sponsor, Tim, and I had finished dinner and an AA meeting. "Marco, how about we take a walk to the Grotto," he said.

I stood and stretched my arms in the air. "Sure, let's go."

We meandered down a well-lit path of one of the many trails that led to the Grotto in silence. Candles were aglow when we arrived, soft and soothing. We took a seat on a wooden bench in full view of the awesome sight.

My thoughts were not on the fabulous scenery. I shook my head and dropped it to my chest. "My life's been hopeless. Living like this isn't worth living. Will the feelings of confusion and pain ever leave me," I asked, looking up at Tim. "I'm weak and nervous. There's anxiety and fear. I'm going to die after living a miserable, lonely and impoverished life. I just—"

Tim shot a 'stop' hand in the air. "I felt the same way. I endured the pain of being sexually abused at a young age. I recovered and came to grips with it."

My body shook as he explained what happened. I couldn't contain the fire building inside. The more he talked, the more the demons of distress rustled and thrashed about in the murky abyss of my psyche. I couldn't take this. He kept going. I cannot—*he's still talking*—take it—*will you please, for God's sake, stop it?*—any longer!

I jumped from my seat in a fit of rage and glared at him. "I was *raped* by my parish priest!" I paused for a moment, my eyes like glazed-over saucers, my hand over my mouth, trying to make sense of what happened. I blew air, flopped my hands to my sides and sat. "Wow. This is the first time I ever said it to an outsider. It was thirty years ago," I said, putting my head in my hands as the visions of the abuse played out in my mind. I rocked back and forth. "I was only ten years old," I confessed with tears streaming down my face, reliving it all over again.

At the end of spewing out all the gory details, I stood up and said, "You know what? I have to go." I turned away and sprinted back to my dorm. One side of me asked how this could've happened to me and how the people in my life could have allowed it. But on the flip side, what a rush it was thinking about the porn and sex that I was made to believe was okay and normal. My heart throbbed in my chest. The urge for perverted sex returned, rearing its ugly, fanged head. The battle inside me raged on through the night. I had to keep telling myself that I was in a good place with the right people around me. Somehow I got through the evening with no incident. Most of the night was spent retching over the toilet.

The next day, Tim said, "How about talking to one of the priests here? Tell him what happened."

"Uh ... umm. Do you mean I should turn to the enemy for help?"

"Maybe it'll help."

"I'll think about."

Earlier, I had confided—while cataleptic—in priests only because, I now realized, I had been unwilling in the deepest recesses of my psyche to fully come to grips with reality: the harsh truth. The abuse I had suffered at the hands of Father McCool was the root cause of my scandalous, self-deprecating behaviors and latent death wishes.

In a *sense* I had known it, had intuited it, and I *had* briefly and tenuously mentioned it to my girlfriend and my stepfather before, but ... not with this kind of finality, this level of veracity as to its quintessential, core cause of my debased condition. And no sooner had I done that, and gotten nowhere with it, I had doubted it again as impossible—cast the wicked thought into the darkness of some remote prison cell deep in the recesses of my subconscious. In my conscious reality I could not entertain such a horrific notion and grant it credence for so much as a minute. I had kept it locked up, secreted away from even myself.

But now ... now that vigorous, impassioned vocal admission had brought to full, lasting light the nebulous, devilish thought ... And to think—believe, now—it was not only him, but also the other priests in the parish, who *had* to have known, and did nothing ...

Damn those bastards ... all of them. Just the *thought* of a cleric made me angry and quiver with affliction over what had been done to me.

Still, I knew I had to somehow get over it. Open to any help I could get, I decided—even though the rage within me screamed against it—to act on his suggestion and set up an appointment with a ... *a priest* ... for later in the afternoon. In my mind, I envisioned the sexual perversion and deception the priest's black cloth and white collar had represented to me since being a young boy. I shook off the repulsion and followed through on Tim's admonition and my promise to give it an honest, open-minded try.

In our session, I not only described the abuse, but also confessed the ensuing sins and wrong doings I had committed. He winced at each wave of descriptive sinful acts I had performed and all the people I had hurt. I broke down reliving the ugliness and insanity of not only the abuse but also the evilness that lived inside me.

"These events that happened to you, Marco, are not your fault," the priest said, holding back tears. "The person I see in front of me is not the wicked being that you're describing. You must report this to the authorities and contact the diocese where the abuse took place."

As I walked away, I realized I had now opened up and admitted the details of the abuse with two others, besides the mere mention of it to my girlfriend and stepfather. I had rarely been able to acknowledge it to myself for more than a passing and fast-dismissed notion. I could finally see with clarity that the derogatory opinions I had of myself were without a doubt due to the defilement. I struggled to hold onto the little glimpse of sanity I had left after reliving the threatening nightmares of my past. I kept to myself for the rest of the retreat.

CHAPTER FIFTEEN
~BEGINNING OF RECOVERY~

I hated living in the Oxford House, sharing my life with six other addicts. I detested the humiliation of bringing my children around, exposing them to my life in a halfway house. I despised living under house rules—being told how many meetings I had to attend each week, having to be in at a certain time, when to clean, cook, and shower. It was excruciating to be present in weekly house meetings where members of the household let their authority go to their heads. I felt inadequate that Louise's parents had to care for my children as well as their daughter, who was in and out of rehab and constantly on binges.

I was sick of people in the program quoting the principles of the *Big Book*. I wanted to scream when I heard, "But for the grace of God." What fucking grace had God given me? And don't get me started on the gratitude list. I had no gratitude. The distress and loneliness made me again consider ending my life. I thought the program was a trick to psychologically prevent me from slicing my wrists. Quotations like "Easy does it," "This shall too pass," "Thanks for sharing," "Keep coming back," did nothing for me but induce intestinal illness. Holding hands and watching people go out of their way to do anything and everything for me made me extremely uncomfortable.

I loathed the closeness and companionship of the people who were working hard for my benefit. The disgrace of not having my own form of transportation, career, dignity, and independence made me resent everything this horrible existence had to offer. I held these feelings inside and operated like a robot going through the motions of living.

I contemplated how to extinguish my mental anguish. Death is what first came to mind. I'd fantasize driving at a hundred miles an hour into a tree, taking a full bottle of Valium or Trazadone, or, better yet, taking a full bottle of *both* drugs and then doing it.

But something inside woke me up, convincing me there was a certain merit, some reason worth living for on this miserable planet. From there, my determination and drive to attain dignity and independence kicked in. I wanted to believe there truly was a good person inside. I wanted to find him.

Insidious images of relaxation flashed through my mind like bright pictures. It was as though all my tension was being released after inhaling a fat line of cocaine while watching porn. The excitement of reliving the act seemed so real that my heart palpitated erratically. I'd get furious with myself for even thinking about going back to that sinister part of my life.

When I returned to the Oxford House after the retreat, I was introduced to a local priest who was in the fellowship for treatment. When I first found out he was a priest, I couldn't stand the sight of him. It disgusted me that people gave him respect because he was a man of the cloth. The fellow addicts thought it was cool they had one of God's errant angels among them confessing his sins of addictions.

Little did anyone know what addictions and sins I was subjected to as a child from a similar 'fallen angel'. I couldn't bear sharing what had happened to me at the group AA meetings—too humiliating. I only shared the secret with a select few and requested it be kept confidential.

More than the special attention the priest received, I was overwhelmed with the eerie resemblance he had to my abuser. His pale freckled skin and strawberry-blond hair made me uncomfortable in his presence. I could feel my abuser's satanic touch when in the same room as that man.

But I was in a mechanical state, staying the course, hoping something miraculous would pull me out of my miring in the past. This perseverance contributed to being the turning point of my recovery, that being when I told him what had happened.

"What's the name of this priest, Marco?" Father Todd said. I told him. To which he replied, "He was arrested for molesting another boy, and he did some prison time."

"I did hear about that, Father," I said.

"You should go to the diocese. They'll appoint a therapist to you. I'll give you the contact names," he said, pulling out a pad of paper with all the information I'd need.

For three years, I had been to doctors, counselors, therapists, drug programs, AA, CA, NA, mental health facilities, and hospitals with no real solutions. I finally was sent to the source of my illness. I needed to go back to the Church for help.

I made the call. The liaison responsible for assigning counselors to clergy abuse victims gave me a list of therapists. Since I didn't have my own transportation, I had to choose one who was easily accessible by public transportation. There was one with an office a couple blocks from the rail line station next to the Oxford House. I took a chance with this counselor and hoped for the best.

The place was in the Historic District in Haddonfield, New Jersey. The building was old, but well preserved. I had to walk up two steep flights of stairs to reach his office. The waiting room had five chairs around two tables pushed together. Magazines were perfectly fanned out so each could be identified. My therapist was on the left of the waiting area; another therapist's practice was to the right. The room buzzed with distracting noise from the fast-food machines against the wall. No conversations could be heard from either office.

I arrived in plenty of time for my appointment. Nature called, and I entered the restroom through an old fashioned door that had a skeleton key lock. In the bathroom were a cast iron tub and a sink with fancy brass handles. I finished my business and went back to the waiting room. Looking over the magazine choices, I found one of interest. But just as I picked it up, I was called in. I neatly set the magazine back to its original place on the table, and stepped into my therapist's office.

I noticed the distinctive smell of Old Bay seasoning when I walked in. The shelves were stocked with books about every mental illness imaginable. Facing forward against the far wall next to a window there was a small antique desk with a phone and fax machine. Between the book shelves and the antique desk there was a door leading to a small kitchenette, where I assumed the Old Bay smell was coming from. On the wall to the right were another window and some potted plants.

After a perfunctory scoping out the room, my eyes focused on the man behind the desk. He was slender, with medium height. His hair was close to his scalp, but not completely shaved. He had a round face and wore wire-rimmed glasses. He was dressed business casual.

He held out his hand. "Hi, Marco. I'm Keith. It's nice to meet you."

I immediately felt relaxed. I reached out to shake his hand. "Nice to meet you, Keith."

"Take a seat wherever you like."

I looked around the room again, observing a small love seat angled in the corner between the desk and the window. On the opposite wall facing the desk were two captain's chairs angled towards each other with an end table between them. I always wondered if choosing any particular seat meant anything mentally or not. Nonetheless, I chose the roominess of the love seat.

Keith struck me as a very well-educated and humble individual. I analyzed his facial expressions while he processed the data I fed him. He came across as being very sincere. I was used to hearing, "Uh, huh. And then what? Okay, go on." My insensitive counselors of the past constantly watched the clock. Their egg timers seemed to ring up more interest in dollar signs than in helping me. Something was special with this one. I felt he believed in his profession and what it stood for. There was an energy there that I couldn't explain at the time. I entered into therapy with this man named Keith, reliving my past all over again.

I told him everything I'd been through and all the people I hurt, especially my precious children. "I've tried hard to suppress and forget what happened to me."

"You must understand, Marco, the shame you feel from the abuse contributed to the awful things you went through and did."

71

Keith verified and solidified the epiphany I'd had after exploding and blurting out to Tim. I knew it then, but ... maybe not for absolute sure? A haunting doubt had still lingered. Could this, in fact, be the truth? I sometimes wondered. His endorsement brought closure, release from nagging ambiguity. Memories from the past were brought to the surface and flushed out in the open. I became regenerated after years of self-medicating. I was furious—thinking that, as a result of the exploitation, my children and I were deprived the full potential that our lives had to offer. After being medically sedated for the past three years, I started to analyze logically and structurally my negative actions with the help of my therapist. I walked down the path of perversion, explaining it to Keith.

After helping me release all the anger I was holding, Keith said, "It'd be difficult to deal with what you have on your plate in a stable environment. This is going to sound tough," he said, taking a deep breath, "but, you still have to be responsible for your actions and pay the consequences as a human being. Even though none of what happened to you or what actions you took subsequent to your abuse was entirely your fault."

"How do I do that when things seem hopeless and unrepairable?"

"You do that by being content with life and living through your true self. The rest will fall in place."

I sensed that he had a game plan by the way he was forcing me to ask the questions rather than him explaining everything to me. "Who is the true self?"

"The true self is the person you were meant to be from the point of your existence. The true self is always good, coming from the energy of creation. That may sound deep, or way out there, but if you have patience, you'll eventually understand. Identify the true self. Use that element of your psyche to orchestrate the various destructive traits and emotions instead of having them instinctively do what they please. These qualities and feelings were developed as a defense against the abuse. The characteristics and emotions you established and are experiencing are the defender parts."

I nodded, slow, thoughtful. "Okay. What are the different defender parts of my psyche that were created as a defense to the abuse?"

Keith held up a finger. "Let's start with the striver part first. This works for perfection, thinking if perfection is reached, your self-image will be satisfied and at peace. This component is beneficial in the inspiration and motivation for reaching certain goals, but peace and satisfaction can never be obtained through this exhausting defensive strategy. When you're burned out from this part is when you're most susceptible to relapsing."

From there, I started to analyze my frustration. I identified and greeted the emotion. I'd ask myself what its purpose was and peel away the many feelings associated with the frustration to get to the root. I went straight to the core of the symptom. This was the part that was trying to get me back into the game of life. But the impatience of this feeling directed its energy the wrong way. Instead of systematically working to chip away at each problem, it was demanding the end result yesterday. This feeling was begging for direction, control, and stability.

From there I worked on my anxiety. What possible benefit could this personality trait play? How was this tireless emotion a defense against my abuse?

"What is the purpose of anxiety, Marco?" Keith said, peering over the top of his wire rims.

My mind went blank. For a moment I paused, thinking. I stroked my chin, looking down, then faced him with my answer. "Fear."

Keith raised an eyebrow and turned an open palm toward me. "Explain."

"The anxiety is instilling in me the impending doom I'd feel if I were to slip back into that ominous world of drugs and sexual perversions."

He appeared satisfied with that much understanding on my part for now and moved on. Depression was next on the list. I gazed into space, at first baffled by his prompting for my interpretation of its purpose. How could this emotion be a protection against the abuse or from the chaos in my life? I couldn't figure out how this emotion was a guardian for the abuse. Was it a reminder of where all the poor judgment and instinctive brainless actions had gotten me? Was it a reminder of all the quality time I missed with my children growing up? I concluded the depression was a psychological mechanism to remind me of the blessings and potential in life I had missed out on.

As I made progress in therapy, it crossed over to other facets of my life. I became interested in studying the meaning of the psyche.

There were glimpses of hope as people and circumstances created positive opportunities for me. My soul was rejuvenated with energetic motivation. I was able to methodically chip away the unresolved issues in my life and concentrate on what I needed to do to get my career back on track. After relentless interviewing and the ensuing progress made, I was finally able to secure an office position as a staff accountant for a state agency. Friends in the program bought me business attire. I put a little money away and was able to start paying my current child support and arrears. My children were now able to spend more time with me. My attitude toward life started to improve. I even cracked a smile on occasion. I now had hope. The demons still ripped at my inner being every day, but I was able to see the light through the slim break in the clouds. Maybe death wasn't the only answer.

CHAPTER SIXTEEN
~A CHANCE AT REDEMPTION~

During this positive transition period, Louise's family asked to get together with me to discuss the past seven years during which they had been primary care takers of Julian and Angel. I yearned for the opportunity to have my two older children living with me again. But I was still residing in the Oxford House with no transportation and nowhere near enough money.

Julian was now fourteen years old and Angel was thirteen. Their mother was in a drunken stupor most days, still addicted to alcohol and drugs. She was living in an apartment, barely able to make one end meet the other.

My prayers were answered when I came up with a solution.

Tim gave me a ride to my mother-in-law's house a couple weeks later. He waited out front. I approached the veranda and took a deep breath before tapping on the door.

"Marco! Thank you for coming," Louise's mother, Debbie, said. "Come in. Come in. It's good to see you." She pulled me close with a hug.

I stepped into the spacious living room where Louise and her family sat on the over-stuffed sofa and chairs. Louise's stepfather stood up and reached for a handshake. "Good to see you again, Marco."

"Thank you, Matthew. You, too."

Louise's sister, Donna, greeted me with a long embrace. "It's been way too long, Marco. Good to see you."

Donna's husband, Laurence, came up with a fist pump. "Hey, Marco. Nice to see you again."

I smiled. "Thanks for getting a hold of me."

Debbie patted the seat next to her. "Sit, Marco. Right here."

I sat, rubbing my hands together. Louise sat in the chair furthest away from me. She glared at me, shaking her head.

"Uh. Umm. I ... uh. I want to tell you how sorry I am for what I put you through as a family. You treated me as if I was your son, and I disappointed all of you. I'm grateful that you took in Julian and Angel during my absence." I paused, needing to divulge my shaming confession, not knowing how to, praying for the words and strength. Looking at the floor, I continued, slow and measured, "I don't want this to sound like I'm making any excuses for my actions, but ... there's something I've never told you, was too ashamed to, and ... " I stopped in a long pause, still searching for the right words, then looked up with reddened cheeks and blurted, "I was sexually abused for a number of years by a Catholic priest when I was a child."

Donna gasped, clapped a hand over her mouth. "Oh, *my God*."

Louise rolled her eyes and huffed. "Huh. Yeah, right," she said under her breath.

I stood ready to walk out. But I composed myself and sat, taking a deep breath and biting my lip. "The abuse made me feel worthless. I self-medicated myself with drugs to suppress the pain and memories. I take full responsibility for my actions. I'll do whatever I can to get the help I need."

I turned to Louise and said, "If you'll go into rehab, I'll move into your apartment and take care of the kids and pay all the expenses."

"Absolutely," her family said in unison.

Louise spit out two words. "No way."

"Listen," her mother said. "Marco's making a generous offer to move in and take care of the kids and bills so you can get the help you need. It'll give you the chance to get well again. You should let him do this."

"Well ... I don't know." Louise looked down, bunching her lips. She shot a look back at me. "You're going to pay all the bills?"

I nodded. "I'll pay the bills."

"Well. Okay. If everyone thinks this is a good idea, I guess I'll let you move in then."

"Yes, Louise. It's the right thing to do," Debbie said.

I got up and thanked them for having me. "I'll get things started as soon as possible."

Debbie walked with me to the door and hugged me good-bye. I walked to the car out front and climbed in. I beamed at Tim and gave him the good news. "Louise agreed to let me move into her place to take care of the kids while she goes into rehab."

Tim looked at me like I was a lunatic. "You're going to do what?"

"I have to help my family."

"I'm *demanding* that you not put yourself in this position." Tim wagged a forefinger at me in rhythm with, "*This* is a *bad idea*." He shook his head. "It won't work. No way. You're setting yourself up for big time failure."

"This is my way of helping my kids live a somewhat normal life. Others have been there for me. It's the right thing to do."

"It's insane." Tim dropped the shift into drive and sighed as he pulled away. "All the progress we've made will be blown to hell." He looked at me and said with the same sternness his expression held. "Don't come back to me after this explodes."

We drove back to the Oxford House in silence. Tim had been there for me over the last eight months, but I knew what I had to do. I'd make this work whatever it took. It was the last time we spoke.

76

* * *

I made an appointment with the intake administrator to interview Louise at a local rehab, but they didn't have an opening for at least two weeks. I was impatient and moved in anyway, hoping to live an independent and dignified life with my children.

The kids had been continually moved around in their short lives. After living with both parents, they had gone to live with their grandparents, and then back to their mother with the boyfriend, Rich, who wasn't allowed to see his own daughter. From there, it was back to their grandparents' house, and then to living with their mother and the convict, Rocco. After that, they were separated. My daughter moved back in with her grandparents and my son lived with his aunt and uncle.

The day I moved into Louise's three-bedroom apartment, Donna and Lawrence dropped off the kids with their belongings packed in garbage bags. I helped them unload their car. When we were through, they shook my hand and said, "Good luck!"

I never could have imagined how bad Louise's situation was. Those two weeks were agony. Louise could barely walk or talk, if and when she'd finally emerge from her room. She would constantly speak hurtful words to the kids and me. I'd take them to the gym, the park, and on errands with me to get them away from seeing their mother in the state she was in.

Eight months out of rehab, my sobriety and sanity were tested every day. But the fire inside kept me strong. Two weeks later she was admitted to the rehab facility.

The next thirty days were glorious. I straightened out the apartment immediately, organizing and bringing her bills current, cleaning every nook and cranny, and stocking the apartment with all the necessary supplies and food. I repaired holes in the walls and replaced towel racks that were ripped off from her drunken rampages. I could get off the couch and sleep in a bed.

My children's lives now had structure. They'd get up in the morning with bowls of cereal and fruit ready for breakfast. I'd leave for work planting kisses on their cheeks and telling them I love them. They'd get a call from me when they arrived home from school with a reminder to keep the apartment in order and to start their homework. Once home from work, we went to the gym as a family. Afterward, we'd have dinner together and they'd finish their homework. I'd clean up, do a load of laundry, and make their lunches for school the next day. Following a quick review of their schoolwork, it was off to bed.

On weekends, my two younger children joined us. We'd do simple things like going to the park, walking around the mall, having an inexpensive meal out, or seeing a matinee movie. I felt bliss and appreciation for this second chance.

Thirty days later, the pleasure in life came to a crashing halt. Louise called me at work. "Your insurance isn't paying for me to stay here anymore. Come and get me. *Now*."

It was like I'd been pierced with a jagged sword through my gut. I told them at work that I had an emergency. I drove to the rehab center. Unfortunately, I got lost and ended up two hours in the opposite direction. When I arrived she was livid and let me know it.

"Where the hell you been? I should've known better than count on you. What an idiot."

"Sorry, I got lost."

"Well, let's get *out* of here."

I packed her things and we started driving. "You couldn't even find your way here," she said. "I thought you were supposed to be cured, but you're nothing but a loser. Always was, always will be."

"Please. I've been through so much, and I'm tired of fighting. Can't we get along? I'm trying my best to make up for what I did to you. You know what happened to me when I was a child, and I'm going through a lot right now dealing with it for the first time."

Louise burst out laughing. "I doubt you were ever abused. You said that for sympathy."

"How can you keep humiliating *me*? This is your second rehab stint in a year. You couldn't maintain sobriety even after eight months in that last live-in facility. You've brought two failed relationships into the kids' lives, and one of those guys ended up in prison. And there's your DUI arrest. Look what you've done, yet you criticize me?"

If looks could commit murder, hers would've buried me alive and twelve feet under. "You're such a piece of shit. You'll never change." She sneered at me, then turned her head and stared out the window.

Her malicious words penetrated me to the core. The humiliation intensified every criticism, whether it was justified or not. She had the power, I realized, to convince me again that I *was* a worthless monster.

At home, I continued the routine with the children. Since Louise's license had been suspended for the DUI, I drove her to and from her AA and NA meetings that were scheduled by the rehab administrator. She was trying to maintain the standard ninety meetings in ninety days.

"I put a roof over your head, you worthless shit." She reminded me in one of our typical heated exchanges.

I was sitting at the kitchen table, and pointed to the stack of invoices in front of me. "I pay all the bills, don't forget." I threw my hands in the air in frustration. "I do all the cleaning, cooking and transporting the kids."

She snorted, finished unbuttoning her blouse and tossed it on the floor, leering at me.

I closed my eyes, counted to ten, opened them, then nodded toward the discarded garment. "Do you think you could at least clean up—pick up—after yourself?"

"Hey, you scum bag, if I was with either of my last two boyfriends, this place would be spotless and there'd be homemade cooked meals every day. They knew how to treat me."

"Oh, sure. If the one wasn't in prison for five years on burglary charges. And racking up hundreds of dollars in collect calls that I pay for!"

"Yeah, asshole, if you don't like it, you know where the door is," she said, running to her room and slamming the door.

I wanted to walk out. But I knew Julian and Angel would be the ones who'd suffer. There's no way she'd be able to pay her bills. I had to take it, and live with her verbal abuse.

Louise emerged from her room, sauntering to the kitchen table. She dropped the latest love letter from Rocco in front of me. This guy was doing time for committing a crime that many assumed my wife was also in on. But he took the fall for her and went to prison.

Her insults ran me over like a freight train. She had a typical addict's attitude, which I once had, that the world owed her everything and she shouldn't have to work for anything.

My therapy sessions switched from dealing with my past to discussing Louise. The sight of her had me trembling, waiting for her to belittle me. I'd vomit on the way home from work at the thought of being in her presence.

Inside, I was boiling over. There had to be relief other than drugs and porn. I attended Mass and talked with priests. I worked out in the gym with the kids five days a week. I appreciated Mary letting me have Jennifer and Brandon on weekends.

I tirelessly fought off demons. They tried to seduce me back with convincing physical symptoms of exciting adrenaline rushes. Images of my sinful acts played like a recording in repeat loop mode in my mind. I refused to give in to the temptations with every gram of energy I had.

I worked for the state to get my career back. The commute was three-and-a-half hours a day. Nine months before, I was in the hospital. Six months ago I was in the Oxford House. I had begun to deal with the real core issues of my past. Feeling a crash coming, I needed a break.

During this time, I was at Louise's apartment finishing my weekend errands when I had a chance run-in with my father-in-law. He had stopped by to visit Julian and Angel.

I heard his thunderous voice coming from the living room and peaked around the corner from the kitchen. "Hey, Paul, how you doing?"

"Great, Marco. Enjoyin' the single life. Hangin' with the guys at the men's club. Life is good." He came over to shake my hand. "How's the living arrangement going? I heard you're workin' hard to get back into your kids' lives. I'm happy to see that."

"I'm trying to be a good father. My children mean everything to me."

"You're doin' the right thing."

Nodding my head, I smiled. "Hey. Thanks. It's good to see you. I'll let you get back to your visit with the kids," I said, returning to my kitchen chores, energized to hang in there and fight for my kids.

Within a couple of weeks, Paul had died in his sleep. His passing made me wonder if he had been mentally and physically exhausted with the constant burden of caring for his daughter and my kids. Now that he knew his grandchildren were okay, he could rest.

Louise got her suspended license reinstated in mid-summer of 2006. From then on it was a daily fight dealing with only one vehicle. I needed the car for five hours a week to take the kids to the gym, and two hours to do the shopping. I had to be dropped off and picked up at the train station for work. Didn't think it was too much time for use of the vehicle each week since Louise wasn't working, but Louise thought otherwise.

"Get your own car, you freeloader."

"Hey. Every penny of my income is budgeted toward supporting the household. There's no excess money for me to buy a car. Can you give me consideration for paying for the gas, maintenance and insurance?"

"Not only don't you have your own means of transportation, you don't even have a place of your own, you shit head. If it weren't for me, you'd be on the street. Or with some hooker. You're worth nothing. You have it made living here, sponging off me and everything I have."

Her words were meaningless. She was still in her addiction. Her existent withdrawal symptoms were clouding her rational thinking and making things difficult for the rest of us living with her. But I wasn't able to take her insults for what they were. They pierced me like being struck by an electrical current.

At the end of summer, with a friend's recommendation, she found a job as a graphic designer for a signage company. Instead of being happy and grateful that she was able to function normally back in society, she said, "They're getting away with murder paying me the measly money I get." She ignored the fact she had nothing more than a high school education—with an abysmal grade-point average—and had been out of work for the past couple of years. "And what a pain in the ass it is to have to work my schedule around getting you to and from the train station."

Before long, Louise started skipping her AA meetings and missing time at work. She began to hang out with old friends and started using again. She lost the job in late fall. There were nights she didn't come home. I would find empty coke and crack bags in her room and in the laundry. I couldn't do enough to appease her, I realized, and ... I felt like a failure.

CHAPTER SEVENTEEN
~TURNING POINT IN THERAPY~

My therapy sessions continued to focus on dealing with Louise and raising my children in a hostile environment. Each week, I'd enter Keith's office shaking. He introduced a new subject that gave me a fresh perspective and outlook on life in a positive direction. It proved to be one of the most significant factors in turning my life around.

I learned that the shame of the past defilement pessimistically distorted my rational about my persona. I had a negative attitude about myself and life. I worried about things I didn't want to happen. I felt like scum. When I looked in the mirror, I saw a hideous creature and thought no one would want to be with me. I thought life was nothing but misery, pain, and heartache from the time you opened your eyes in the morning until the time you put your head to the pillow at night. My anxiety raged with cumbersome worries that stormed about my skull.

When would the IRS or creditors garnish my wages because of the mammoth debt I owed? Would the IRS put me in jail for back taxes? Would I be able to pay back the mountain of child support I owed? Would my employer find out about my financial and personal problems? Would I be fired? Would my children be happy and healthy? I agonized that something bad would happen to them. Along with these torments, I thought I would be bitter, debilitated, and restless for the rest of my life. I believed I would have to work until the day I died only to live in poverty. Images of no future, no hope, with no possible life of abundance were etched in my mind.

"You're attracting negativity in your life through the type of energy and thoughts you're emitting," Keith said. "All the depressive thoughts and ill feelings you have about life and yourself are physically being transmitted out into the world."

"Like bad aura or vibe to people?"

"Exactly. Like attracts like. Good people and good things attract other good people and things. Bad circumstances create more bad situations."

I thought he was *nuts*. This is some kind of psychological trick to get me out of my pessimistic doldrums. But the more I thought about it, the more it started to make sense. I attempted to understand this theory more.

Before I could devote my energy to putting the method into practice, I had to have a logical understanding behind it. I learned that quantum physicists called the theory the "Law of Attraction."

I built the base of my understanding: all things had come from one thought, and from that thought, an energy source had been created. From that energy source, particles had been created and so on down the line until everything we see and don't see had come to exist or not.

The Law of Attraction purports the hypothesis that the energy source that exists in all creation operates at different frequencies, and those similar frequencies are attracted to each other. A miserable, anxious, and depressed person is operating at a low frequency and attracting similar feelings, events, and people into their life, making them even more miserable, anxious, and depressed. The opposite holds true for people who are happy and content with life and themselves. They are attracting more opportunities, events, and others into their lives that are making them even happier and more content with life and themselves.

The law also states that if you ask the universe for something and transmit the feeling and gratitude of already receiving it, it will come to be. My interpretation regarding this part of the law is that the Universe is God in the Holy Trinity. And the thought and energy that created existence came from God. But, the Universe can be whatever your heart believes. The Universe, Jehovah, Allah, Hara Krishna, Mother Nature, or whatever the source of your faith is the starting point for you asking, believing, and receiving.

My therapist suggested I see the documentary that discussed this topic, titled, *The Secret*. While researching the quantum physics of this topic, I came across an article stating the documentary had been put into print and was currently in circulation. I fully intended to obtain and read that, but sadly, once again, my therapy for the real issue, the abuse, had to be put on hold. I was having intense problems at home. Keith worked on calming my crisis with Louise and the negative thoughts I was transmitting.

Louise had become more addicted than ever. She ravaged her way through the apartment like Godzilla, knocking everyone down in her path. Her usual repetitive verbal assaults on me would morph me into a pathetic puddle of saline.

She'd go on drug binges and then sleep for days. The kids and I would find her drug paraphernalia throughout the apartment.

Keith worked to keep me from losing control. "I've never seen anyone with as much determination and drive to get better and improve their family's life as you have," he said. "It's tough enough for someone in a perfect environment to overcome what you went through. And here you're doing it with no support from your immediate family or friends, while in an immense financial hole and a hostile, addictive environment. You're a miracle, Marco. Truly amazing."

I could not take what he was saying to heart. I still felt like a creature at the bottom of the pyramid. *God* could have been in front of me telling me these things, and I would feel He was full of crap.

While trying to control the anxiety when I was at home with the help of my therapist, I requested another conference with Louise's immediate family. "The kids and I are living in hell since the relapse," I said, once we were all seated. I shook my head and sighed, stroking my chin. "And Louise is unbearable to live with. I'd appreciate it if I could use Paul's car left behind after his death. I truly believe it'd relieve some of the stress, and it'll help me get back on my feet to get sole custody of the kids."

Debbie and the others agreed. We drafted a contract to enable me to take the vehicle now and pay for it later. When I was able to come up with the funds and reimburse the Blue Book value, the proceeds would go into the family's inheritance fund. I finally had a way to have transportation again.

Louise flipped when she found out. "You fuckin' moocher. Couldn't get your own transportation so you suck off of my inheritance for your own needs? That car belongs to *me.* You have no right driving it, you loser. I can't stand you living here!"

The day had come. It was a weekend in February, 2007. I had completed my normal rituals of cleaning, shopping, taxiing the kids around, and running errands. I was fatigued from a week of work. No big deal in any normal environment, but to have to do it with an ill-tempered, abusive individual in the mix really wore me down.

"Why can't you at least attempt to lift a finger to straighten up or cook a meal for the kids?" I said.

"If you don't like it, you know where the door is," Louise said, stumbling out the front door. I was tempted to pack and leave, but I didn't.

A couple of hours later while de-stressing at the gym, my cell phone rang. Angel was crying. "Dad. I can't believe she's doing this to you. Mom's calling the police to escort you out of here. She wants you to leave. She told me to call you. I don't want you to leave, Daddy."

I knew it was a lie. This was Louise's way of torturing me. It wasn't right to put the kids through this.

"Honey, it's okay," I said. "Don't worry. I'll do everything in my power to get on my feet and get custody of you guys. As soon as I can. Please don't cry."

When I got back to the apartment, Louise wasn't there. Julian wore a long face and Angel sobbed while I packed my things. It had been eleven months of living there. Louise's family kept a close eye on the kids while they continued to live with their mother.

Not knowing where to go, I began driving closer to where I worked, crying along the way. I felt relief that I wasn't burdened anymore from Louise's mental pressure, but enraged that my treasured children had to suffer at being secondary victims to my exploitation.

"Fuck you, God! Where are you now?" I choked and coughed at the strain on my vocal cords. "Why must you make my life a constant conflict? Why are you doing this to my children?" The veins in my face bulged, intensifying a fiery heated sensation. "You're a fucking jerk-off to me! Where are you, Jesus? You're supposed to be my brother! Where are you now?" I turned my anger back to God and screeched, "Bring it on! Bring everything you got on! I'll take it all and then some!"

I thought for sure I had bought a one-way ticket to hell for eternity. My body shuddered. I broke down, weeping in sorrowful remorse. My mind replayed the pitiful looks on Julian and Angel's faces when I was leaving. It brought back the same sick feeling when forced to leave Jennifer and Brandon after screwing up my chances with Mary. It was all too much. I had to pull over to compose myself from the wailing.

After a few moments, I continued on my search. I had remembered there was a hotel right next to the train station where I caught the train for work every morning. It was only fifteen minutes away from the kids — adding to the allure. I checked it out and decided to move in.

As soon as I opened the door to my room, a shock wave of emotions hit me like a tsunami. I stepped in and my memory flashed back to preparing for a night of binging on drugs and sex. All my senses were stimulated at once. I was back in the past at the height of my addiction. I could literally see drug and sex paraphernalia throughout the room. Audio of a porn feature blared from the TV, while sounds of wild intercourse rang in my ears. The aroma of crack and sex permeated the room.

My heart had begun to beat violently. I thought it would explode. I had become physically and sexually excited. Paranoia overcame me as if I was using again — pacing the floor and peeking out the window. My eyes focused on the floor and images of white crumbs and ripped empty blue bags entered my mind. I began going through the same ritual I had when I ran out of drugs. I moved dressers, night stands, and lifted the mattress looking for a prior occupant's leftover stash.

When I awoke from the trance, I was rocked with gloom, as if I had actually committed the act. I had to get out of there. There was a restaurant a couple of doors down where I could regroup.

The first week's stay had me in distress. On the train from work, I repeatedly dry heaved until I reached the point of vomiting. Memories of the binges kept flooding my senses. My heart would undulate and bring me to sexual arousal.

I tried to keep myself occupied by going to the gym and then out to eat, but I would become too physically drained from the barrage of emotions. To make things worse, I would see drug transactions taking place among couples staying at the hotel. Everything was in place for me to fall back into my past routine. I refused to give in.

The second week got better, and I began to function somewhat normally. The gym became my number one priority after work. On the way home from the gym, I'd pick up takeout and head to the room to eat and sleep, avoiding any human contact. I repeated this routine every day of the workweek. On weekends, I'd stay busy by going to the gym, visiting my four children, and spending quiet time in places like parks, bookstores, and church.

That worked for a while, but then I'd again slip into the negativity that had gripped me countless times before. The situation at the hotel didn't get any better. Numerous drunken domestic disputes would break out nightly. There were parties, drug dealing, and prostitution all around me. Everything was in position for the right time and circumstance to pull me down.

One evening the phone rang. Thirteen-year-old Angel was hysterical, trying to catch her breath. "Mommy ... blood-shot eyes ... empty baggies!"

When I was able to decipher her words, I thought Louise had overdosed, and Angel had walked in on her. But Louise had passed out with empty coke bags tossed around the room.

I sprinted to the car, rushing to pick up Angel. She was watching for me through the apartment window and raced to my car as soon as I pulled up. "This wasn't the only time," Angel said. Julian had, she informed me, also found drug paraphernalia in the apartment. We drove to the hotel room to rest for a few hours.

"I promise you," I said, looking into her saddened and frightened brown eyes, "that I will get on my feet and get custody as soon as I can. I want to give you the life you deserve." Angel hugged me close before I had to release her back to Louise's apartment.

CHAPTER TWENTY
~CONFRONTING THE DIOCESE~

It had become obvious to many people close to me, who knew of my sordid childhood experiences, that clergy sexual abuse was the cause of my unstable mental state. People I had talked with suggested pursuing legal action against the Archdiocese of Camden. Through a friend, I had contacted and retained a lawyer. He offered to take my case and receive payment contingent upon, and commensurate with, a financial settlement with the diocese.

The attorney, Tony, discussed strengthening our case by attempting to solicit a confession from my abuser. He researched an Internet site that listed past sexual offenders and located my abuser's address. He asked me to draft a letter to Father McCool saying I was in therapy for what he did to me, and my therapist thought it would be beneficial to my recovery if I wrote him questioning him why he took advantage of me.

I tried to confront the pedophile, but my head spun from the thought of him touching the same paper that I touched. When Tony realized my fear, he drafted the letter, and I copied his words in my handwriting. We mailed the letter, and I checked the mail daily for his response.

Every night I'd gather and organize my medical, financial, employment, and legal records to build a case and support my claim of the damages caused by the defilement. My mind was tested, trying to chronicle my admittance into the numerous medical facilities and mental health drug treatment programs.

I accumulated and calculated my financial records. The thousands of dollars squandered on drugs and porn alone devastated me. Again, despair set in ... realizing how much I'd lost due to my reckless actions. Humiliation inundated me as I gathered and reviewed the court documents, judgments, and warrants for child support and collection agencies. I was mentally and physically exhausted seeing the tangible evidence of the damage caused by the abuse and the destructive emotions associated with each aspect of my life.

At each meeting with Tony, I'd emotionally break down while reviewing the documentation. By now, he had become more of a friend than my counsel. With each requested record delivered to his office, our case against the diocese became increasingly stronger. It was blatantly obvious that the problems I incurred throughout my life were a result of being abused, and the diocese had been negligent in protecting me from one of their priests.

In addition to the monetary damage, it was evident the crime had caused an immense amount of pain and suffering in my life and the lives of those around me. The only obstacle we had to overcome was the statute of limitations. We had to prove, within three years prior to filing the lawsuit, I had been unaware that the damage and addictions in my life were a result of having been exploited.

CHAPTER TWENTY-ONE
~THERAPY WITH PRIESTS~

While pursing my case against the diocese, in addition to my normal therapy sessions, I went back to church and talked to a priest once a week about the sexual violation, in addition to my normal therapy sessions. For a year, I basically used each priest that I talked with as a punching bag, releasing my mental anguish and frustrations on them.

One particle priest said, "Sometimes in life, Marco, we must put aside all the hurt and anger, and take a step forward. Try to move on."

I snapped. "How would you like to live your life with the memories of the disgusting acts done to me in the bedroom of the rectory while fellow priests, exactly like you, sat in their bedrooms a few feet away? Could you turn it off like flipping a light switch, Father?"

Nothing the priests said to me could put me at peace. Another priest said, "Marco, you must appreciate the little things in life, like sunsets and birds singing."

I stood up and got in his face. "How the fuck is a bird singing during a sunset going to heal my pain?"

Certain priests did seem sincere. "You're not a piece of trash," another said. "You're doing everything possible to heal your wounds and the wounds you caused other people."

They prayed for me. Some of them worked hard to put me at peace during our sessions, attempting to convince me there was hope, love, and joy in the world. It was a struggle to have faith in their words. I tried to notice and savor what they thought was happiness in life, to no avail. I was only going through the motions. My hardened heart and frigid soul felt nothing but misery and seclusion.

The pleasantries they told me to think about were converted to images of perversion. Even in God's house, my mind manufactured images of the woman in front of me bending over the pew while being violently entered from behind, and the man in front of her stuffing himself into her mouth. I envisioned the priests molesting the altar boys or girls. Images played in my head of the two women to the right of me or the two men to the left of me having sexual intercourse. It was difficult to find the stop button ... or even the pause button. Most the time I only had one button: repeat.

I'd have these deviant images in simple conversations with a stranger, meetings at work, in the gym and grocery store. I couldn't look at any female without vulgar images playing out in my mind. To me, women were vessels used to exploit my sexual urges. Deep inside, I wanted the companionship, friendship, and love of the opposite sex, but that yearning was overpowered by my conditioning. I started to switch gears in my therapy to deal with these photographic issues.

CHAPTER TWENTY-TWO
~REPROGRAMMING THE HOPELESS MIND~

In an attempt to occupy my mind and not regress to sinister thoughts, I drove to the local Wal-Mart. While browsing the store, I passed the book section. The book, *The Secret* by Rhonda Byrne, jumped out at me. Keith had mentioned this title as a CD. I recalled reading an article that said it was recently published as a book explaining the Laws of Attraction. I was curious and purchased it.

I took the book with me to the laundromat the next day. I thought that using the theory to actualize material things like new cars, houses, parking spaces, and checks in the mail were ridiculous. But it did help me rotate a hundred eighty degrees my attitude and thinking about life. The book's strength in programming the mind to feel confidence, gratitude, peace, love, joy, and happiness made it an imperative healing tool for someone like me ... and still does.

Over the next two weeks, I read the book through four times, pausing after each section and meditating on it. I would visualize walking into a room full of people with confidence and the ability to look everyone in the eye. I would imagine being friendly, outgoing, and have people looking at me without judgment. I would concentrate on having an unblemished heart, mind, and soul with pure thoughts and righteous desires. I envisioned living a peaceful, comfortable and secure life with all my financial and personal problems satisfied. I pictured myself living in a home filled with my children's smiling faces, and a wholesome down-to-earth wife who was compassionate, loving, kind, and caring. Okay, and beautiful too. I could see myself living a gracious spiritual life with an abundance of family and friends.

After finishing the book, I implemented a systematic list to meditate on throughout the day and keep the Law of Attraction always fresh in my mind. I would repeat each item on the list until I actually felt the emotion of experiencing each trait my inner self wanted to be. I would repeat daily that I was a massive vibrating frequency of positive energy. I would force myself to feel a connection of being one mind with God. I would then repeat, "I am a bright, spiritual light; shining inspiration out to the world. I am strong, confident and stable, like a rock. Yet humble, patient, well-mannered, loving, kind, caring, compassionate, friendly and outgoing, generous and gracious. I am physically fit and healthy. I am attracting all good things and people into my life. I am attracting an abundance of financial security and peace. I am attracting a good home with nice things filled with happy children, friends and family. I am attracting a beautiful woman who is wholesome, down to earth, compassionate, understanding, loving, kind, and caring." I would then meditate on the joy and gratitude of the blissful feeling of experiencing these positive emotions and realities.

I repeated this drill throughout the day and, after awhile, I noticed my spirits rising. I observed that when I went through the list, I would stick out my chest and lift my head high, as if I *did* have confidence. I started to appreciate the things I had rather than bemoaning the things I didn't have. I was overjoyed and grateful beyond words for having my wits back and being able to communicate again. I was thankful for getting my sanity and sobriety back. The gratitude for the balance of having a job, transportation, a bank account, and being able to see my children, brought tears to my eyes. All of a sudden, it wasn't so bad waking up in the morning.

Following a month of programming my mind and outlook on life with positive feelings and thoughts, I was blessed with a wave of fortunate events that changed my life for good.

It started out with a promotion at work to a senior-level position in operations. The excitement that hit me when I received the news was so intense I had to close my office door so no one would see me jumping up and down. The gratitude brought tears to my eyes. In a year and five months, I was given the position over people who had been there for years.

For the first time in a long time, I felt proud and good about myself. This was what I needed to get my children's lives back on track. I was a long-dead car battery jump started back to life. Maybe I finally had found out the *secret.*

CHAPTER TWENTY-THREE
~THE DIOCESE'S HEARTLESS RESPONSE~

During this mental transition, my pending case against the diocese appeared to be going well. With each document review meeting, Tony was increasingly positive for a favorable settlement.

Our case was strengthened when I received a letter in the mail that had sloppy handwriting on the envelope. It didn't hit me what was in the envelope at first because the handwriting looked like that of a child. Then in an instant the preprinted return address stamp with the name, *Father McCool*, caught my eye. My heart gunned into overdrive again. The "Father" part of the return address had been scribbled out with only his first and last names legible. I tore open the letter and read it. His confession and apology made me smile.

I thought for sure the diocese would consider the letter as undeniable evidence that the abuse had indeed happened and they would do the right thing to ease my family's pain and suffering. I called Tony and drove to his office. I could see in his face he was thrilled for me, and probably also happy for his firm's bank account.

But my positive outlook became short-lived when he called a few days later. "I have bad news. After reviewing documentation from your psychologist in New York, there were detrimental details in his report."

The energy drained from me. I fell to my knees. "Am I cursed?"

"I'm sorry this isn't going your way. The psychologist's prognosis confirmed what all the other doctors and therapists previously documented. He stated that he believed all the stress, anxiety, and problems you accumulated throughout your life were a result of the shame and guilt from the abuse. He reported that he saw true heartfelt merit within you by the concern and love you had for your children, and also the sorrow you communicated to him for your misconduct toward your loved ones. But in the document he also quoted you as saying that you did not hold the Catholic Church responsible for the abuse."

"I said what?" I had to sit. Stunned.

"You did not hold the Church responsible," Tony repeated, his voice softly trailing off.

"I don't even recall speaking about the abuse with that therapist."

"Unfortunately it's here in black and white, and I had to share it with the Church's lawyers."

"What does this all mean?"

"This occurred a little over three years prior to the lawsuit. With that comment, the Catholic Church is legally exonerated. The diocese attorneys picked up on it immediately and sent us a letter confirming the lack of legality of our case."

I went to his office the next day. We sat and weighed our options.

"I'll represent and support you to the end," Tony said. "But, in my professional opinion, our case has little chance of winning."

Hanging my head, the tears flowed, leaving welts in my cheeks. "How can this be fair? How can I be held accountable for a comment I don't recall making? How can I be responsible for something I said while on a multitude of psychiatric medications and illegal drugs? I barely knew I was breathing at that time. What about the letter?"

"Unfortunately the letter is immaterial. I'm going to have to contemplate our next move."

I could barely put one foot in front of the other when I trudged out to my car. I cried some more when I sat inside.

A few days later, the diocese sent my attorney a letter offering one hundred fifty thousand dollars for my pain and suffering and a limit of five years additional therapy sessions. Tony called me to his office.

Storming through the front door, I screamed, "What audacity. That small amount for a lifetime of pain? That's about a hundred thousand less than the financial debt alone that I presented to them. Are you serious? They're only offering a hundred fifty thousand? That's mere pennies for what my family and I went through." I broke down in tears once again. "What about my kids? I'm trying to gain custody. They're in such a horrible position."

"It's tough, Marco, I know. But as it stands, we most likely can't win this case."

"What about my kids' future needs?"

I grabbed the raggedy expandable folder I carried around with me. It was filled with my life's legal documents, bills, calculator, and checkbook. Pulling at the frayed strand holding it together and opening the vessel bulging at the seams, I took out the calculator and a pad of paper.

Tony stared at me while I punched the calculator keys and wrote down figures.

"Look at what they're offering," I said, slamming the pad of paper on the table. "After we deduct your legal fees, the settlement comes to approximately three thousand dollars a year from the time the abuse started to this day. This equates to fifty-eight dollars a week, eight dollars a day, and thirty-five cents an hour for the infinite amount of torturous pain that my family and I had to endure. And that's not taking into consideration any future issues that my family and I will have to deal with. Show this to that pompous bishop so he can review it in his nice plush office, or as he gorges his lazy fat ass with meals specially prepared for him in his lavish living quarters. I'm sure he didn't get that big fat ass by fasting. And a time frame limit on my therapy? Are you kidding me? How the fuck can you put a limitation on getting someone help that had been injured by a member of his organization? Does this organization have any ethics at all?"

"I'll write the diocese and ask them to reconsider an amount of two hundred fifty thousand. I'll tell them that this figure will put you in a better position to establish residency, attain custody of your children, and be able to negotiate a settlement with your creditors, tax agencies, and child support enforcement divisions."

The diocese came back with a counteroffer of two hundred twenty-five thousand dollars.

The unmitigated arrogance of the Church. It was to me incomprehensible. How could they not take a good look at my case on a compassionate level? They treated it like a bargaining item. Split the difference, a pedestrian gambit, like I was a used car, bartered back and forth from crooked car salesman to naive consumer. They had absolutely no sympathy for the distressing anguish my children and I were experiencing. It was simply a monetary transaction to them with no concern for our welfare. Like a pack of hungry wolves circling its prey, the diocese was feeding on my unconscious comment and vulnerable state of mind, using it against me to get out of their responsibility to rectify the damage their organization had caused.

Mentally exhausted and disappointed, I gave up the fight and accepted their offer. I started the painstaking task of fighting for custody of my children and settling my debts. Even Tony saw the Catholic Church's lack of compassion for my situation and gave me a slight discount on his fee. When all was said and done after legal fees, tax judgments, child support arrears, and wage garnishments, I was left with a hundred thousand dollars. This would enable me to establish residency, attain custody of my children, reimburse my wife's family for the car, divorce my wife, negotiate with my creditors, and purchase everything my children and I needed when we left their mother ... with nothing but the clothes we were wearing.

CHAPTER TWENTY-FOUR
~THERAPEUTIC RECOVERY:
WORKING ON A LEVEL PLAYING FIELD~

Within two months of moving out of my wife's apartment, I was fortunate enough to get out of that awful hotel room and acquire a place of my own. I could settle my child support arrears and gain custody of my children with a twenty-six-thousand-dollar payment to my wife.

I negotiated with the IRS and state tax agencies, filling out the stack of paperwork necessary to submit my bid amount for an offer of compromise. My mind was at ease knowing my wages wouldn't be garnished. There would be a review and possibly the interest and penalties would be exonerated. I was able to settle a lesser amount owed with the majority of my creditors and made progress negotiating with the remaining stubborn collection agencies.

My confidence was restored as my independence and dignity returned. But there were internal forces at work, brewing up trouble. It seemed like I was in a constant panic state. I felt like something was trying to sabotage my party. Getting on medication crossed my mind. The force was powerful.

Immediately, therapy sessions switched to dealing with this issue. Through subsequent visits, I came to understand that the shameful parts created from the abuse would attempt to pull me back into the disgraceful lifestyle I had been used to. It was exhausting to understand and get through this period. Through perseverance, I was able to get past this phase and continue the process of getting on with life.

A euphoric feeling of freedom now existed. It felt like I was standing on a level playing field, concentrating on the therapeutic work of unburdening the remorseful and culpability-ridden perceptions I had of myself. I could now work on healing my damaged psyche.

Keith reverted back to reviewing the therapeutic logic of the true self and the defender parts. He said, "Remember, Marco, the key to all of this is to first identify and acknowledge that your true self exists within. The next step is to understand and identify when the defender parts are stepping in to combat the situation and which ones they are whenever you are confronted with a crisis or harmful emotional moment. The most important key at that point is to get space between the true self and the damaging defender parts. Those parts need to be conducted by the true self in the manner they were reprogrammed after they had been unburdened of all their troubles and false impressions of themselves.

"If the damaging defender parts are left to their own devices, they will run you into the ground. In order to achieve this synergy, the damaging defender parts need to gain trust so they can be relieved of their shame, guilt, worries, pain, etcetera. This frees them so they can follow the orders of the true self. The way to do this is to simply give them a shoulder to cry on so they can be rid of their burdens, and let them know they are understood. It is at this point of understanding that the defender parts gain trust in the true self and can be reprogrammed to be conducted by the true self and perform in a healthier manner. Which negative emotion or false perception of yourself would you like to deal with first?"

"What a dirty, perverted, ugly, disgusting and obese monster I thought I was. My entire adult life I've physically seen that image every time I looked in the mirror."

"You were looking through the eyes of the shameful part," Keith said. "It wasn't who you really were. Your self-perception was like individuals with anorexia who view themselves as fat even though they're nothing but skin and bones."

We first identified the physical symptoms of the defender part that made me feel like a hideous creature. "What do the physical symptoms I am experiencing have to do with what's going on in this sick head of mine?"

Keith chuckled. "Your defender parts are activated by an event or thought. The physical symptom you are experiencing from that event or thought is that particular defender part coming in to combat or guard you from what it falsely thinks is harming you. Do you remember, Marco, when we first tried to identify your various emotions as an exercise early in your therapy?"

I gave him a look. "Listen, I'm lucky I remember my own name with all the stuff I've been through and what's spinning in my head."

He again laughed. "Marco, remember early on when we discussed your frustration, and you determined that it was the defender part that wanted you to get back into the game of life? And that your anxiety was your fear-based defender part that was alerting you of the impending doom if you slipped and went back to your inappropriate behaviors? Or how about when the depression part stepped in, and you resolved that it was a reminder of your past actions? These are the physical symptoms of the defender parts."

I felt that if a light bulb was hanging over my head, it had now lit up. I was impressed with Keith's memory of what I had said and the affection in his tone. At this moment, I trusted my therapist implicitly— he was the real deal.

"Marco, identifying the defender part's physical symptoms first is key to acknowledging when that part is coming in to control a situation or thought and identifying which one it is. Catching the defender part at this point is crucial to prevent it from starting to control the situation in an unhealthy manner or overwhelming your emotions with negative judgments."

After Keith's summary of the logic in identifying the defender parts, we went back to the hideous creature I thought I was. Whenever I was overcome by this defender part, I had a feeling of great disappointment and nervousness in my gut. I wanted seclusion. I thought the world viewed me as the lowest of life forms. This part also made me feel physically ill and drained the energy from me.

I then visualized getting space between my conscious true self and the repugnant defender part, and attempted to feel a connection between the two. Once I felt a connection, I tried to view the hideous part with the eyes of my true self. Then I asked myself how I felt toward that part. I started to feel compassion and sorrow. I had destroyed any sense of self-worth and confidence in being a normal participant in the human race, and identified how exhausting it was.

"The next step, Marco," Keith said, cleaning his glasses with a soft cloth, "is finding out whether or not that part could accept and sense the true self's feelings toward it."

I paused. "I'll have to think about it," I said, staring into space in a vegetative state.

After a minute, Keith said, "What's going on? Your concentration seems to be straying."

"I'm confused. It's like I'm in a mentally numb state."

"Could it be another part coming in? It's a common thing when identifying the various defender parts from abuse. The parts don't want to be messed with when they think their protective means are being sabotaged."

"Ah," I said, with the light of recognition dawning in my head. "It's the two different parts working in conjunction with each other, preventing me from getting to the root of the part that made me feel inadequate."

The easiest part of the two to decipher was the one that placed me in a state of confusion. It was the first line of defense for protecting the other defender parts created from the defilement. It didn't want me to go through the pain of reliving any past memories of being exposed to the sexual perversions.

The second part was the next line of defense for protecting the various defender parts. Breaking through the state of confusion, the blank state of numbness, protected me from feeling the painful emotions. I started to realize that this part was born very early following the abuse. This part worked extremely well at deadening the pain and shame. It also contributed to the numerous problems and difficulties I experienced throughout my life. In the past, whenever I was confronted with any form of conflict, difficulty, or stress in life, this part would kick in and attempt to alleviate any anxious feelings I was experiencing. My problems were numbed out and forgotten by this particular part, thinking that if the memories were out of my mind, they would go away on their own. This way of thinking was the major force in compounding all my issues to the point of causing my breakdown.

"Can the two respective parts step aside, Marco?"

"I have a hard time concentrating through the state of confusion and focusing past the numbness. I need a break to think about things."

CHAPTER TWENTY-FIVE
~DISCOVERING THE TRUE SELF~

It took two more sessions to get past the first two protector elements of my psyche. I had to get the true self reconnected with the inadequate part. I took a step back to summarize where we left off prior to the first two defender traits coming in. I identified their physical symptoms of disappointment, nervousness, and wanting seclusion, greeted them, and created space between the parts and the true self.

From there, I viewed the inadequate part through the eyes of the true self and asked myself how I felt toward it. As before, I started to feel compassion and sorrow for that portion of me that felt so inadequate and disgraceful. I then switched to the inadequate part to see if it could accept and sense the feelings from the true self. I envisioned two images facing each other in my mind. The true self appeared to be a motherly-type, consoling the inadequate image. I began to feel the reassuring, soothing sense of the true self's compassion toward the inadequate part's feelings.

"Now," Keith said, "ask the inadequate part what it wants from the true self."

I thought for a moment. "Are you really what you appear to be? Could you be an insignificant being not worthy of any delight and love in this life?"

But I couldn't find the answer within my true self. There appeared to be another ego lurking within, preventing the true self from reassuring the inadequate part that it was not the shameful disgusting creature it thought it was.

"How the fuck do I know the reason I can't concentrate," I snapped, jumping up from the wooden captain's chair. I paced the room, stopping in front of Keith. Gripping the edge of his desk, I leaned forward, getting in his face. "Am I stupid, or do I have some form of mental deficiency? Did I do physical damage to the brain cells I destroyed from the massive quantities of drugs and psychiatric medications I ingested throughout my lifetime?" I stood back, shaking my head. "I can't see how it's possible to heal these scars and unburden myself of the painful memories of the abuse, the sins I committed, and the life I wasted. I've been living in anxiety and paranoia with an overpowering burden of mental pressure." Blood rushed to my face. I pursed my lips. Pounding my fist over and over again on Keith's desk, I screamed, "I've had to live in perfection, trying to secure the perfect life, never losing at anything, never catching a red light, never dropping or spilling anything, or else I'd explode with a furious temper tantrum. I don't see how it's possible to get over this past abuse and live at peace with life and myself."

Keith came from behind his desk and put his arm around my shoulder. "Calm down, Marco," he said, leading me to the more comfortable love seat. "There's an un-blending process happening here. The various defender parts have a positive intention in defending against the pain from the abuse. It just happens to be in an incorrect manner."

Keith returned to his seat and leaned back in his chair. He took a deep breath. "When you're concentrating on one particular personality trait, the other parts work in conjunction, in different combinations with each other. They try to prevent you from getting to the core of the respective trait and having to relive the pain and shame from the abuse." He leaned forward, punctuating his words. "The key ... to un-blending ... the defender parts ... successfully ... is to understand each attribute ... as it steps in to do its job. They protect you from the harmful emotions that are associated from the abuse." Gazing at me over his wire-rimmed glasses, he said matter-of-factly, "Getting the defender parts to step aside so you can concentrate on the characteristic you want to address is the un-blending process. Once you are able to get through all the various defensive parts that get in the way of dealing with the core part, the true self is now able to answer the part in question in a divine loving place."

I sat, pulled on my ear while thinking that over for a moment. "So, the true self is present to bear witness to all the feelings, beliefs, memories, and experiences of the inadequate part."

Keith smiled. He leaned forward, resting his elbows on the desktop, his chin perched atop his clasped hands. "In essence, the past is being stirred up so all the associated burdens, pressures, and pain can be released and relieved. Following this unburdening process, the respective part can be cleansed. It can then be recomposed in a more constructive manner—similar to wiping a virus-infected computer hard drive clean ... then reprogramming it with anti-virus protected software."

I stood up. With a few deep diaphragmatic breaths, I cleared my mind. While attempting to decipher what part came in and threw me off course, I sucked in my lips, vigorously shaking my head. Skepticism came in as a defensive part. I got back in Keith's face. "This psychological un-blending is full of shit. The defense against the abuse is another trick to get me to believe that this crap actually works." I flung my hands in the air. "How is this going to unburden the weight I carry on my shoulders every moment of the day? All my deficient personality traits are a result of me being a dirtball loser." I shook my head. "I'm not worthy of the slightest bit of solace or happiness that this punishment called life has to offer."

Keith took a deep breath in and a longer breath out. "Marco, you're a miracle. A remarkable good-hearted human being. You're the most determined individual that I've come across in my thirty years of practice."

I shook my head and slumped back in my seat. The negative thoughts took over my brain. Folding my legs, I rested my elbow on my knee, fist holding up my head. "How do I know that I have a true good self," I asked, without waiting for an answer. "How do you know that the shameful sins I committed were a conditioning from the abuse and not a result of me being evil?"

Keith took a breath to answer. But I interrupted. "How do you know that these various parts were created from the abuse?" Again, he tried to speak, but I asked, "If this work that we're doing is not full of shit, how do you have faith in it."

Keith leaned back, rested his palms on the desk. "Being skeptical and questioning everything will eventually lead you to the answer."

"Oh. I get it. By me questioning everything surrounding what I am seeking, I am logically eliminating those doubts. How do I know my true self is good and not the monster that I believe it to be?"

"Have you ever heard the statement, 'What you are seeking is causing you to seek'?"

I closed my eyes and meditated on it for a short while. Soon, a feeling of understanding overcame me as I flashed back throughout various stages of my life when I was in the grip and power of my contemptible behaviors.

As a child and in the midst of the sexual abuse, I would envision myself as a star athlete and perfect role model. When I was a young man running around with whores and doing drugs, I envisioned myself as a patient, well-mannered, athletic, successful and spiritual individual. In the psychiatric hospital, brain wasted, and on massive quantities of psychiatric medications, I visualized being a family man with a beautiful, practical wife, a nice house full of happy children and Sunday dinners after a day at church. I began to see how throughout my life I had a quintessential, but remote and latent desire to be respectable, righteous, benevolent, and caring.

My confidence was again restored in my therapy, and I was able to connect with the skeptic part within. I could see that the positive intention of the cynic was to divert my concentration from getting to the core part and reliving the memories of the abuse. Its sole responsibility was to convince me that all this work was a festering crock of hooey and to give up.

After fully understanding the reasoning behind my skepticism and the enlightenment in regards to my true self, I began the work of un-blending the various defender parts. I hoped to bear witness and unburden the inadequate self-perceptions that I had about myself.

I asked from the viewpoint of the true self what the inadequate part wanted. What I felt inside was that the inadequate part wanted reassurance that it wasn't the appalling creature it thought it was. As my concentration and understanding became more focused, I was able to break through the defender's first few lines of defense.

I could answer the inadequate part in the divine loving place of the true self. I was able to visualize the true self making it clear to the inadequate trait that it was not the terrible disgusting person it perceived itself to be.

I then switched gears to the inadequate part and concentrated on whether or not it could acknowledge the true self's perception. I sensed that I *could* feel the understanding from the true self.

"Marco, does the inadequate part want the true self to know anything else?"

Again, the light bulb went high beams. "Yes. I want the true self to know how loathsome I was. I wasn't able to carry anything through to completion. Every glimpse of confidence was devoured by disappointment and inadequacy."

I continued repetitiously to blurt out each negative emotion the inadequate part felt, and concentrated on the true self, understanding and absorbing the pain and destructive way of thinking of the inadequate part.

After some time, I finally could not think of anything else to say to the true self. I closed my eyes and leaned my head against the back of the love seat. I took a deep breath ... and then slowly released it. I meditated on what just happened. Keith quietly waited for me to return from the trance I was in. There was relief and satisfaction that some part of me finally understood the pain and mental anguish I endured for the past thirty-three years. My closed mind opened and things started to become clear.

I was now able to logically decipher my behavior and analyze my actions. I understood all the conditioning that the exploitation and disgrace had in creating the different personality parts and behavioral traits that dwelt in my depths. I started to understand how criticism and insults painfully intensified my ignominious impression of myself, causing me to take everything personally.

The numb, confused, and skeptic defender parts now made sense to me. I could see how they contributed to the various problems I incurred throughout my life. I comprehended why I mistrusted and did pernicious things to loved ones — for fear they would do them to me first. The need to self-medicate made sense.

I began to recognize the urge for porn. The need to commit acts of perversion was a result of my adolescent mind being manipulated and programmed to believe it was acceptable. I perceived that the reason why I wanted to be humiliated sexually was because the shameful part from the humiliation of the maltreatment wanted to be reinforced. The logic of it all—how all the parts fit together, their roles and reasons for being—became apparent to me.

I opened my eyes for a brief moment. Keith was leaning forward with his right elbow resting on his leg, his hand supporting his chin, staring at me as if he was trying to analyze my thoughts. I gazed off in a distance, remembering my numerous misbehaviors. I could trace the main contributing factor for why I acted the way I did to the resulting ignominy from the desecration. But the most significant understanding I had was, that even though it wasn't my fault, I was still responsible for my behavior.

My lengthy musings came to a halt when Keith said, "Marco? Where are you now ... tell me what you're seeing, thinking."

I proceeded to explain to him my current revelation. "Excellent work, Marco," Keith said, cracking a smile. "Now think about your next step."

My next step was to cleanse and reprogram the inadequate part. I closed my eyes again and began to concentrate. The only way to accomplish this was to create a tangible picture in my mind of the inadequate part being exorcised of all its imperfect characteristics.

Once I was able to concentrate on this step, I looked up into his gaze. "I see myself overlooking a canyon during a sunset. As the sun descends, I envision its rays reflecting off the sparse layers of cloud cover, creating a beautiful multi-layer spectrum of blazing colors. I imagine a cool breeze flowing across my body, as a warm illuminating light from above shines on me and creates a white-out effect that is the cleanest, brightest white I can imagine. I picture the whiteness as a soothing cleansing treatment for the blackness within. I'm feeling as pure and clean as the brilliant color itself."

"And now how do you want to orchestrate the inadequate part?"

I stood up and puffed out my chest. "I want it to be the exact opposite—confident, strong, and stable. It should be at peace with itself and not paranoid about what other people think." Sitting back down, I folded my hands over my crossed knees. "I don't want to feel as if I have to worry about working to exhaustion in my personal life. On the job, or in the gym, I shouldn't feel I have to be perfect in order to be accepted in society. I want to move past that. I want to feel good and proud of myself. But most of all, I want to feel morally acceptable."

I now had a better understanding of the inadequate part, its defender parts, and what they wanted. I was able to see the un-blending taking place within me. The unburdening and bearing witness process got me to the point of reprogramming the misconception that the inadequate part thought about itself. I could go straight to the visualization technique of cleansing and reprogramming the part whenever I felt its symptoms coming on.

The most exhausting part that haunted me with unrest, nervousness, worry, and fear had to be tackled. It was a part that created such turbulence in my life that it wore me down mentally and physically. It created internal anger, sending me into explosive tantrums of rage, causing massive migraines. This trait brought such a terrifying panic of paranoia and chaotic disorder that I'd seek self-medicating remedies and actions to extinguish the internal fire. It was so persistent that it weakened my stability to where I didn't think I'd be able to go on living. This element of my psyche was the anxiety that lurked close to the surface.

When I contemplated the anxiety's physical symptoms, I began to realize that, even though they were progressively more intense, it was the same feeling I experienced during the abuse. When it was happening to me I had the distinctive gut feeling that 'something was not right.' I was petrified I was doing something wrong and was going to get caught. Because of what was being done to me, I felt that bad things would continue to happen to me. I waited for the wrath of God to punish me. I couldn't shake the feeling, even though I did nothing wrong, trying to be a good-hearted, law-abiding citizen.

I'd wake up feeling good, but this part would overpower me with negative thoughts, certain that trouble lay in wait. It was as though none of the good things I did existed or mattered; it was all about the one wrong thing I did.

In my next therapy session, as I walked up the stairs to Keith's office, I organized my thoughts. When I settled into the love seat, I explained what I thought was a new part I discovered, and detailed the characteristics.

Upon further discussion, Keith said, "The part you're actually describing is the shameful feelings that were conceived from the abuse and the ensuing conditioned reprehensible actions that followed. It was the feeling of shame that brought on the anxiety and all its feelings of guilt."

Following my understanding and ability to distinguish the shame versus the anxiety and the shameful part's origin and roots, I went back to identifying its physical symptoms.

"I get overtaken with restlessness and remorse. It paralyzes me with fear. There's tightness in my chest. My breathing becomes heavy, sometimes to the point of hyperventilating. When I get a feeling of unrest I'll pace, fidget my leg up and down, sometimes my face will twitch."

As I identified the shame's physical characteristics, I could recognize its obsessive and perfectionist parts that came in to defend against the past's painful memories and self-perceptions. It made me squirm in my seat.

"I thought the obsessive part's purpose was to divert the energy of my shame's reactions of anxiety, fear, panic, and paranoia to something that would put my mind at ease, convincing me I was doing nothing wrong. Following the abuse, I developed an obsessive-compulsive disorder to expunge the shame's guilty feelings and divert its energy into developing a perfectionist self-image of what I thought was innocent, admirable, and morally acceptable. In my youth, I'd neurotically work at proving myself in athletics, obsessing that I would be the next Mike Schmidt, Larry Zonka, or Dan Gable. In my early twenties, I took bodybuilding to the extreme by training so hard I would literally get sick in the middle of workouts. I dieted so strictly that every calorie, fat content, and macronutrient was measured down to a science, obsessing that one day I would be Mister Olympia."

I continued on, spreading out on the love seat, leaning forward with elbows resting on knees, explaining to Keith my obsession to be perfect in all areas of my life—including therapy, working feverishly on the steps to unburden the disgrace. In my mind, I had now un-blended the obsessive and perfectionist defender parts, getting them to step aside. I realized I needed to get my true self connected with the shameful part so it could bear witness to all the burdens and painful memories. From the true self, I asked the shameful part what it wanted.

I jumped up, pacing as I explained myself. "I relate the shameful part to being like a child who had done something wrong—sent to his room—waiting for his father to come home and punish him." I stopped in front of Keith's desk, bending toward him. "It's frustrating." I rested both hands on the desktop, shaking my head. "I can't latch onto one good deed or intention to convince myself that there is decency within."

At this point, I became physically exhausted. I plopped into the love seat and spread my arms across the back of the chair.

Keith made a minor adjustment to his spectacles with a forefinger pushing its bridge, then let the finger make its way down his nose as he thought, looking down. He looked up, fixed his eyes directly on me. "The anxiety part jumped in to prevent you from having to relive and experience the pain that the shameful part was carrying."

"And," I said, leaning forward, "if I connect with the anxiety and ask it from the true self what it wants, the answer is rest, peace of mind for body and soul."

Keith slowly nodded his head as I continued. "It wants to live without stressing over everything and anything in an attempt to achieve perfection. The anxiety put me in a survival mode, pumping me up with adrenalin, putting me on guard, alerting me that there was danger ahead. I understand how the anxiety feels. It doesn't have to worry anymore. There is no more danger ahead. The true self is now running things. We are now going to be able to take a deep breath, relax, and be at peace with ourselves. I'm so thankful that I now won't be burdened with the nonstop torturous uproar of emotions."

Being in a more relaxed state, I was able to un-blend the anxious part and have it step aside so I could finish my work with the shameful part. I revisited painful burdens the shameful trait was bearing, understanding the reprehensible and guilt-ridden emotions it was experiencing. From the true self's viewpoint, I assured the shameful emotional component that it was not the creature it appeared to be. It didn't have to feel guilty anymore. I guaranteed that all of its subsequent actions were a direct result of acting like the shameful creature it was sculpted into from the awful atrocity that was committed.

From the shameful part, I meditated on receiving and getting connected with the true self's assurance and understanding. I was able to direct my true self to ask this trait if it needed anything else and how it wanted to release the degradation it held in.

It wanted the disgraceful memories erased, as well as removing the chill and sickness in its gut when they flashed instinctively and uncontrollably in its mind. It sought to have all the unmanageable sexual images of its imagination controlled and reprogrammed with normal thoughts. It wanted to feel like it was not a consenting party to the abnormal sexual perversions that were forced upon a young child.

The shameful part within me wanted reassurance that the creature I thought I had become was the result of a young mind being molded from wickedness thrust upon it during peak developmental years. It wanted to stop having to always look over its shoulder thinking it had done something wrong. It wanted to wake up in the morning at peace, not immediately expecting the worst. The shame within wanted to stop feeling like bad things were going to happen in life because it was not a good person. It wanted to feel it deserved to be happy and worthy of receiving the good things of this life.

After relinquishing all the burdens of the shameful part and communicating what it wanted from the true self, I continued meditating on the connection of the true self's understanding and the shameful part's acceptance of that understanding. I visualized unburdening the shame like the outer tarnished skin being removed from a banana, envisioning the negative self-perceptions of myself peeling away and exposing the true clean, white, sweet goodness within.

CHAPTER TWENTY-SEVEN
~REPROGRAMMING THE PSYCHE~

As I was meditating on this unburdening method, the muscular tension I was holding in my body began a gradual dissipation, beginning from my temporal lobes and working its way down through my feet. Simultaneously, I focused on deep breathing and then exhaling all the toxic anxiety I was holding in.

I could now wake up in the morning and live the day with no resistance or turbulence, instead of being on guard like a soldier defending his position. My mind became focused on all the good I was doing in life rather than being fixated on negative things I did in the past or the human imperfections I had.

A sense of relief overcame me as I realized I was not the horrible monster I had thought I was. I could logically comprehend that I had my wits regarding the exploitation, justifying the reproachable actions instead of believing I committed them because I was flat-out evil. I also knew I was still ultimately responsible for my actions.

Now that I understood the nature of the stigma and had the ability to unburden its hurt and negative self-perception, I had to reprogram how I wanted it to feel and act. To achieve this, I went through the process of stripping away its tarnished unfavorable self-perceptions until I attained a state of clean, sweet goodness. I meditated on the relaxing sensation of all the shame's tensions and stressors being released.

When I established a state of cleanliness, I realized there was a blank new part that could be programmed any way I wanted. A sense of excitement blew me away as it dawned on me I could take the intense energy that wore me down over the past thirty-three years, and apply it to a positive intention.

I began the technique of downloading all the traits I wanted in my clean part's hard drive. Peace, tranquility, and patience were the first things that came to mind. I wanted a sense of serenity that could free me from the chaotic battle between all the abuse's defender parts and shame that I had been tormented with. I wanted the part to know it was not being judged and had a sense of child-like freedom.

I pictured images of my own children smiling, skipping, running, and doing leaps of merriment and happiness for no reason but the pleasure of existence. I longed for the new part to feel that way. I wanted that feeling of absolute trust in the world, not worrying about punishment. I yearned for the new part to live carefree without sweating the little things. I wanted freedom to trust life, people, and most of all myself.

I visualized the new part as friendly and outgoing, able to walk into any room with its head held high, looking people in the eye. I wanted the new part to attract good people, friends and family into my life; unlike most of my life where it sheltered me from any type of normal interaction. I wanted its gloomy self-perception that sent me into seclusion expunged permanently.

I hoped the new part would make me feel good about myself, telling me I'd done a good job, prevailing over tremendous odds and succeeding. I wanted it to feel proud and fulfilled that it had accomplished something, seeing and recognizing all the positives in my life, rather than only focusing on the negatives. When people asked how I was doing, I desired to use words like 'fantastic', 'great', 'wonderful', and 'couldn't be better'. I wanted to open my eyes in the morning and look forward to living the day.

CHAPTER TWENTY-EIGHT
~THERAPEUTIC INTERRUPTION:
SON'S DOWNTURN~

In the midst of making tremendous progress dealing with the past, I was confronted with additional trials that tested my patience and faith in therapy. Besides the normal responsibilities that fatigued and drained, I transitioned from being a psychiatric patient to a single parent, caring for two children full time, and four children on weekends.

I was challenged with parenting duties that tested my mental strength and endurance. Even in a stable environment, this isn't an easy task.

Keith had to reinforce in me that I was in the developmental stages of seeing the beginning of the healing process. He told me many times how amazed he was that I was able to stay driven with the stressors surrounding me. I didn't see it that way. I still battled with thoughts that I wasn't doing enough.

Julian had become progressively more distant during our transition of becoming a family unit. He was always in a fog, and had an abnormal delay when communicating. He stopped going to the gym and eating dinner with his sister and me during the week. He exhibited almost no motivation to do much of anything. He took on a grungy appearance and started spending a lot of time at his mother's apartment—where there was limited supervision. He didn't want to be with me, like he had in the past. No more movies, dinners out, or watching a ball game together.

I didn't approve of the kids he was hanging out with. He became disrespectful and wouldn't follow any rules I put in place. Even when I grounded him, he'd look me straight in the eye and walk out the door. He didn't care about school or his grades. He constantly lied to me. I could tell he was numbing himself, and soon he was doing nothing more than occupying space.

I tested him with a home drug kit and discovered he was smoking pot. A lot of kids smoked pot when I was his age, including myself. But he was smoking all day long, which was obvious from his continual staring into space. I was sickened as I flashed back to being his age. Could he be dealing with anything like what I went through?

My first reaction was that it was my fault. One morning before work, I sat with him at the kitchen table. "You're at an age now where there's a fork in the road, and you have a choice of which path in life to take," I said. "Do you want to take the path leading to struggles and pain, or one that leads to peace, happiness and security?"

There was a blank stare as I paused for a response.

"I think you're starting to make some wrong choices," I said. "My first-hand experiences can be an advantage to show you how your current choices in behavior can lead to awful consequences. You can't do what you want because life dealt you a bad hand. You have to play with what you've been dealt. You're responsible for your actions."

"Yeah, whatever," he said, staring at me with glazed-over eyes. He stood up and walked away.

My frustration grew. I may as well have been talking to a telephone pole. He wasn't getting it no matter how much pleading, advising, reprimanding and disciplining I did. The harder I worked at getting through, the more distant he became.

To add to my internal strife, the shameful part decided to join forces with the obsessive perfectionist. Those elements of my psyche attempted to revert back to the appalling being I was thirty-three years ago. My irritation mounted. The feelings of failure intensified because my son was not a perfect straight-A student, star athlete, clean-cut looking, and church-going kid. Not only was I primarily concerned for my son's health, well being, and future, but I was sure I was to blame for failing him as a father.

One night when I awoke in the early morning hours to find him not at home, I panicked. I called his number—over and over—only to have my call continually dumped into voice mail. Who does he think he is? He's only sixteen years old. He's still living under my roof. It was the middle of the summer, and my two younger children were with me for a two-week stay. I couldn't start searching for him until they woke up.

At a more decent hour of the morning, I started calling his friends. The more numbers I called, the angrier I became. Then I started to worry. I packed up my two younger children and went door to door to my son's friends' houses.

Finally, one dad helped me by locating his son. As that father interrogated his son, I found out there had been a party.

I got the friend's number who held the party and left a message, "If I don't get a phone call back in five minutes, I'm getting the police involved."

I anguished that maybe he overdosed or was in an accident. Five minutes later, at two in the afternoon, Julian finally called, acting like nothing was wrong.

As I was driving to pick him up, my anger escalated. By the time I got to the house, I was in a rage. I moved up the walkway to the porch, each step a little quicker—a little more determined. Trying to compose myself, I took a deep breath when I reached the door. That didn't work. I pounded on the door.

Julian answered. "What's up?"

Almost blowing out my vocal chords, I screamed, "What do you mean, what's up? I didn't know if you were dead or alive. You do whatever you want ... and it's not okay with me." At this point, my hands were flailing in the air. "I demand respect. You call me when you're not coming home. Do you understand me?"

He laughed in my face and said, "What's the big deal? I didn't have my phone on me."

I glared at him. "Then what's that in your pocket?"

"Oh, I found it."

Still playing along with his game, I yelled back, "And what? The house you were in didn't have a phone?"

"My friend's father wouldn't allow me to use it."

I stopped trying to rationalize with him as he continued to insult my intelligence. It was one lie after the other, thinking he was a big tough guy that could say and do what he pleased. When we got home, I immediately sent him to his room and grounded him.

Sometime later that evening, my son emerged from his bedroom, showered and ready to go out for the night.

"Where do you think you're going? Don't think you're going to stroll right out of here."

He looked me eye to eye and said, "I'm not grounded. I don't care what you say. I'm going out."

"If you walk out that door, I'll take away all your privileges, which includes the roof over your head."

"No problem," he said, handing me his key and walking out.

I stared in disbelief at the closed door. I had the little ones with me and didn't want to cause a scene.

At three in the morning, I heard a loud noise coming from Angel's bedroom. She was spending the night at a friend's house. I was startled, stimulating an adrenaline rush. I jumped out of bed and rushed to her room. Jennifer and Brandon woke up and scurried behind me. Julian had broken the window to get into the apartment. I tried to physically remove him, but the little ones started to cry. I walked away to gain my composure. I let him stay the night.

The next morning after I got the two younger kids up and ready for summer day camp, I shook my son awake. "Pack your bags. You have to leave."

After dropping the kids at camp, I passed the apartment on my way to work. Julian was sitting on the bleachers at the baseball field across from the apartment complex. He looked depressed. Was I doing the right thing?

I asked his uncle, grandmother, my therapist, and a friend at work whose son had similar behavior problems if I was doing the right thing. They all agreed that I was right.

My next therapy session was devoted solely to the matter. We discussed the issue and decided that it was best for Julian to take the hit now and pay the consequences, instead of later when it'd be more difficult to overcome. I made the decision that he couldn't stay in my home if he didn't follow the rules.

I was hoping he'd have no place to go. But his mother took him in. My plan to teach him a lesson backfired.

Julian grew more out of control, with a free pass to do as he pleased with little supervision. His behavior and appearance steadily deteriorated. He grew dread-locks and a scruffy beard. He pierced his ears and got a tattoo. He started smoking cigarettes in addition to the pot. He was now experimenting with hallucinogenic drugs and cocaine. The cashier drawer was regularly coming up short where he worked at a gas station in a nearby strip mall. I was friendly with some of the merchants there who told me Julian was hanging out with guys who were bad news. They even asked what was happening to him, saying he looked horrible.

My shame up-shifted into high gear. I had totally failed my son and was a horrendous father. I envisioned my wife blabbing and laughing to everyone that I was a disgraceful, hideous and awful parent. I was overwhelmed with paranoia. I thought people were whispering in shadowy corners that I was a loser for not having the perfect family. I even thought my family was sitting at the kitchen table laughing at me. I mentally regressed back in age to the period when I constantly held my head down, unable to look people in the eye.

Julian's issues worsened while living with his mother. Angel woke me up one night and said Julian was arrested. It was all over the Internet, as friends spread the word through instant messaging. He was in a car with three of his friends when they were pulled over and the officer smelled marijuana. Upon a more thorough search of the car, a quarter pound of pot was seized. All night and into the morning, I frantically tried to call his phone.

When I reached him the next afternoon, I asked, "Can you please come home so we can deal with the situation."

I was totally amazed when he said, "Am I going to be grounded?"

"You need to come home. And yes, you will have to serve some time being grounded."

"Then I'm *not* coming home."

His insolence was unfathomable. He still thought he'd done nothing wrong and didn't have to pay the consequences. A crushing sense of irritation overpowered me. I felt my head was going to erupt. I had lost control of my son. I had failed at fatherhood.

Over the next two weeks, I convinced Julian to come home. I tried to find a happy median between being the headstrong, forceful enforcer and being a lenient, nonchalant father.

I took him to a counselor once a week and tried to follow the therapist's advice. A good part of my own therapy sessions switched from my issues to dealing with my challenges with Julian. I tried to let him do somewhat as he pleased, while advising and pointing out the consequences of his actions.

"I'll get you an attorney. But this is your one 'get out of jail free' pass. I do love you. As long as you're being productive, responsible, and working for a goal, I'll support you. I'll put a roof over your head, clothes on your back, and food on the table for you. But, if you're doing the same thing in a year and a half when you turn eighteen, you'll have to leave."

"Okay, I get it," he said, with a vacuous stare.

I could tell that he didn't get it ... at all.

CHAPTER TWENTY-NINE
~THERAPEUTIC INTERRUPTION:
SINGLE PARENTING TRIALS~

While feeling the sting of Julian's poor choices, Brandon was running into problems as a result of his developmental issues. He was diagnosed with bipolar disorder at the age of three, as well as high anxiety and ADHD. He wasn't able to maintain the same pace as other children his age, and was put on psychiatric medications for three years to stabilize his drastic mood swings and erratic behavior. His doctors experimented with a variety of different concoctions and dosages, trying to stabilize his behavior. They added and adjusted various medications until Brandon began to have hallucinations.

When his mother called, explaining what had happened, I was furious. "Is this the way these fucking doctors are dealing with our little boy? They send you on your way with any and every scrip possible, pushing you out the door. I'm pissed that he has to go through this while the doctors can't figure things out."

"Marco, calm down," Mary said. "They're doing what they can for the little guy."

I flashed back to my own hospital stay, strung out on massive quantities of chemicals. I was in a comatose state of despair and hopelessness. Reliving the gloominess of wanting my life to end, I hoped Brandon wasn't feeling the same way.

Brandon was taken to Children's Hospital, and the specialists immediately took him off all medications. Over the next couple of months, I began to notice withdrawal symptoms when he was with me on weekends. Adverse effects from the drug removal made him a full-time project. He developed sporadic twitches and his speech was slurred. He was unable to interact with his siblings and other children. He became extremely frustrated and angry whenever he was unable to accomplish or understand something, resorting to hitting or kicking at times. If he didn't get his way, he'd go into a violent convulsion of temper tantrums, making a scene wherever we went. I love this kid. But the anxiety I felt dealing with my own issues and Julian's problems made it difficult to go out in public.

The doctors adjusted his medications from the psychiatric mood stabilizers to ADHD stimulants periodically over the course of the next few months. They attempted to increase his attentiveness, so he would be able to mature developmentally to match other children his age. The withdrawal symptoms finally dissipated, and his behavior problems became manageable.

During this trying period of dealing with my two sons' issues, Angel's boyfriend had broken up with her. She was an emotional wreck for weeks, unable to attend our weekday gym sessions or enjoy a night out with her friends. Her heartache ripped through my soul like a chainsaw through paper. I absorbed her depression and pain as if they were my own. I felt helpless, wanting to take it all away. I tried to comfort her, but she wanted none of it.

I had flashbacks of my inability to get close and secure in a partnership. I had believed that a relationship was only physical and sexual. I never felt like I was able to satisfy my partner. My distortion created insecurity and jealousy, eventually leading to my heart feeling like it was ripped in half.

While Angel struggled, I wanted to help with her chores. I went to her bedroom for her dirty clothes. As I was filling the washing machine with her things, I found the ripped off top of a condom package mixed in. I began hyperventilating. My daughter's too young. She couldn't be having sex. I charged into her bedroom, shaking the evidence in my hand. "How could you be having sex at fifteen years old?"

"It's not mine," she said, her face a bright red. "Really, Dad, I don't know where it came from. It's probably my girlfriend's when she slept over this weekend."

"Am I really supposed to believe that? Is this what you want people to think of you? An easy lay? And if it's not yours, where were you when all of this was going on?"

"Thanks for thinking of your own daughter as a *slut*. Thanks for making me feel *worse* about myself than I already do."

I took a step back. Why was she thinking badly about herself? Softening my tone, I asked, "What's going on, honey."

She collapsed in my arms, crying. "I don't know what's going on. I'm so confused."

I felt something bizarre and familiar at that moment, but I dismissed my baleful intuition. I convinced myself to believe her at first. Then I began rationally talking with Angel, advising her of the consequences and complexity of having meaningless sex at such an immature age. She listened, but didn't offer a response. She wanted to retreat to her room and cry. All I could do is go back to the laundry.

The parenting stressors I had with my other daughter, Jennifer, were not as complex as they were with the other three kids. I love all my children equally, but my younger daughter has the potential to be the most talented and anchored. It helped to have a grounded mother in her life, tirelessly working to get her involved in a multitude of activities. Jennifer played on two traveling soccer teams, was on the school's basketball team, ran track, sang in the choir, played piano, took gymnastic lessons, and went to Catholic school. It was easy to care for her.

My two older children needed attention because of the dysfunctional lives they had to experience, while the youngest required special consideration because of his developmental concerns. When I tried explaining this to my ten-year-old daughter, she wasn't mature enough to understand why everyone else got more attention than she does.

During this period, it was almost impossible having Jennifer and her eight-year-old brother together. She spewed a high-pitched, piercing scream at Brandon that sent a spine-tingling shock wave throughout my body. By the end of the weekend with these two, not only were my vocal cords exhausted, but also my mental stability.

Mondays were brutal at work. I could barely put syllables together, let alone function productively after the chaotic weekend of caring for all four children. It'd take me two days to recuperate from the grueling task of keeping the two younger ones from killing each other and the two older ones in line.

I was exhausted mentally more than physically. My guard was down, and my defense against the various defender parts seemed to surrender. I switched back to survival mode once again. My life seemed to be nothing but stress, hard work, problems, and loneliness. Even though unjustified, my psyche reverted back to believing I was an irresponsible, no good, obese, ugly, piece of shit that was doing something horribly wrong and deserved nothing good out of life. I'd have to work twenty-four hours a day, seven days a week, three hundred sixty-five days out of the year for the rest of my life to make up for the evil I had done and the hurt I had caused in the past.

I was beaten down from the financial uncertainties that were still pending: the divorce, the IRS, the credit agencies, all that and more. Would there be any money for the kids' education, any kind of retirement for me, anything left to leave behind for my children when I pass?

From there, I went into self-pity mode. I was tired of having to work so hard at everything. The stress from parenting left me exhausted at night. I was frustrated by my two eldest not taking my advice on the importance of maintaining good grades and completing all their homework. I was aggravated that they didn't understand they needed to start right now to improve on their academics so they could go to college. I constantly explained to them how tough it was out in the world. A good education with a decent career would make their lives a whole lot easier.

It upset me that they wouldn't do their chores or respect my rules. No one was allowed to have friends in the house when I wasn't there.

They were supposed to return home at a set time, keep the house in order, and take care of the dog—that they begged for until I gave in. The little Toto-looking Karin Terrier destroyed every pair of shoes in the house and soiled the rug to the point of my needing to disinfect it every day. I felt they had no respect for me and, as a result, I lost respect for myself.

I yearned for the companionship of a woman's presence. I longed for the peaceful security and relaxing comfort of holding a lover in my arms at the end of the day. I craved the refuge, tranquility, and reassurance that someone had my back, and I had theirs. I desired the sexual intimacy of being connected as one. I wanted to show the person I loved the physical pleasure of my deep, desiring love. Most of all, I wanted to love someone and have someone love me, sharing and benefiting from the lessons I had learned in life.

CHAPTER THIRTY
~THERAPEUTIC INTERRUPTION:
A MENTAL STEP BACKWARD~

I was almost at the point of giving up on finding the companionship of a friend, lover, and soul mate. The confusion of why such execrable events happened to me as a child and having to pay for it from now until the grave tested my faith in everything.

The defender parts took control, concealing happiness and appreciation for any good that happened in my life. My perception of the world was clouded, creating a pessimistic attitude. I was primed for a relapse in my mental wellness.

I accumulated an immeasurable amount of anger and hurt that tunneled my vision. I couldn't understand the point of living with its torturous mental anguish of pain and disappointment. I was regressing to where I was when first released from the hospital two-and-a-half years prior.

My exasperation was first directed at the Church and its so-called leaders and teachers. Fury overpowered me, as I would faithfully continue to sit in church on Sundays, listening to the priest's sermons. This imperfect human had the audacity to lecture that we were not doing enough. As I listened to him preach, I got so disgusted I could've chewed up his sermon notes and spit them down his goddamn throat. *We* weren't doing *enough. We* needed to do *more.* What did *they* do when one of their own was corrupting a wholesome child with filthy porn, trying to sodomize a ten-year-old boy a few feet away from them?

I found it difficult to remain seated in the pew as I thought how they sipped their scotch, gorging their stomachs in their own bedrooms down the hall, well aware that something wasn't right. What did they do to prevent and report the atrocities that occurred over the years to scores of young, innocent youth? What the fuck did they do to make things right and take care of God's shattered children? They hid behind attorneys, statutes of limitation, taking the quickest, easiest and cheapest way out. What did the motherfuckers do to help multitudes of family members who were devastated as a result of the cowardly acts and perversions of the pedophilic, chosen-by-God priests?

My wrath then switched to God. I had to leave Mass.

Even though the majority of my issues were a result of bad decisions I had made in my adult years, my scar-ridden soul knew that my decisions had been a result of the torturous abuse. The indignation I had for God sent me to a gloomy, lonely, and scary place.

I overheard a rock song that added fuel to my fiery rage. When I first heard it, I repeated its words over and over in my head as I ran the treadmill at the local gym. I'd pound away at a rapid race, testing my endurance and strength, as I ran seven miles in less than an hour singing the tune. The words energized me and pumped my adrenalin to the point where I wasn't breathing as heavy as I usually was.

At first, I wasn't paying attention to the words until I heard sporadic phrases of, "Man of God, hypocrite, confess it all away, do you remember the child I used to be?" I wasn't sure, but I wondered if it was about clergy sexual abuse.

I looked it up on the Internet the next day, and sure enough, there was a song. It was titled "I'm Not Jesus." The words I'd heard did include phrases such as: "I thought you were a good man. I thought you talked to God." The lyrics turned accusatory: "child abusing, turn satanic." I was stunned by the lines: "Do you remember me? The kid I used to be."

The words were chilling. It was as if they were plagiarized from thoughts in my mind about my own abuse. What further pumped me up was its chorus about not being like Jesus and forgiving it away.

I only heard the song on the radio for a few weeks, and all of a sudden it wasn't aired anymore. In the back of my head, knowing the tactics of the Catholic Church to limit their monetary damages, I wondered if the diocese offered the group money to stop promoting the negativity of the Church.

It is said that you sometimes have to take a step backwards in order to take two steps forward. I had taken a gargantuan leap backward in my therapy, and it would take a whole lot more than two steps to get me going forward.

The relentless stressors in my life could have sent me into another breakdown. But there was something inside that had gotten me this far, enabling me to gain composure and regain health and stability, not only for myself, but also for my children.

Determined to pull myself back onto the path of recovery from the latest emotional setback, I devoted the therapy sessions solely to issues surrounding the abuse rather than dealing with the external stressors in life. It was going to be a fresh start, and to kick things off I needed to vent.

"Why the fuck do I have to work so fucking hard? I try to contain and control the motherfuckin' wild beast inside me, but the motherfucker fights endlessly to sabotage any little glimpse of goodness in my life. It fuckin' drives me into the ground." I continued until I exhausted all the blasphemies and obscenities my vocabulary could think of against God. Pausing a moment, I then looked my therapist in the eye and said, "Okay I'm done. Now let's get back to work."

With eyebrows raised, he and I laughed. "I've been telling you all along that your issues are a direct result of the shame from the exploitation," Keith said.

"My humiliation feels like it's coming from the acts I committed following the perversion and not from the actual abuse I received."

"Yes, that's true. But the injustice that occurred in your life was unquestionably a major contributing factor in you subsequent diabolical acts."

I sat back in the chair, relaxing for a minute, relieved that I wasn't some heinous person. Maybe the defilement really did have something to do with my reprehensible actions. But the critic within commenced to convincing me that my therapist was full of shit, saying those things to trick me or brainwash me into believing my despicable deeds were a result of the violation.

"I don't understand how someone came up with all this shit about true self, defender parts, un-blending, bearing witness, unburdening, and cleansing," I said, leaning forward in my chair. "I don't see how it's feasible that mankind could possibly interpret something that was inside someone's mind and understand it, let alone fix it. I don't see how this process could possibly take away the tormenting pain and restlessness that haunts me every moment of my life."

We worked together at greeting the critic, recognizing it was a defender part from the hurt. It was trying to distract and derail me from reaching the core of the shame. When I understood this, I was able to get the personality trait to step aside so I could continue working on the wrongdoing.

While struggling to connect with the part of me that was holding in the disgrace, the beast took over, fighting and tearing at my inner psyche. It was on a quest to possess my soul, and not going to let me rest. The creature relentlessly tried to deceive me into believing that if I didn't work nonstop toward perfection, I was a vile animal and complete failure.

"It's exhausting," I said. "I have to battle this part along with the sense of frustration and hopelessness it creates. It's so tough and strong that it seems undefeatable."

"What does the overburdened restless part want?"

"It wants someone to bring it under control to rest and have peace. It's like a hyperactive fidgety child, pacing back and forth, crying for someone to make it stop."

I was having trouble connecting my inner true self to the stressed part because of the intense energy it was creating. Keith guided me by helping me communicate with the stressed part. I needed to make it understand that by stepping aside it would allow the healing process of unburdening the emotional component that was holding in the shame. Without the burden of the disgrace, the anxious, stressed-out, perfectionist, striver part would not have to work so hard to compensate for its self-perceived shortcomings.

Furthermore, relieving the humiliating burdens would bring rest, tranquility, and peace. The intense energy could then be orchestrated in better ways. At this point, we ended our session. I left his office once again annoyed and uncertain, wondering if I was ever going to be able to live a normal peaceful life.

As I meditated on the session during the week, I understood what my therapist was explaining. I visualized fast-forwarding directly to the ultimate goal of un-blending the various multiple defender traits from the abuse. Getting to the root of the therapy and healing process of dealing with the disgraceful iniquity was my goal.

I had trouble believing whether or not my logic in understanding the process was correct. It seemed too simplistic to me at first. I envisioned confessing all my scandalous deeds and desires for the world to know. I imagined no more secrets or lies and eliminating the need to masquerade with a phony façade to hide the atrocious creature I thought I was.

Instantly, I was buoyant as helium. The crushing weight from the wicked acts was lifted from my shoulders. The mortifying and disgusting impressions I had were no longer there. I was able to get a brief glimpse of the divine true self. For a moment, I physically felt what life could be like while at peace with myself. Happiness and comfort engulfed me at the possibility of living a life free of judgment, low self-esteem, anxiety and paranoia.

While in this good frame of mind, I became aware of all the goodness inside of me and the decent things I was doing in life. My human flaws appeared to be minor bumps in the road rather than being amplified into major roadblocks. I began to see how I pulled myself out of mental illness, addiction, and sexual perversion. I became conscious that I survived sexual abuse at an early age and persevered by holding it together.

I was imbued with a sense of accomplishment. I now comprehended and conquered the difficult therapeutic work of dealing with the harmful emotions associated with bringing the misconduct to the surface.

I thought about having being housed in a mental institution and sedated on numerous psychiatric medications. I was able to regain my wits, dignity, and independence. The comprehension of where I was mentally and physically now compared to where I was a few years prior, shocked me with amazement.

I began to grasp how I, unyielding, had strived to regain my career, working at a physically demanding manual labor job in the hot summer heat. I was fresh from the hospital while dealing with medication and street drug withdrawal. The awe of little things mystified me, like being a productive part of society, having my own transportation, my own place, and custody of my two older children. I grasped the miracle of my heart, soul, and mind being transformed from a bottomless murky pit of perverse sexual acts to a high plane of clean thoughts with righteous desires.

I was joyful. I had a clear perception of what the meaning of life was: love. Nothing else mattered but love. Love of my children and for my children. Love for the ability to right what was wrong, for forgiveness, and second chances. Love for the peace that life can offer and the beauty it radiates.

I had definitely made a major breakthrough in my therapy. All those two-steps forward with one-step backward had built up my fortitude and backbone, strengthening my mental stability. With the ability to visualize and sense living at peace with myself, I was now able to focus on, and have reliance in, my therapy.

CHAPTER THIRTY-TWO
~THERAPY: UNBURDENING THE PAST~

Each ensuing session progressed a little further than the previous one. I understood the various defender parts that orchestrated my personality and behavior. I was able to improve on the techniques of unburdening the enormous amount of disgrace imprisoned inside with faith, confidence, awareness of my issues, and therapeutic work.

At each subsequent session, I went directly to dealing with my shame. When I was able to connect my true self with the loathsome part, a fervent feeling of sorrow would come over me. My eyes would fill, lips would quiver, and a lump would develop in my throat as I contemplated what the disgraceful part wanted the true self to know.

The shameful part wanted someone to understand how it had been suffering for the past thirty-three years. It wanted it known that the reprehensible actions it committed was not its fault, and not who it really was. As with the other various parts, the shame wanted peace from the multitude of ill self-perceptions it had of itself. The pitiful part wanted to stop feeling like the adolescent child who had done something wrong. It wanted to feel that it was not a consenting adult in the sexual perversion. The shame wanted freedom from the bondage of remorse from not only the abuse but also from the subsequent discreditable events it was involved in.

Initially, the different defender parts immediately attacked the process of entering the shame. Confusion, followed by insentience, tried to overcome me. I became adept at identifying the first and second lines of defense. Eventually, it didn't take much effort to break through their defensive stance and get back to the process of connecting with the shame. The next two protector parts were more difficult to break through and required more determination and time to defeat.

Whenever I gave credence to the notion that I was a consenting adult during the sexual molestation of a child, I'd be overcome with an onslaught of furious rage, diverting me from entering the place of shame. Once I would pause and meditate on this belief, exasperation would take over, sending me into a tantrum of heated emotions and verbal obscenities. How could a grown man, a priest nonetheless, do such revolting things to a child? The thought of an adult raping a child infuriated me to the point where all I wanted was vengeance.

I fixated on the idea that my youngest daughter was the same age as I was when my innocence was taken from me. Once I exhausted the fury within, I was able to decipher the anger's intent to throw me off track from dealing with the corruption. I was able to have it step aside and get back to the point where the degrading part felt a kinship with the true self.

As soon as I was able to feel the connection of the sorrow and understanding between the shameful part and the true self, the next defender part that stepped in to sidetrack me was the skeptic. I concluded that it was my resentment at the slow process involved with therapeutic work in unburdening the shame that activated this part. I wanted to be free of this annoyance of restlessness I had within my exhausted psyche. My skeptic would bring up possible scenarios in an attempt to convince me that therapy was worthless.

This repetitive cyclical process of connecting with the shameful part and then being distracted by the defender parts continued for some time in my therapy. My affiliation with the shame was longer with each session. The skeptic's intensity was the first defender part that began to dissipate as my association to the shame became more concentrated. I understood and felt the benefits of relating to the mortification. My confidence was building in the therapeutic psychological ideology that Keith was feeding me for the past two and a half years. The more I developed reliance in the psychological theory of the mind's method of defending against traumatic events, the more the skeptic started to fade.

Conversely, my irritation was prominent, still distracting and preventing me from permanently connecting to the shame so I could unburden it. Unable to get the resentment to move aside to concentrate solely on the shame, I decided to go through the un-blending process to relieve it of its burdens. I needed to organize the anger to understand it and attempt to prevent it from showing its ugly face whenever it pleased.

From the place of the true self, I meditated on how I felt toward the rage. As with the other intense defender parts, I felt overtaken with sorrow and compassion for it. I envisioned consoling the anger, conveying to it a sense of understanding why it was so outraged. I encountered a sense of grief and sympathy that it hated its existence. It was holding the abuse responsible for the emotional and physical pain and suffering it endured, in addition to the bad decisions that led to a life of hardship and depression.

I became extremely troubled as I started to relate to the part as if it was one of my children. I wanted to ease the anguish and unrest that the anger endured. I concentrated on communicating these emotions in an attempt to let it know there was someone out there who understood and cared.

Switching over to the mindset of the angry part, I meditated on whether or not I could sense the true self's emotions toward it. I intensely contemplated receiving the true self's sympathetic understanding of the source of the agitation. I was bowled over with a sense of relief as I connected to the true self, knowing there was finally an open line of communication with somebody. I was able to vent in an organized way. The repetitive cyclical rage that instinctively and spontaneously occupied my mind was now under control.

CHAPTER THIRTY-THREE
~THERAPY: MOVING FORWARD~

Starting at the top of the list, I vented on the animal that ruined over thirty years of my life and the lives of my family. I became more irate at the thought of a grown man luring, befriending, deceiving, seducing, and then forcing himself sexually on an innocent child. The anxious frustration exhausted me in reminiscing missed opportunities, loss of pleasurable memories, and the permanent damage. My hatred for what this man had done sent me into a deep, indistinct psychological abyss.

Following my enraged rampage against the predator, the Church was next on my long list of combatants. I was appalled at the acceptance and tolerance the majority of religious sects had in the solicitation of young children for their perverted sexual desires. Shocking memories incensed me, recalling the entries and exits from the bedroom at the rectory like spinning around in a revolving door. The other inhabitants accepted my presence as an admissible and normal practice.

An inundating sense of antagonistic resentment for the Church beleaguered me. I sensed the frozen coldness of the Church's officials when I approached them with what had happened.

"What do you want from us?" Typical responses like that made me want to grind my teeth down to the gums. The cowardice of the Church hiding behind the veil of the statute of limitations infuriated me.

The Church officials held the position that I was mentally coherent well before the statue of limitations expired. They accepted no responsibility for what the Church had covered up, nor for the addictions and psychological problems I had developed. How did they know what coherent was? Were they the ones bearing the burdensome weight of the filth and sinful self-perception that I wasn't even good enough to be dog shit on the sole of someone's shoes? Were they the ones who needed to find every means possible to satisfy the burning perverted sexual desires programmed into a child's mind, as if it was an endorsed and commonplace part of life? Were they the ones who needed to find any and every means possible to extinguish the intense pain and humiliation of the negative self-perceptions caused from sexual abuse?

When I had exhausted my seething toward the Church, I vented the fury I had at God for allowing unspeakable things to be done to me by an animal representing His organization. I cursed God for the torment I had to live with. I was engulfed with rage for having been taught that God was always with me in times of trial. If that was the case, then God must be one sick, perverted fuck.

Subsequent to my blasphemous tear into God, my fury was switched to those who should have protected me and prevented the trauma I endured as a child—my so-called family. I had an immense hatred for my stepfather, as I thought about his selfishness by seeking his own pleasures rather than protecting a child. The only conscious memories I have during this period are of him working all week and rushing home on Fridays to spend the weekend with his friends, getting drunk at the local men's club. I recall the fighting between my mother and him over the little time he spent with his family. I'm astonished at the disregard he had in allowing a child to be trusted alone with a basic stranger for hours, and even overnight at times. Even when the notion entered his mind that maybe something strange was going on, he never followed up with it, stashing it under the bed, never to be brought up again. He continued to allow the pedophile to come around our house.

Consequent to venting my resentment toward my stepfather, I tried to evaluate my mother's role in not preventing my abuse from continuing over a three-year period. For some reason, which I cannot explain, I could not find any anger in my heart for my mother. The inflamed part of me blamed my stepfather more so than her. He was more concerned with his own recreational time, while my mother maintained the household, raising two babies and me. I could see that she was also operating in survival mode, as I had found myself operating with my own children. Memories of her awakening in the early morning hours to exercise, preparing breakfast for the kids, and then making sure I went to school with a freshly made lunch, replayed in my mind as I tried to be upset with her. She'd then spend the day cleaning and running errands before I'd come home from school. She'd make sure my homework was finished before she started dinner. She'd clean up after dinner and go to her night job in the local mall. I understood her loss of reality dealing with a self-centered drunken husband while doing all she did.

My outrage continued with my family for their failure in trying to understand my psychological and addictive illness, abandoning me during my time of need. I never heard from any of them after my final breakdown. I was the sick one, the victim, the unconscious one operating in a robotic way to defend against the abuse mechanically. Who were they to hold my involuntary actions against me? The resentment within me solidified feelings that since I was nothing to them, they were nothing to me.

Finally, after I exhausted all my infuriation for the external variables, I turned my displeasure upon myself. How could I have let this insane individual molest me? The appalling feeling of filthiness swept over me. My tantrum continued to escalate thinking about letting him take away my childhood purity. The bitterness was smothering when thinking about the arousal I experienced as I was lured and seduced with porn into the priest's sick world. The fury continued to escalate at the idea that my prominent childhood thoughts were of distorted sex rather than riding a bike, eating ice cream, playing tag or hide and seek.

I stopped midway through blaming myself, recognizing that I was ten at the time of the abuse. I pictured my ten-year-old daughter's angelic face, crying as I realized that I had shared her virtuous persona before I was violated. Thinking about what had been done to me at that age again incensed me.

I concentrated on the true self understanding what the angry part was experiencing. Sorrow washed over me as I absorbed the vengeful energy. A feeling of grief besieged me for all the unhappiness the angry part was experiencing. The compassion was so great for the anger that I wanted to do what I could to extinguish the anger's torment, much like I would for my children.

I switched to the angry part's acceptance of the true self's sympathy and love. A great sense of relief descended upon me. I understood and had a connection to a soul mate. For the first time since the abuse, I felt loved and cared for. I was not numb to affection. So many times in the past, my striver attempted to force love upon me. I was never able to experience the magic of true love for myself until now. As with the unconditional love for my children, I now felt that kind of love for me.

This wonderful part that loved and was full of compassion and understanding existed inside of me. I was the true self and responsible for my own happiness. For so long in my therapy, I was viewing it as an outside physical entity. I found the seeker that was causing me to pursue the morally acceptable lifestyle I had always dreamed of having. I reverted back to the analogy of the tarnished ripened skin of a banana being peeled to expose the pure white sweetness of its inner core. It was a euphoric feeling to finally recognize there was goodness inside of me.

This epiphany enabled me to easily go through the next process of cleansing the agitated part. I encompassed the anger with the realization of the true self within and expunged any hostile emotions as a result of living from the place of my shame. Once I came to the realization that I was the true self, my shame and anger disappeared.

I felt good enough about myself and what I had accomplished that I was able to not only think, but also feel how I foresaw the shameful part's new role. As I meditated on visualizing how I wanted to foresee the new role of the old disgraceful parts, the emotions of what I was meditating on began taking over. An immense sense of gratitude came over me as I realized how happy I was.

The list of emotions and character traits that I desired and recited daily were once only words to me. Now they had meaning, infiltrating the once unyielding armor of my psyche. I finally felt that I was not the gruesome creature I had perceived myself to be. I was an inspiration who was strong, confident and stable; yet humble, patient, well-mannered, loving, kind, caring, compassionate, friendly, outgoing, generous and gracious. I was a good father who had accomplished a tremendous feat in overcoming trauma, mental illness, and addictions to get back into my children's lives.

I had a feeling of bliss that brought out a smile so wide it felt like my facial skin would tear. I felt physically fit, healthy, and attractive. I sensed I was drawing good things and people into my life. Best of all, I felt free from the abuse's bondage that had imprisoned me.

For the first time since beginning therapy with Keith, I finally understood what he had been telling me existed all along. By discovering the true self, I realized the shame had nothing to do with me. The humiliation seemed to dissipate more easily with each therapy session. I started to relate this revelation to a tangible matter containing a foreign substance, like the clean water in a swimming pool with leaves floating in it. With the realization that I was indeed the true self, it was as easy as plucking out the leaves, or in this case the shameful parts, from the water. I was not going to hell for events that happened to me in the past. Bad things were not going to come back to me for things I did previously, as long as I kept doing what was right.

CHAPTER THIRTY-FOUR
~LIFE'S TRIALS:
OLDEST SON'S TROUBLES~

During this sudden intuitive leap of understanding, I was affected with events that tested my strength and character. The hectic holiday season from Thanksgiving to New Years was upon us. Julian's errant behavior and addiction to drugs, more than just pot, escalated. He was constantly high, cutting school, and failing every course.

I came home from a grueling day at work. As I got close to the front door, the smell of marijuana wafted from the apartment. I growled under my breath. After fumbling with the keys, I finally got the door unlocked. Julian and six of his friends were in the living room, lounging on my couches, playing X Box, and ... eating the snacks I bought for my younger children that weekend.

I stood in front of the TV screen, pointed to the door, and screamed, "Get *out* of my house ... *now*."

No one moved. They gazed at me with bloodshot eyes. I repeated, "Out. Now." The guys stood up and moved to the door. Flailing my hands in the air, I finished with, "And don't come back!"

Julian tried to follow them out the door. I grabbed him by the arm. "You're not going anywhere," I said, dragging him to the kitchen table and plopping him in the chair. "You *know* how I feel about bringing low-life characters here when I'm not home. It's got to stop."

"They're my friends."

"These are not the types you want to hang with. You," I said, getting into his face, "need to make new friends."

"I'm not going to make new friends. I like my friends."

"I've set house rules. You have to respect those rules. These characters are the ones that got you in trouble in the first place."

Julian shoved his chair back and stood up. "I don't *care* what you think. They're my friends. Deal with it." He strutted out the door. I was dumbstruck.

Every day became the same old ritual. I'd come home from work to more hoodlum-looking characters in my apartment. I'd throw them out, telling them to not come around again. But the next day, they'd be back. Sometimes I'd even find kids hiding in the closets when I'd surprise them by coming home earlier.

No form of positive reinforcement *or* punishment seemed to work in persuading my son to change his ways. I tried every possible means I could think of to get him to understand what he was doing wasn't right.

I resolved to stay focused on my own career for the family's welfare, but I was distracted by what was happening at home. I was on the phone throughout the day at work, trying to coordinate with various people to assist in keeping Julian on the right path. At least once a week, I'd have to ask his grandparents to drive over and pull him out of bed. Sometimes they'd find him hiding in a closet and would take him to school with force.

I was on the phone and communicating via e-mail with the assistant principal, academic counselor, child-study counselor, drug counselor, therapist, and mentor, pleading for guidance. I'd ask for suggestions on what I should do to help Julian.

I attended child-study team evaluations, academic review board hearings, joint therapy sessions, and state funded programs. I enrolled him in an after-school outpatient drug program. Nothing and no one seemed to get through to him. In his mind, he didn't have a problem and was doing nothing wrong.

Things worsened when Angel called me after coming home from school one day. She was hysterical. I couldn't understand her at first, but when I calmed her down she said, *"Everything* is gone."

"What do you mean?"

"We were robbed. It's all gone, and there are knives stuck in the wall."

"Call nine one one. And wait outside until the police get there."

I called Debbie, asking her to pick up Julian from the after-school outpatient drug program, and left work immediately. When I arrived home, Laurence, Debbie and Matthew were at the apartment with Angel and Julian.

My jaw dropped when I walked in and took a quick glance. I felt blood race to my face. Storming up to Julian, I screamed, "What the fuck happened? This is *your* fault. How could you keep bringing those shady characters around when I wasn't home? I told you this would happen."

"Fuck you," Julian said, bolting from the apartment.

The place was ripped apart. All my personal belongings were flung on the floor. The new clothes and boots, still in the bags from my recent Christmas gift purchases, were gone. No more big-screen Plasma TV in the living room. Missing were my Apple computer and the LCD flat screen TV from my bedroom. I was cleaned out for seven thousand dollars worth of goods. None of it was insured. I had been cutting corners, one of which included rental insurance, so I would be able to purchase a house once my lease was up. Bad decision.

The anguish over my son's disrespect and disobedience overshadowed any favorable emotions I had for him. I felt helpless. Julian had to know he was responsible, but he wouldn't cooperate with the police and give up the names of possible suspects. Julian was out of control.

"If you continue pulling this shit, Julian, I don't want you living here. Do you think you can support yourself making seven fifty an hour pumping gas? If you're going to continue abusing drugs and disobeying my rules, maybe you should drop out of school ... find somewhere else to live. Then I wouldn't have to stress, worrying whether or not you made it in that day. I wouldn't have to wonder who's in the apartment when I'm not there ... or whether or not you're even alive."

Julian shrugged and gave me a deadpan stare. Nothing stimulated or produced any rational thought that may have existed in his mind. Whether it was positive or negative, it didn't work.

A law enforcement official called me at work the next week. "We're looking for your son for questioning in the attempted robbery of a pharmacy. We'd like you to examine a picture of the suspect that was in the local newspaper to see if you think it could be your son."

"Yes, I'll pick up the paper and take a look." When I viewed the hooded image, my heart pounded and sweat gathered at my temples. I called on relatives for their opinion on whether or not they believed it was Julian in the newspaper. They all concurred that the image did appear to be him. I finally called Lawrence, who was a retired lieutenant in the precinct where the robbery occurred, for advice on how I should handle the situation. We agreed the best thing to do was for me to turn my son in rather than risk him getting hurt if the police were to attempt to apprehend him.

I found out Julian had cut school that day, and was unable to reach him. I left work in a panic, attempting to find him before the police did. I called home over and over. He finally answered the phone when I was about five minutes away. In an effort to prevent him from getting scared and fleeing, I told him the courts made a mistake from his previous incident when he was arrested for marijuana possession. We had to appear in municipal court right away.

When we arrived at the precinct, the juvenile detective and Lawrence were waiting for us. The confusion on my son's face sent a pain into the pit of my stomach. I sat him down and said, "I love you. I brought you in myself because I didn't want you to get hurt. You're here because they want to question you about an attempted robbery of prescription drugs at the Sears pharmacy."

"I was at Sears," he said, scrambling for a story. "But I didn't try to rob the pharmacy."

"Is this you?" I said, pulling the picture from my pocket.

He quickly glanced at the picture and said, "Yes."

I began weeping, almost passing out. The detectives and officers in the area attempted to calm me down, pacing back and forth at my side.

The ache was deep. Even though we were butting heads and not getting along, I still loved him. I didn't want him experiencing agony or suffering. All I could imagine was him being locked up in a juvenile detention facility over the holidays, feeling alone and scared. The heartache of being a failure as a father also enveloped me. I felt like I was to blame. I was in shambles, but I needed to pull myself together for my son.

As I regained my composure, they began the interrogation. At first, it appeared that Julian was guilty. He had stayed overnight at a friend's house in the area of the attempted robbery. He had admitted to being at Sears, and the image in the surveillance picture was his. He didn't have an alibi during the time frame of the robbery, and he also gave up the gender of the pharmacist before it was divulged to him. In addition, a barrel-less paintball gun was used in the attempted robbery, which my son happened to be missing. I knew there was a paintball gun barrel in our closet at home, which was found when I went through our belongings following the house robbery to see if anything else was missing.

Julian maintained his innocence throughout the entire interrogation. The officers informed me that they believed he did it but didn't have enough evidence to book him on the charge. Julian and I then consented to a DNA test to be matched with some clothing found near the robbery scene, which was used as a disguise. After about four to five hours of questioning, we left the station and went home.

I had to wonder. Is the boy I'm supporting and allowing to live in my home with my other children actually the monster the evidence pointed to? Rumors were floating that a certain friend of my son robbed my house—one that he owed money for drugs.

I couldn't sleep at night worrying if Julian could in fact do such heinous things. I was restless when I was away from home wondering what would be missing next. I had to move the kids' Christmas presents to their grandparents' house or the trunk of my car. I walked around checking the windows on a regular basis, making sure they were locked. My paranoia, disappointment, and agitation became more acute as I stewed over the recent events.

It was the morning of Christmas Eve, 2007. The investigating detective in the robbery called with the news. "We've apprehended the suspect. He confessed to the attempted robbery."

"Oh, my God. Thank you for this good news."

"Although your son is innocent, he's hangin' with some bad company. You got some issues there. I've been involved personally in narcotics for some time in your neighborhood. And, uh, your son and his buddies are well known at the precinct."

"I'm aware of my son's issues. I'd appreciate any advice or help you can give me."

"Like I said, he needs to get new friends. But I want to thank you for your cooperation. Good luck with everything."

I was somewhat relieved that my son wasn't guilty and wouldn't have to be detained in a facility with hardened criminals. At the same time, I was also a bit disappointed. What may have been an opportunity to get him help and teach him a lesson—when nothing else had worked—was no longer possible. I pleaded and tried to persuade him to go to a treatment facility for three to six months. But he'd have to adhere to the strict regimen, and he was stubbornly against the idea.

My strength and hope deteriorated as I shifted into a status-quo mode. I waited and prayed that something would happen or someone would come along to help with this family crisis.

A call came in one Friday afternoon from the juvenile detective from our township. He told me there was a warrant out for Julian's arrest for not appearing in court for his drug case.

I called my attorney right away and left a message, asking what was going on because we never received notice for the trial. He called back and said that the hearing was transferred back and forth from the neighboring counties. The notice had been sent to his mother's old address, but she was evicted from there. My attorney tried to get the warrant rescinded by communicating the correspondence that he had sent to their prosecutor's office. But at four on a Friday afternoon, the prosecutor wanted to hear none of it and left the warrant in place. This meant that I had to keep the kid in check all weekend. Then I'd have to explain to my place of employment that I would be late coming in Monday morning because I had to turn my son in at the courthouse because there was a warrant for his arrest.

When we arrived at the Hall of Justice on Monday, a juvenile court officer called us into his office. The officer was a husky, hardened-looking man. Julian's eyes darted around the room. He sniffled continuously and bit his lip. The officer sat us down and started in on the questions. "Do you go to school? How are you doing in school? Do you have a job? Do you know your social security number? Do you follow your father's rules of the house? Do you have a curfew?" Julian lost the color in his face. His answers weren't the ones the officer wanted to hear.

He then turned to me and started with the questions. "What are you doing for your son? Do you eat dinner together? Do you spend much time talking and not yelling at each other?"

"We used to go to the gym and have dinner every night together. He used to maintain employment. I tried getting help through the school and an individual therapist. I attempted to get help from the state through Value Options for Children, and I've even enrolled him in a three day a week outpatient program called the Princeton House. Nothing seems to get through to my son. He won't cooperate and check in to get help. He puts in no effort to use the advice or treatment programs I offer him."

"Can I spend a little more time with you?"

"Sure."

He walked out the door. A couple of minutes later, he came back with a booklet filled with current inmates' names, race, and why they were imprisoned. At least ninety-five percent of the names viewed were either black or Hispanic, and the majority of that percentage was in for murder.

The officer then turned to Julian. "How do you think you're going to survive in an environment like that? In a little over a year, when you're eighteen, your father won't be able to do anything to get you out of trouble." After finishing his scared-straight speech, he sent us on our way with a new court date.

Julian had nothing to say as we were leaving the Hall of Justice. We drove home in silence. I was optimistic that Julian would realize the severity of his current behavior this time, hoping he'd straighten out his act.

Each time Julian would cut school without my permission, I would report him as truant with his academic guidance counselor. Louise would obtain a doctor's note, excusing him for the day. I disciplined him with in-school suspensions and met with the school district's superintendent to ask him to mandate a drug treatment facility, following with a specialized school. Louise advised Julian against going to a drug rehab, telling him that he'd learn more there about doing drugs and getting more contacts to buy them, rather than learning to stay sober. It shocked me that he'd think his mother was giving him good advice. She'd lost custody of her kids while passed out with a crack pipe in her hand.

Louise acted like an authority on drugs with years of sobriety. But she was coming up on charges of robbing houses and pawning the goods for drugs. Her expert advice to him was that he needed to go away when he was ready, and not when anyone else wanted him to.

Julian's issues took a toll on my job, therapy, and personal life. At work, I often had to leave for appointments with school officials, child-study teams, therapists, drug counselors, attorneys, and family court officers. My therapy was all about how to deal with the stress of my son rather than my own matters. The stressors he was creating compromised my tenuous happiness and faith in God.

CHAPTER THIRTY-FIVE
~LIFE'S TRIALS:
YOUNGEST SON'S PHYSICAL HEALTH~

During this same time period, my younger son, Brandon, who was eight at the time, had health concerns that needed immediate attention. He was rushed to the emergency room with stomach pain, vomiting, and a high fever. It was determined he had a urinary tract infection, which is rare for circumcised boys. Upon preliminary ultrasound and x-rays, it was presumed that his urine was refluxing into his body from a deformity between the bladder and kidneys. A small bubble had formed in the urethra and was causing the reflux. The preliminary procedure was to go in with a scope through the penis, and burst the bubble to allow the urine to flow properly from the kidneys to the bladder and out through the penis. More detailed tests needed to be conducted by a urologist at Children's Hospital of Philadelphia to confirm the initial diagnosis and to determine the next course of action.

The first of two tests was to determine whether or not Brandon had sleep apnea. If so, it would cause complications with the anesthesia when he needed to go under for surgery. The test consisted of Brandon being wired with multiple sensors and monitored throughout the night as he slept. He handled it well, and he was cleared for surgery if need be.

The second and final test was called a VCUG (Voiding Cystourethrography) test. I gasped when I read the description of the procedure. Brandon would lie on a table with an imaging camera over him, as a catheter was inserted into his penis that pumped fluid into his bladder. He'd be put in various positions so the doctors could capture the imaging of the reflux from numerous angles. When this process was completed, he would have to urinate out through the catheter.

Mary and I sat with him in the room where the procedure was going to take place. I held the little guy on my lap as he fidgeted, trying to keep him calm. I stroked his head, and caressed his pale face. "It's going to be okay," I said.

"I'm scared, Daddy. What are they going to do to me?"

A staff official came in with toys and animated storybooks, explaining what would happen during the tests.

"Mommy, I'm scared. Is it going to hurt?"

Mary held him on her lap and said, "It's going to be fine. It might be a little uncomfortable, but you're a big boy and can handle it. I'm so proud of you."

My mind was spinning. Flashbacks took over my psyche, triggering bad memories of my childhood. Brandon jumped from his mother's arms to play with the toys. I pictured someone touching, defiling, and corrupting my son's innocence. I was enraged by thoughts of him suffering in life. It took tremendous determination to keep my composure so he wouldn't feel fearful.

Brandon came through the procedure well with only a few brief uneasy moments. We met with the doctor in his office afterward. He explained that the problem was more complex than originally thought. The VCUG test showed a tremendous amount of urine refluxing from the kidneys. He'd need major surgery to correct the deformity.

Brandon went in for surgery on a Wednesday morning. My anxiety intensified to levels similar to when I was ill, but I kept myself under control, sensing his fear and not wanting to fuel it. The hospital personnel did a wonderful job keeping Brandon busy with toys, and his mother and me comfortable. When the nurses came to take him to the operating room, I gave him a hug and kiss. "Daddy loves you more than anything in the world, Brandon."

"Love you, Daddy. Am I going to be okay?"

"You're going to be fine. Mom and I will be here when you come back."

The surgery took five hours. When Brandon was transferred to the recovery room, Mary and I went in and sat by his side, waiting for him to wake up from the anesthesia. I sat in awe of his spotless smooth skin and beauty, touching his face and hair.

I strayed off again to images of my own abuse. I was furious thinking of my own childhood beauty and innocence being corrupted into a filthy decaying corpse. I stared at my son and started to cry, not only for his current physical pain, but because I didn't want him to ever have a glimpse of the mental suffering and misery that I experienced.

Brandon woke up from the anesthesia looking uncomfortable. In a raspy voice, he said, "My ... throat ... hurts."

"You had a tube in your throat that brought oxygen into you during surgery," I said. "Let me see what I can get you for that."

I found a nurse in the hallway and asked for a cherry-flavored ice drink. Brandon smiled when I walked back into his room and handed it to him. I wanted to bear all the pain for him if I could. The once numb and emotionally dead state of mind that existed for most of my life was no longer prominent.

When my son was transferred to his hospital room, he asked me for another cherry ice. I walked to the other building where the operation took place and brought back another iced drink. His face lit up as he reached out for it. I kissed him on top of his head.

The next few days were heartbreaking. Brandon's stomach had been sliced from one side to the other, catheterized with tubes coming from his insides. He was on a constant morphine drip.

We had to get him to sit up in a chair, and eventually to walk. His mother and I took turns staying overnight to be by his side. Four days later, he was discharged and went home with everything functioning properly.

CHAPTER THIRTY-SIX
~LIFE'S TRIALS:
OLDEST DAUGHTER'S DEPRESSION~

Angel's emotional state declined in concert with my two sons' problems. She was sleeping a lot and acting more irritable than usual. She stopped going to the gym and having dinner with me. One day after school I confronted her, subsequent to yet one more wordless and flippant dismissal of my request that she accompany me to the gym—she just rolled her eyes and walked away. I caught her by the arm, turned her toward me. She had tears in her eyes.

"Honey, tell me what's wrong. Let it out." I eased my grip on her arm, gave her a tender stroke on the shoulder.

She bit her lower lip and shook her head as more tears dripped down her cheeks. "I don't know what's wrong, Dad. I can't stop crying."

She was having breakdowns in school, needing to be picked up in the middle of the day. She'd stopped maintaining her room and taking care of her hygiene. This was major depression, I recognized—and I was frightened.

"Is it your mother," I asked, holding her in my arms. I could feel the moisture from her sob-induced saline penetrating my shirt—and heart. "Your old boyfriend?"

"No, Dad. I don't know what it is. I feel horrible all the time." She sniffled and buried her head further into my chest.

I stroked her hair, looking heavenward, asking for some kind of help here, please God? "Life will get better, Angel. You won't always feel like this. The darkness you're experiencing will dissipate." I wanted to tell her about my own horrifying abuse to reassure her that it's possible to escape, but I couldn't bring myself to telling her yet.

I felt it best to get her professional help in an attempt to get her to open up. I scheduled an appointment with Julian's past therapist since she knew our family situation and history.

After numerous sessions with her therapist I wasn't seeing much improvement. I discussed with Keith the possibility of telling my daughter what happened to me as a child. He concurred that it'd be beneficial to discuss my experiences with her, not only in assisting her to deal with depression, but also in understanding some of my own past erratic behavior. I then suggested it to my daughter's therapist. She agreed.

The session went well with my daughter. It was more difficult for me to tell her than for her to have to hear it. My daughter's therapist helped me explain the traumatic events that happened in my life as well as the ensuing mental isolation and hopelessness it eventually led me to.

"I'm sorry for my actions, Angel. I'm not the person that you saw leaving the family ten years ago."

"It's okay, Dad," she said softly. "I don't blame you for anything."

"I hope you understand why I'm telling you this."

"I'm okay with it, Dad. Really."

"I love you so much." Tears filled my eyes. "I wanted to tell you my story to prove that even though when life is tough and doesn't seem worth living, it does get pleasurable and wonderful again if you hang in there."

"Thanks, Dad," Angel said, putting her arms around me and squeezing tight.

I felt like there was something she wasn't telling me.

CHAPTER THIRTY-SEVEN
~ABUSE'S RIPPLING EFFECT~

As I contemplated on our joint session, the same repetitive rage came over me once again. I kept thinking about the rippling effect of the abuse, like the infinite waves expanding outward from a pebble thrown in still waters of a peaceful lake. It affected and caused agony to many people. I was again enraged at the Catholic Church's lack of responsibility. I looked at my children's damage as well as the physical and mental anguish others had experienced from my actions. I dry heaved while thinking that not only the Church, but God himself, would allow such misery to happen.

My older children were suffering. Julian was heavily self-medicating and disregarding any respect for authority. Angel was in distress, crying during the day for no apparent reason, and barely able to lift her head from her pillow in the morning.

Louise was full of hatred, resentment, and addiction from the rippling effect. She couldn't see past her own illness to perceive that I was doing everything possible to be responsible for my actions.

I could only think I was somewhat to blame for her current illness and behavior. She was addicted to drugs and committing acts I had never thought she was capable of. Our children's bank accounts were cleaned out. She was caught robbing her best friend's house, who happened to be providing her with a place to stay. She stole her friend's deceased mother's jewelry, her children's piggy banks, and her husband's tools, selling them at local pawnshops for money. When her car insurance expired, she altered the expiration date and was caught. I had to surmise the shady path she had taken, so similar to my own, was a direct cause of side effects from my own abuse and consequent aberrant behavior to which I had exposed her.

In addition to Louise and the children being affected, Louise's family members suffered. They were burdened with having to take care of my two older children for a number of years while they sought help for Louise's issues, as I was mentally and emotionally out of commission. My younger children's mother struggled with single parenthood. She dealt with the developmental and health issues of my youngest son. She had financial burdens that I contributed to.

And the families that I disrupted with my sexual affairs. It broke my heart. I found it hard to fathom that I was once that repulsive, inconsiderate, self-centered monster. The thought of all the lives I negatively impacted in the past caused so much anxiety and pain ... I had to stop thinking about it.

My plate was overflowing. I was still trying to obtain a divorce from Louise, and it was getting hideous. As I was dealing with my children's issues, Louise was inflicting as much pain and misery as possible. She even told Angel that all she wanted was for me to suffer.

Coinciding with coping with the multiple divorce proceedings and issues, I had Julian's hearing on the matter of his possession of marijuana to deal with. My attorney was able to get the charges reduced to a loitering misdemeanor. But there were strict probation terms. There were the normal conditions of probation, such as no drug use, reporting weekly to his probation officer, and not getting in any additional trouble. He was also court ordered to maintain daily attendance at school, with no unexcused absences, obtain acceptable passing grades, follow my rules of the house, and abide by set curfews for both weekdays and weekends.

From the minute we walked out of the courthouse, Julian had no intention of following even one of the conditions of his probation. He didn't attend school, and therefore was unable to maintain passing grades. He rarely came home before curfew, continuing to use drugs, and seldom followed the house rules. I tried everything to get him on a constructive course. I communicated with every party involved in his life, including his guidance counselor, drug counselor, probation officer, my attorney, his mother's family, my personal therapist, and anyone who would give me advice. Nothing worked. Even taking him to probation in Camden, New Jersey, in a room the size of a closet, filled with dysfunctional and violent individuals waiting to report to their own probation officers, did nothing in persuading my son to go straight.

I was wrought with fear and anxiety for him, unable to function normally for a week. With everything compounding and coming to a head at the same time, I shut down—unable to go to work, the gym, or do household chores. I stayed in bed exhausted from the multitude of exacerbated dilemmas.

My employer questioned my absenteeism and the need to come in late or leave early so I could take care of the plethora of issues that existed in my life. I had to do something quickly before I lost everything I had worked so hard to attain.

CHAPTER THIRTY-EIGHT
~ABATING THE ABUSE'S RIPPLING EFFECT~

I reported Julian to his probation officer for violating the probation terms. I wrote a letter pleading for them to help my son. I informed them of his dysfunctional family upbringing and let them know I was desperate to get the proper mental health and drug counseling for him. I explained the vast amount of programs and help I provided for him; also making it clear he was a mild-mannered kid and would not benefit from going away to a hard core juvenile detention facility. In addition, I wanted something done quickly before he turned eighteen and got himself in trouble when I no longer could help him.

The outcome was grievous and expensive for me. I ended up having to take two additional days off work, one to file for assignment of council and another for his pretrial. I didn't qualify for a public defender, so I was required to retain council for another fifteen hundred dollars.

During my application to file for a public defender at the courthouse, I noticed, behind the information counter, the juvenile officer who tried convincing my son to straighten up. I expressed to him I had researched residential drug treatment facilities provided by my insurance company. I hoped the court would enforce my son's admission to one of those facilities. The officer took both of us into a back room of the courthouse.

"You're going to be given a drug test," he said to Julian. "How's it going to turn out?"

"It's going to come up hot."

"I want you to choose whether you want to go to one of the residential facilities your dad's providing, or go to a juvenile detention facility."

Julian hesitated in answering.

"Take out your earring and give me your jacket," the officer said.

Julian's face lost color. The officer handcuffed him and took him to a lockup room. When he returned to the room I was in, he said, "We'll let him sit in a cell for an hour to think about things. You can come back in an hour to pick him up."

I took a deep breath and shook my head. "Thanks." There was a diner down the street, so I headed out for a cup of coffee and to gather my thoughts.

An hour later, I walked back to the courthouse. When the juvenile officer noticed me, he nodded and went to the cell area. A few minutes later, he stepped back into the room with Julian and said, "I'm going to turn you over to your father because he pleaded for your release, and you said you'd go to the rehab facility."

"Thank you," Julian said without hesitation, rubbing his wrists where he had been handcuffed. "I'll go to rehab."

The next week I was able to get him on a waiting list at a top-notch facility that not only supplied mental health and drug treatment programs, but also provided services to get Julian caught up with his education.

The waiting period was a few weeks, during which Julian partied with his friends every night. It was a dismal time.

My next step was getting Angel additional help for her depression. I maintained contact with her therapist, voicing my concerns so they could have a dialogue in their subsequent meetings. On occasion, we would have joint conferences. I took the therapist's advice and maintained more frequent sessions for her, making an appointment with one of their staff psychiatrists for medication monitoring. After the initial assessment, she was put on Prozac.

Within a month, the results were dramatic. Angel was happy and energetic. I thought she needed something to calm her down. She was maintaining daily attendance at school, and her teachers told me she was making a miraculous recovery with her grades. She was now able to function, socializing again with her friends and able to find a boyfriend. Everything was coming together on that front.

Next up and of major importance in rectifying my past was the pretrial for my divorce. On April 7, 2008, I entered the courtroom for the fourth time in a year. Louise had postponed the prior three dates one after another.

First it was due to her showing up without counsel. The second was upon request of her attorney, whom she had retained that same day and had needed additional time to put together a case. And the third—well, this one was not her doing, I'll admit—was because of a scheduling conflict by the courts that had not been communicated to either counsel.

During the day of our pretrial, Louise's attorney had presented to the courts documentation accusing me of running up her bills and using her credit cards to accumulate over ten thousand dollars of past-due balances.

As I waited for our case to be called, I glanced through the supposedly incriminating paperwork. What I was seeing was beyond my comprehension. Not one of her bills had anything to do with me. She had submitted bills for tax preparations, attorney fees, and at least nine statements from collection agencies attempting to collect on bad checks that she wrote to various vendors. I was surprised that her attorney would allow her to submit the documentation. Once the judge reviewed the affidavits, she dispensed with the pretrial, scheduling our divorce for final trial on the thirtieth of the month.

A few days later, Julian and I attended his pretrial for violation of probation. I had already submitted to my attorney a multitude of correspondence showing the help I tried to get him and the support from the professionals. In addition, I presented informational material and insurance approval for the rehabilitation facility where he'd be admitted. My attorney was able to convince the court not to go to trial and make part of Julian's revised probation conditions that he completes the curriculum in its entirety. The judge and prosecutor agreed, and Julian was court-ordered to enter the program once a bed was available.

My problems and issues from the abuse and subsequent irrational choices seemed to finally be coming to an end. I was in a sound mental state. I had attained my dignity, freedom, and independence, coming out of a six-figure financial deficit. My career was back on track. I had the love of my children, and they were back in my daily life. Angel was coming out of her depression, and Julian was on his way to getting healthy. Adding to that, my divorce appeared to be coming to a close by the end of the month. I began to bask in the moment and rejoice in what I had overcome, when I was rocked with some shocking news that sent me back into a frenzy of anxiety and depression.

It was April 10, 2008. The eve following my son's pretrial for his violation of probation. Angel's grandmother had taken her to her weekly therapy session earlier that day. That evening when I had come home from work, I took Angel for her follow-up session with her psychiatrist to monitor her medications.

On the way there, I noticed she started to sniffle. "What's wrong, honey?"

"I ... uh ... Dad ... my therapist ... uh ... told me ... ahm ... to talk to you about something."

My stomach twisted into a giant knot. I feared she was going to tell me she was pregnant. "We're just pulling in. Can it wait 'til we get out?" I patted Angel's hand, and she nodded. "We better get inside."

We hurried across the parking lot. I had to take things one at a time. I pushed the ominous thoughts from my mind. If Angel tells me she's pregnant, I'm not sure what we're going to do. But first, we have to get through this appointment.

We took our seats inside the psychiatrist's pristine office, sitting next to each other on wooden chairs. Angel stared at the beige carpeted floor. My chair squeaked from my squirming in it.

"It's good to see both of you," the psychiatrist said, fingering through the paperwork on her desk. "How is everything going, Angel? How are your medications working out?"

"I'm feeling good," Angel said, barely lifting her head.

"She's responding well to the medications," I said, leaning forward in my chair. I'm happy with the results. I don't think anything has to change."

"Good. Then we'll see you next month."

We left the office and ambled across the parking lot. Angel kept her eyes on the pavement, not saying a word. My thoughts were all over the place ... what was it that had her so down? I bit my lip and shook my head, worrying how we were going to handle the possible pregnancy.

When we got into the car, I asked with some anticipatory trepidation, "What was it that your therapist said we need to talk about."

Angel started to cry, her shoulders heaving, unable to get any words out.

"Honey, it's okay," I said, putting my arm around her. "You can tell me anything without fear. We'll deal with whatever it is you're experiencing."

"Dad," she finally blurted out, looking at me with reddened eyes, makeup running down her face. "I was sexually molested."

I shrieked, my eyes wide with revulsion. "You were what? Who did this to you? When did this happen?"

She put her head down, her voice as soft as her face was sad. "By Mom's first boyfriend, Rich. For three years. I was eight when it started. I can't erase it from my mind." She wept, furiously shaking her head, her hands grasping her temples. She squeezed her eyes closed and whispered, "I'm so ashamed."

My body shook as I struggled to hold my composure and not further upset her. "Oh, my God," I said, pulling her close, patting her back, stroking her hair. "It's not your fault." I had to press my eyes closed to hold back the tears. "You're going to be okay. I'll take care of you ... I'll protect you."

"I w-want to ... g-go home," Angel said through a torrent of tears.

We drove home, my hands clenched on the wheel, knuckles white. Pictures in my head flashed back to the time when my stepfather thought something was not right with the relationship between me and my abuser. He went into a raging rampage, threatening to kill him. But then did nothing, allowing him to come around our house. I didn't want Angel to feel the way I did back then, fearful that the world would know her secret and view her as a freak. I spent the rest of the night settling her, centering her, reassuring her she was safe and it was *not* her fault.

I was drained. The obstacles were coming at me too fast. How could God put this in front of me? My world was one of relentless chaotic disorder. I lived in a state of unrest, on edge, waiting for the next incident.

I wanted to rest and take a deep breath, smile, relax, and be able to revel in one good moment for an extended period of time. I was run down and exhausted from the bipolar-like symptoms of experiencing brief glimpses of hope and happiness only to be shattered with negative after effects. It was contemptible that I wasn't there to protect my child from the same atrocity that happened to me. I felt hypocritical that I had the audacity to have resentment toward my family for not protecting me.

At home later that night, I had a talk with Julian. "Did Rich ever touch you inappropriately? Was he physically abusive to you?"

"Nah. He never touched me," he said, shaking his head.

"You were young. Did you feel helpless with this guy?"

He shot me a firm look. "I told you. He never touched me."

I wasn't convinced but didn't want to keep pressing him. It was like looking in a mirror. I was petrified of anyone knowing that something as atrocious as child abuse had happened to me, fearing that I would be viewed as a deviant queer. It made sense why Julian was acting out in the negative manner that he was. He appeared to be holding a secret.

One that he wasn't ready to talk about.

All my instincts could do over the next week was operate in survival mode. I felt like a robot tackling the issue with the best mechanics it was programmed with. I used my own past experience of being abused for the benefit of my daughter. I gave her what I thought I needed when I was her age but didn't get. I inundated her with assurances that she was safe; I'd protect and take care of her. I told her everything would be kept confidential, and she'd decide who would know. I scheduled a joint session with her therapist to come up with a game plan on how to proceed in her therapy. The plan included eventually prosecuting and suing her perpetrator.

The following week, with my daughter's approval, I contacted the prosecutor's office and gave them the specifics. We discussed how to proceed in going after my daughter's abuser when she was healthy and ready. With Angel's knowledge, I discussed the issue with Debbie, Donna and Lawrence. Having the support of her family, I had hoped she wouldn't feel alone—as I had when I was abused. I didn't want her to feel the estrangement that I endured throughout my adolescent years that made me want to die. I would have discreet but open discussions with her about the matter, reassuring her that I understood everything she was experiencing because of the same thing having happened to me.

After the shock dissipated, a raging tempestuous wrath exploded in me like a C4, shrapnel-laced bomb. My children had had to pay the price and take a hit as an indirect result of my exploitation. An intense burden of anxious guilt overpowered me to where I wanted to give up, but ... that was not who I was now.

Composing myself, I knew I had a purpose. My family and I were experiencing these atrocities for a reason. The story needed to get out so that the masses would know the horrific shock waves that affect not only the abused, but those close to the one violated.

It was at this juncture that I began forming my writings into a story. Through Keith, I was able to ascertain an editorial contact. After he reviewed my manuscript, I was encouraged to attempt to proceed in soliciting a literary agent with a book proposal. His critique was brutally honest. A great deal of work needed to be done to my manuscript to be able to present it to a publisher. He said that it was difficult getting into the publishing industry and it offered little success. He warned me of the ramifications of getting my gruesome, yet astounding, story out in the open. Life would never be the same. He did recognize that my story was extraordinary and offered encouragement. With determination, I retained his services and proceeded forward.

At this time, the Pope was visiting the states, spewing his phony propaganda regarding the Catholic Church being sorry for the abuse scandals. I immediately took pen to paper and vented my anger at the bishop of the diocese where my exploitation took place. I wasn't asking for money, but was hoping for compassion.

I mailed the letter the next day and then accompanied my daughter to the Child Advocacy Center. The historical building had high cathedral ceilings, and finely-detailed trim outlined each room. The waiting room had an aquarium filled with turtles. Boxes of cuddly stuffed animals were stationed throughout the area, free for the taking. Children's toys, books, magazines, and pamphlets with child abuse information lined the walls of the facility.

The interesting sea life, fun loving items, and bright-colored literature were a distraction to comfort the pain and humiliation child abuse victims are forced to somehow come to grips with. I experienced great grief as I realized the age group the decor was targeting.

I had no pleasant childhood remembrance after being taken from Poppy and Nanny. No playful memories of having fun with what was in front of me. Angel must be feeling the same way, I thought.

The officers and officials at the center were courteous and professional. They kept my daughter and me at ease throughout the interview. I was brought in first to disclose the details of my daughter's abuse. Angel remained in the waiting area.

I sat on an armchair in front of a tidy desk. Looking the officer in the eye, I said, "Mine is one dysfunctional family. I confessed to my daughter that I was abused by a priest as a child. After that, she told her therapist about what had happened to her. Her mother's boyfriend molested her when she was eight years old."

Following my interview, the lieutenant in charge of the case escorted me to the waiting area. He took Angel to be interviewed alone. They talked for forty-five minutes. Afterward, the lieutenant asked for a few more minutes of my time, so he could go over my daughter's interview. When I went back into the office with him, there were two other officers and a social worker in the room, who had viewed the interview from another area.

As they discussed the details of the abuse, my bottom lip quivered. I was astonished by what they told me. I needed to put to use the practice techniques Keith taught me. I took deep breaths from my diaphragm, choosing peace instead of anxiety.

Concluding our discussion, I walked back to Angel with the lieutenant. He said, "Angel, would you be willing to solicit a confession over the phone?"

"What? Oh. Wow. Uh ... I don't know. Oh, my God," she said, breaking down into tears. She put her face into her hands and cried uncontrollably. I sat down next to her, putting my arm around her shoulders, pulling her close to me.

"I'll have her therapist discuss it with her tomorrow and get back to you," I said.

The next day, Angel and her therapist agreed that it was too soon for her to experience another traumatic event in her life. I called the lieutenant and he understood. He'd proceed to prosecute my daughter's abuser anyway.

* * *

A couple of months passed. I picked up the mail, and there was a letter from the bishop. I ripped it open, hoping his words would console me. I envisioned soothing spiritual psalms of guidance to lift my spirits and give me strength in the fight to rectify the damage created by one of his corrupt disciples.

I pulled the stationery from the envelope and started reading. The bishop's words showed no consideration for my family's situation. He did nothing to sooth my mental pain in any way. He defended the Church's position, carefully not admitting to any responsibility in the matter. Once again, the Catholic Church did nothing to heal the pain of the sexual abuse scandal. The letter must've been written by the Church's attorney.

The bishop said he recognized the crisis my family was in. He also stated the Church had added more money than what was originally offered to me.

I felt like my bowels were infected. I'd only asked for twenty-five thousand more than what they had counter-offered. The Catholic Church again treated it like a business transaction to limit their monetary damages and reputation.

I gave up on the Catholic Church after that. Not on God, but the false institution that pompously postured to represent Him.

CHAPTER FORTY
~REHAB ADMISSION STRUGGLE~

It was mid May, 2008. New Hope Behavior Health Rehabilitation Center called and said there was a bed available for Julian. I scheduled the appointment for his intake the following week.

He was by now more unmanageable and out of control than ever. His lack of respect for me had reached new heights. His defiant demeanor raged havoc on his sister and me. We were prisoners in our own household, scared to leave for fear that Julian would steal our things for drug money. He was wasted every day, trying to get as much partying in as possible before his admittance. I was fearful he'd overdose if his hell-raising continued at its current pace. I had trouble eating and sleeping.

The day of his admission was an all out brawl the moment it started. Behind my back, he was scheming with his mother to run away and stay with her. But she was kicked out of her apartment the night before.

My entire day at work was filled with panicked phone calls from Julian, begging me to reconsider, or at least postpone, the intake until the end of the month. I had my daughter and a neighbor track his every move, keeping me posted on his whereabouts. They sensed that Julian was ready to run and called me. Right away, I called the house and he picked up. "I want to let you know, Julian, that I'll be picking you up later today. Make sure you're ready." After hanging up, I left work.

I called Angel when I got close. "Is he still there?"

"He left for Buddy's house a little while ago."

I knew where his friend lived and headed straight to the house. I called the guy while driving. "Hey, Buddy. Is Julian there?"

"Uh, yeah. Oh, Julian? No, he's not here."

"Is that Joe I hear in the background? Can I talk to him?"

There was a pause. Then some shuffling noises. "Hello," Joe said.

"Joe, is Julian there?"

"No, he's not here. I swear."

But I was pulling up outside the house. I got out of the car and knocked on the door. Julian and his normal entourage were hanging out. Every one of them had a stoned glaze in their eyes. I locked eyes with Julian. "Get in the car."

"I'm not going with you." Julian crossed his arms.

I pulled out my cell phone. "Very well, I know you're all high," I said, with a sweeping gaze around the room getting everyone's attention, "and I'm calling the cops."

Opening my phone, I pretended to make the call. That snapped them out of their give-a-shit stupor. They all grabbed my son and threw him out the door, with him flailing and shouting curses. I had all I could do to force Julian into the car, pushing and yelling.

"We'll stop at home to pick up your things," I said once we were on the way.

"I'm not going. Mom's on her way to pick me up."

"Then I'm taking you straight to rehab and I'll drop off your things later tonight."

He opened the car door, trying to jump out while I was going thirty-five miles an hour. I snagged his long dreadlocked hair, yanked him back with enough force to make him holler and held on. He burst out crying.

"Dad, I'll go. Let go of my hair. I'll go to rehab."

I released my grasp, and he sat back in the seat. "If you think I'm going to let your mother come and take you away, think again."

"She's coming to say goodbye."

When we arrived home, I shadowed him every moment as he paced the front of the complex waiting for his mother to arrive. My mind regressed to when I was in his situation a few years prior. I knew what he was going through.

I was again angry with God for my children having to pay for the sins of my abuse. Inside I was weeping for my son, but I maintained my composure. He tried a few times to make a run for it, but I would catch up and restrain him.

The neighbor who had helped me keep track of him during the day came out and sat on the sidewalk with him. She gave him a cigarette, hugged him, and in a soft-spoken tone, calmed him down. "Your dad loves you," she said. "He's doing the best thing for you right now even if you can't see it."

Julian hung his head and whimpered. As I contemplated my faith, I tried to convince myself that it could be worse. There are parents who have to watch their children physically suffer or even die right before their eyes. There wasn't the slightest comparison between the two scenarios, but I felt his anguish and grief, questioning God's purpose.

After an hour, his mother arrived. I stood close, prohibiting Julian from entering her car. He smoked a cigarette with her, and she gave him a quick hug and kiss goodbye.

We packed a duffle bag with his belongings and took off down the road. The hour-and-a-half ride seemed like hours. Julian's body shook the whole way, as he chain smoked one cigarette after another. Our conversation with each other became repetitive.

"You know that this is the best thing for you," I said. "And I love you."

He grunted and stared out the window. Turning his head my way, he said, "I don't need this, because I *don't* have a problem."

"It'll clear your head and teach you the benefits of sobriety and living a healthy life. You'll be able to catch up on your schooling so you won't have to repeat your junior year. Try and make the most of the program. Three to six months out of your life is but a moment in the grand scheme of things."

"Yeah, right," he said, glaring at me. "That's a lifetime for me."

"When you complete the program, you'll get your privileges back. You'll have your cell phone, driver's license, and special favors again. We'll work hard together maintaining sobriety. I'll work with you to improve your education and finding a job. We can work out in the gym together, do activities and have meals as a family again. I love you so much."

"I'm moving in with Mom. You don't love me. You want to get rid of me."

"I do love you. And I'll be there to support you. I'll never abandon you."

"You're trying to bust my balls."

We pulled into the facility's parking lot. Julian sat for a moment, staring ahead. His hands were shaking. He finally stepped out of the car. We walked through the doors into the waiting room. From my own past experiences with rehab centers, I could empathize with him.

Taking a seat, he bounced his leg up and down. This was it, he knew, no longer would he be able to get high. We joined the others waiting to be admitted.

As we sat in the waiting room, I could see pain, anger, and exhaustion on the faces of the parents sitting next to their kids. The emotionless expressions showed evidence to lives of havoc and heartache that filled the room. Each parent's profile appeared to be carved with scars of disappointment and distrust.

The children, on the other hand, hung their heads downward. Some covered their faces with hooded sweatshirts or buried under the collars of their shirts. The girls and boys with long hair, including Julian, draped their hair over their faces. Whatever method used to veil their faces, I knew from my addictive past that it was a technique to hide from the reprehensible life of drugs, theft, and immoral behaviors. I understood what each half of the family was going through. My compassion went out to both parties.

We waited for the intake officer to call on us. Julian often exited the facility to smoke a cigarette, knowing that he'd have to kick that habit, too. After forty-five minutes, his intake officer motioned for us. We were in his office for another forty-five minutes, filling out paperwork and signing consent forms for everything imaginable. Julian continued his periodic exit to get the last inhale of nicotine. When we completed processing the paperwork, we were sent back to the waiting room.

It was nine at night on a Wednesday, which was visitation night. The parents whose children were already in the program began exiting the building. Most of the relatives and friends appeared elated from the visitation. Some were depressed or angry. As the parents exited, they first glanced at Julian, and then at me with a slight smile. I took it to mean that everything was going to be fine. When everyone was cleared from the building, we were the only ones left in the waiting room. There were no more words to say between us, so we sat in silence until the nurse called on Julian for his physical at nine thirty.

At ten, he was finished, and the nurse gave him permission to smoke one more cigarette before being taken to the residential wing. I stood with Julian outside the doors.

"It's only three to six months out of your life," I said. "What harm can come of it?"

Julian stared off into space.

"You'll get the proper mental and physical help that you need. You'll get your education caught up. I do love you, and I'm doing this for your own good."

He finished his last cigarette, dropped the butt to the ground, and stomped it out. I reached out and gave him a hug.

"I love you, Son," I said.

"Love you, too, Dad."

He walked back inside, and we waved at each other. It was ten thirty, and I dreaded the hour-and-a-half trip home. But once I began driving, the ride was one of the most serene times of my life. My son was in a safe place getting the help he needed.

I had thought there'd be guilt in abandoning him. But it was the opposite. I opened the window, feeling the cool night's breeze streaming into the car, relishing in the peaceful ride. No longer was I burdened with worry about his safety, as well as my daughter's well being because of his actions.

When I got home, I flopped onto the sofa. Ah, peace. I slept well that night.

CHAPTER FORTY-ONE
~REHAB PROGRAM~

The following Wednesday, the first week in June, 2008, I was nervous. I didn't know what to expect visiting Julian for the first time. I left work early to freshen up at home. It was a three-hour commute leaving from home.

There was a strong thunderstorm that night. I was running ten minutes late. I had to call a special number to let them know. It was a lock-down facility and visitors, I had been informed, had to be led inside all at once, following a brief tutorial in the lobby regarding visitation conduct. The person I talked to on the phone informed me that, even though I would be arriving late, I would be allowed to attend. This time. When I arrived, an attendant was waiting to let me inside. He directed me to where the group was meeting.

As I was walking down the corridor, I could see everyone sitting in one big circle. The youths were sitting across from their parents in a semicircle. Counselors were outside the circle, observing and maintaining order.

When my son's peers saw me walking toward them, they called out, "Juuliiaan." It was an affectionate playfulness. I grinned. Julian was accepted by his cohorts.

My eyes made contact with Julian's bright blue eyes. A warm smile emerged. I was touched—grateful to see a genuine smile beaming from the same countenance that for the last unbearably long time had exhibited anger and resentment toward me. A face that had shown apprehension now radiated satisfaction that I was there to support him.

My ill feelings toward Julian and his actions were at once erased. Gone were any and all traces of anger for his disobedient behavior. Images flashed through my mind of his toddler years. Memories of when I used to take videos of my first two babies while still in diapers played like tapes in my head.

That two-year-old boy could barely say *Daddy*, stumbling toward me on chunky legs with a big grin. His chubby red cheeks jiggled with each shaky step. He had pushed a new toy snow shovel around the living room one Christmas morning long ago.

I was now looking at my son as an innocent and pure child. Disappointment no longer flooded my thoughts. Feelings of pride touched my heart.

I arrived during the family program portion. Most of the children's statements were like they were reading from the same script. "Hi, I'm so and so and I am an addict. I am feeling fine today, and I'm looking forward to my stay."

The angry ones said, "I'm fucking pissed. This is fucked up that I'm here. I hate that my parents put me here. I can't stand the fucking rules. I can't wait to get out of here."

There were a few who *were* happy and gave a unique introduction and inspirational message of hope. From my own experience I was able to correlate where each group was in their recuperation. I could also relate to each emotional stage of the three groups.

The children who showed little emotion and were repeating the same generic message were at the most crucial point of their recovery. Like the median point of a graph, they were at the midway period of their rehabilitation. Balanced on a fence, teetering side to side, they were at a juncture where they were either going to succeed and recover, or fall back into the grips of addiction. This group had broken through the irate stage and succumbed to the purpose of the program.

The agitated children were either in the beginning stage of their recovery and experiencing the side effects of withdrawal, or they didn't want to get help. They were mandated to be there, either by their parents' ultimatum or by enforcement from the judicial system. I noticed that many of the ones who didn't want to get help had little parental support at the facility.

My heart grieved for these children. I wondered if they were given a fair chance at life. They may not have had the proper tools with which to build their moral character because proper parenting and a support foundation were missing.

The adolescents who were emotionally buoyant were the patients who understood the benefits of the program. They were overjoyed at being unburdened from the vile contrition and arduous physical demands that drug addiction has on an addict's mind and body. I could feel their anticipation to go out into the world to attain their goals and dreams. Also I sensed fear of possible failure because of their physical incapability and mental incoherency.

The few who understood the importance of sobriety had another chance to live an innocent teenage and young adult life. They had succeeded in breaking through the barricade that the other two groups were experiencing. I hoped and prayed that Julian reached that phase of healing and would be able to recoup what precious years he had left as a young person before entering the already far-too-jaded world of adulthood.

When it was Julian's turn to introduce himself he appeared timid, hanging his head so his long hair would cover his blushing face. His voice was stifled. He recited the line of the patients who were at their indecisive point of recovery. "Hi. I'm Julian. I'm an addict and feeling fine today. I am looking forward to my visit with my father."

He caught me by surprise by lifting his head, showing me his stunning blue eyes, and launching a smile that said, *Thanks for being here for me.*

Once the kids were finished with their statements, the parents did the same. The majority of the family members introduced themselves, whom the child was they were seeing, and then ... would burst into tears as they explained their feelings. The absence of their children in their lives caused an abysmal pain. Not only the women, but also some of the tough-looking, burly men showed the emotional effects the disease of addiction has on a family's life. As these parents broke down, their children wouldn't make eye contact, hanging their heads.

I tried to learn from the other parents' behaviors as I waited my turn. I didn't want to embarrass Julian. Because I had inflicted irreparable mental anguish and physical damage on my loved ones, I felt it'd be hypocritical for me to burden him with hurt.

There were parents who were thrilled at the sight of their offspring. As the parents described their pride, delight and gratitude for the program's results, I noticed their children's expressions of happiness and appreciation for their parents' love and support. I wanted to achieve that same state of synergy.

There were a few parents who were infuriated with their children. They were accosting in their accusative demeanors, inflicting feelings of reprobation and blame for their offspring's wasteful and wicked transgressions. I winced and wiggled in my seat listening to their insensitive, cantankerous attitudes. I wanted to hug the kids whose parents vented in front of their peers, counselors, and other families in the room.

As I sat listening to the parents who failed to understand what their teenager was experiencing, I became annoyed as the drug-addicted adolescents were bashed for being selfish, inconsiderate, and rotten for the pain they caused their families. These parents seemed to take no responsibility for their child's stumbles that led them off the path of morality and emotional wellbeing.

I had to hold back. They didn't understand. Addiction is a disease. Self-medicating is a method to suppress symptoms—the pain and anxiety from a mental disorder, dysfunctional upbringing or post-traumatic events. My heart palpitated in my chest. I wanted to reprimand the adults who didn't understand. These poor kids were programmed with a deadly virus. They were acting on information plugged into their minds during their early developmental years.

I did recognize there were adolescents in the program who may have succumbed to the coerciveness of peer pressure and had become addicted to their drug of choice for the purpose of getting high for a good time. I acknowledged the fact that there were parents in the group who had done their best and were perfect role models. I realized that some of the parents had a legitimate beef with their children's inconsiderate and selfish actions, having every right to be angry. My turn came.

I kept my introduction simple. "Hello. I'm Julian's dad, Marco. I'm here to support him to the fullest and help him to not make the same mistakes I did at his age."

My son sat there in silence and smiled to acknowledge my encouragement. His counselor said to Julian, "What do you have to say to that?"

He sighed, and a small but gracious smile appeared. "I'm happy that my father is back in my life and supporting me when others in my family are not here today to do so."

Next on the agenda was the family group therapy session. This portion of the program was designed to have the parents and youth interact with each other as a group. This would attempt to provide therapeutic treatment, to help mend the broken bond, and reunite the families. This segment would assist in dealing with the consequences of misconduct.

My first assignment with Julian involved reversing roles. We were to stand up and explain how we would act and handle the present situation. About three quarters through the program, the head counselor invited me to share my thoughts on the matter. I walked to the front of the group.

"I need an open communication connection between us," I said, as if I were my son. "I would be open, honest, and express my feelings without any concern for judgmental perspectives. There would be complete confidence that I was loved for being me. I'd feel free to discuss my issues, often asking questions, searching for advice and guidance to learn from my father's past experiences. My family would be loved and appreciated by all of its members. The household rules and contents would be respected. I would strive for success, giving it my best effort to improve on my education and work toward an enjoyable career. Goals would be set to stay motivated, reassessing the long-term goals when the shorter goals are met. My main goal would be to work on a healthy state of mind and body by staying active, striving to do healthy and pleasant activities, without the need of getting high to enjoy them."

When I finished, the head counselor asked Julian for a response. I was proud of his courage to express his opinion and draw attention to himself in front of the group. The boy I knew a few weeks before wouldn't have been able to stammer through a poorly structured sentence, let alone present his thought processes in an organized manner.

Julian began by saying, "I'd be more understanding of my son's feelings, patient and supportive in whatever he wanted out of life. If he was in trouble, I'd do whatever I could to help him, but be more strict and tough so he wouldn't get into trouble in the first place. If the rules were broken, there'd be a fair punishment. I would love my son no matter what."

As I listened to his words, I became flush with embarrassment. Did I handle the situation with my son in the proper way? I had thought I *had* done everything I could to help him. I felt awkward in front of the group, thinking that everyone was staring at me, assuming I was a lousy father.

My cognitive skills took over, and I realized my son was reciting everything that I *had* done for him. Maybe I hadn't been one hundred percent understanding and patient, but through my experiences with the disease of addiction, I was confident that I had acted in the correct manner.

When Julian had nothing more to say, the head counselor said to him, "Do you think that your father portrayed any of the characteristics that you would've shown if you were the father?"

"Yes," he said. "My dad supported me with all of the qualities I mentioned. But, he could've been a little more patient and understanding."

"I *could've* been a little more patient and understanding," I said, walking up to Julian and giving him a hug. "I love you, and I'm very proud of you."

"I know, Dad. Love you, too."

After we finished, everyone huddled with their arms around each other and recited the Serenity Prayer. From there, the families separated into various sections of the room for a half hour of individual visitation time.

Julian and I sat on folding chairs facing each other. For the first time in a long time, we spoke to each other in a connective manner. "I can't believe how good you look," I said, looking into his clear eyes. "I'm so proud of how far you've come since arriving here. It's nice to be able to sit and talk without stress."

"I know what you mean," Julian said, smiling.

"You've made tons of progress since you've been here."

"I get along with everyone here in the program. Even if they're kind of ghetto." He laughed. "You know, wearing their pants hanging on their asses, hooded black sweatshirts, and crooked baseball caps. Most of them like rap music and say things like"—he adopted a raspy, street slang slur—"*ya feel me* or, *y'see what 'm sayin'* between almost every sentence."

"A bit different from your long dreadlocks, scruffy face, and hippie clothes," I said, with a playful tug on his hair. "How's the food around here?"

"Don't care too much for the food, Dad. It's all starches and very greasy."

"What'd they serve today?"

"Breakfast was tasteless," he said, wrinkling his nose. "Runny eggs. And for dinner they fed us some kind of mystery meat on a stale bun. But lunch wasn't too bad. How do you mess up peanut butter and jelly sandwiches?" He laughed again.

"And that's another reason to not do drugs," I said with a chuckle. "Not quite what you're used to eating at home. So, what do they have you doing all day?"

"I have different therapy programs through the day. Right now the educational program's on break, but next week I'll start some online classes. We get to go outside in the courtyard and play basketball."

"Do they have chores for you to do?"

"Oh, yeah. Some of my favorite things," he said with mock sincerity. "Like cleaning the bathrooms, mopping the hallways, rearranging the group chairs, and cleaning up after meals." We both chuckled.

"Good character-building projects," I said with a wink. "What's your primary counselor like?"

"He's a good guy. Easy to talk to. My favorite part of the day is when he lets me chill in his office and listen to music on his iPod. We like the same kind of classic rock music. Everyone else here likes the rap shit."

"I'm glad that you have that in common with him. It's important to have good communication with your counselor and that you feel comfortable with him."

"Yeah. We both like Bob Marley and Pink Floyd. He's got some cool oldies downloaded."

After a half an hour of alone time, the head counselor announced that the family portion of the program was over, and we needed to wrap it up.

"You look good," I said. "I'm so proud of you. Keep up the good work."

We both stood up and hugged. "Love you, Dad."

"Love you, too," I said, trying to keep my composure.

By the time I got out to my car, I couldn't hold back the streaming tears of joy. As I drove home, there was now contentment within me with regard to his progress and his coherent demeanor. I yearned for him to be back in my life

CHAPTER FORTY-TWO
~FINAL DIVORCE~

My divorce hearing was supposed to take place during the same time as my son's rehabilitation. The final hearing that had been scheduled for April 30 was postponed by the judge for an indefinite period of time. She had two open divorce cases and didn't want to have a third one open in tandem. This was the fifth time the trial had been rescheduled.

As each hearing was cancelled over the past year and a half, my attorney's fees escalated. Because of a scheduling conflict, the June date was postponed—delaying the hearing for the sixth time. Whatever, I thought. By now I was callous to the whole frickin' thing—cancellations didn't bother me. When my attorney's assistant called to tell me that a final hearing was scheduled for July 28, I had to let out a sarcastic chuckle. *Right*, I wouldn't bet on it. I wondered if I was cursed. Would I always be legally attached to that woman?

During this time, Louise's addictions and problems took another turn for the worse. Each time we thought she had hit rock bottom with nowhere to go but up, she would set a new masochistic standard of what was considered her lowest point.

Following eviction after robbing her friend's place, a wealthy family affiliated with a local Baptist church took Louise in as a nanny to their children. She had, prior to being accepted into their household, confessed her drug abuse to the family: the cheating, stealing, and pain she inflicted on her loved ones. They felt convinced she was a good person and deserved a chance to straighten out her life.

Once she had moved in, they told her she wouldn't have to steal from them because they would provide anything she wanted or needed. They paid all of her expenses, including the legal fees for the divorce, warrants associated with the theft of her friend's belongings, and unpaid motor vehicle fines. They provided a roof over her head and a place to bring our children so she could spend time with them. Louise had a fresh start at life, but her illness was too overpowering. The family gave her numerous chances to stop stealing from them and using drugs but, after six months they had had enough and asked her to leave.

Louise went from house to house, using everyone she had prior contact with to provide shelter. She would last about a week at each house before she was kicked out for either drug use or stealing ... or both. It was hard to believe that she was capable of doing the things that I was hearing about. It was at this point that I began to have compassion for her. I saw her as an ill person, acting out her issues.

A few weeks before the final hearing for the divorce, the law firm representing Louise notified my attorney that the lawyer in the case had quit and was not communicating with them.

When the chief partner of the law firm reviewed the case, he questioned Louise regarding her allegations that I ran up her bills and used her credit cards without her consent. He told my attorney that Louise was not cooperative, and that his firm was dismissing her as a client. As soon as the court found out that she had no representation, my petition for divorce would be terminated. I would have to start the proceedings all over again.

I was creeping back into a despondent, pessimistic mental state. It seemed like nothing was good in life. Even though we had a good home, food in our stomachs, and clothes on our backs, the mental anguish blinded me from the fact that things could be much worse.

I made an effort to gather my sensibilities. My children and I were healthy. I was thankful for that. I reaffirmed all the good that we had in life to break through the depression. I was able to maintain composure by concentrating on positive affirmations and continue to fight to change my mental outlook while dealing with the divorce crisis.

My attorney convinced the courts to not delay the scheduling of the final divorce hearing. Louise's law firm agreed to wait until the divorce proceeding before requesting to be relieved of their representation if she didn't cooperate and attend the hearing.

The final hearing went as scheduled on July 28. Louise didn't show up. There were outstanding warrants for her arrest. The court granted the law firm's request to be relieved of their representation of her. The hearing proceeded with my attorney and me. At last, something went in my favor. I was granted the divorce. My now ex-wife was court ordered to pay me child support and reimbursement of attorney fees because of the extra expenses involved with her false accusations. Although my attorney and I knew we weren't going to collect a cent from Louise, the fact that the hearing went well was satisfying for the moment.

CHAPTER FORTY-THREE
~REHAB PROGRESS~

August came. I had been making the three-hour round trip every Wednesday to visit Julian after work. Although the same family program was held on Saturdays, it was too demanding for me to make the drive while having my two younger children.

With every visit, Julian showed improvement at an incredible pace. When I thought he couldn't get any better, he'd surprise me every time. His enthusiasm to succeed and his will to live a normal and healthy lifestyle intensified with each visit. Our conversations became more meaningful as we discussed our plan of action when he was able to come home.

When he was under the influence of drugs, I wasn't able to hold a conversation with him for more than a minute. Now, we were participating with each other in family therapy sessions. He was able to understand the past advice I had given him, like a hard drive on standby just booted up. He recognized the comatose mental state he had been in when using. He knew what he had done wrong and understood why I nagged and pleaded with him to change the direction he had been heading.

Every Wednesday morning I found myself waking in a great state of mind. It was invigorating. I looked forward to seeing my son.

As the adolescent patients progressed in the program, they earned certain levels based on their behavior and improvement. In return, they were granted certain privileges. After a month and a half, Julian reached the level of a two-hour furlough with me after an hour family session with his primary counselor.

During this session, Julian was honest and forthright about everything he had done. It wasn't like he had said anything I didn't already know, but he wasn't lying or trying to manipulate me into thinking I was the one to blame. It showed me that he had changed and was doing even better than I perceived. He admitted everything—the different types of drugs he took, who he did the drugs with, the disrespect and destruction of the apartment, stealing from people's cars and his sister, the fights, and police altercations that I didn't know about.

He continued to plead his innocence with respect to the robbery of the apartment. He said he knew who probably had done it, and that he was to blame for his poor judgment of whom he let into our home. He maintained that he had nothing to do with the robbery itself. After his being blunt and sincere, I believed him and put that issue to rest.

In return, I was honest about things I did in the past and apologized for having a part in his deterioration. I felt he was ready by now, and I wanted to tell him what had happened to me and why I acted the way I did. I asked if he wanted to know. He became disconcerted and declined.

We discussed what we wanted our life to be like when he completed the program. We both wanted, in his words, to *chill* with each other, start working out and having dinner as a family again. We agreed to go to Narcotics Anonymous meetings together. It was nice to see my son with the same attitude I had when I was in rehab. He was fortunate to be more than twenty years younger than I was when having my awakening.

The visit during his furlough was harmonious. I took him to the local mall, and we walked around talking. I let him pick out a couple of tee shirts, a pair of shoes, and a CD of his favorite band, The Disco Biscuits. He couldn't wait to play the CD during his one-on-one time with his primary counselor.

We lost track of time. The two hours went by like it was but a moment. Since we couldn't sit down for a nice meal, I bought him a couple slices of pizza. We rushed to get back in time.

* * *

A few months into the program, there was an incident at the rehab facility that required disciplinary action. They wouldn't disclose what the incident was. For almost three weeks, the entire facility population was on Loss of Privileges (LOP) status.

I didn't find out about this until it was announced during the family visit on Wednesday night. The program proceeded as usual with the normal greetings and feelings session. After the greeting stage, the kids were unable to visit one on one with their parents, and were sent to their rooms. The parents proceeded with the family session without them.

The following two weeks, I didn't make the trip because I was unable to visit with Julian alone. The LOP delayed the patients' completion schedule by a month. It was unfortunate that everyone in the program was unilaterally held responsible; each one demoted at least one progression level based on their involvement—even if there was no involvement. They had to earn their levels back by completing various delegated chores and assignments.

When I did see Julian next, I was glad to see he had continued to improve at a steady pace. After the LOP was dropped from the entire unit, he advanced to the next level where he was able to come home for an eight-hour furlough. And happily, since we lived so far away, he was allotted twelve-hours.

I picked up Julian on a Saturday morning in late August, 2008. We stopped and ran errands before arriving home. First stop was for a haircut. Julian's hair was comparable to an old, worn out, raggedy wet mop. His hair was well past his shoulders, as thick as a bush. He looked like Grizzly Adams. We debated for a while in front of the stylist on how short to cut it. I was surprised how civilized our debate was and how he accepted my terms without backtalk. I gave him a break and told the stylist to cut it to the bottom of his earlobe. After a half an hour, I could see Julian's radiant face.

His siblings were waiting for him at the apartment. Brandon and Jennifer ran to Julian with smiling faces and hugs when he walked in. Julian tousled their hair and playfully rough housed with them. Angel cracked a slight smirk, seeing her brother for the first time in three months. She nodded her head, punched him in the arm and said, "What's up?"

He responded with a grin, nodded back and punched her in the arm. "What's up with you?"

This was an amazing turnaround in their relationship. In my eyes, it was as if the two were joyful, hugging and jumping up and down with excitement because they missed each other. Before his rehabilitation, I don't think either would've cared if the other had died.

We all relaxed for a while in the apartment, hanging out. Jennifer had a soccer tournament later in the day and Mary picked her up. An hour after Jennifer left, the rest of us piled into the car for the two-minute drive to my ex-in-laws' house for lunch.

They had a picturesque lakefront home that was maintained by the neighborhood association. The lake was one of a series that were dammed. Before and after the summer season, they were drained so property owners could maintain their bulkheads and docks. The debris around the property was cleaned up in order to maintain its beauty. Public access points for bathers were stationed around the water. It had docks with slides and diving boards, a picnic and playground area, which were monitored by life guards. Canoes, sailboats, and rafts floated up and down the lake throughout the day. All day, families would fish, swim, or relax by the water, delighting in the scenery.

Even in the winter when the lake would freeze, various properties had spotlights shining out on the frozen lake. Families could be entertained with a night of ice skating and making fires to roast marshmallows. When there was snowfall, the homeowners would shovel a squared area in the form of an ice rink to promote ice hockey games. Julian and Angel spent most of their adolescent years here with their grandparents.

We were greeted on the dock with appetizers and iced tea. The sun was shining and there was a slight breeze. The kids' grandfather, Paul, had designed a pond with a series of waterfalls that trickled down to the lake, putting us into a tranquil state of mind.

While we waited for lunch, Julian showed Brandon how to swing from the rope like Tarzan. His grandparents had attached it to a large tree next to their dock. After twenty minutes, Brandon was tired of swinging into the lake. Julian dragged out the fishing poles and showed him how to fish.

Angel watched the two guys from a lounge chair overlooking the pond. She laughed at Brandon's reaction to catching his first fish and his victory dance. I wished Jennifer would've been able to take in this intimate family moment, too.

We were served hearty cheeseburgers cooked on the grill, which exploded with flavor in every bite. Fresh rolls from a local bakery complemented the burger, along with crisp lettuce and ripe tomatoes. Condiments would have ruined the taste of the luncheon entrée.

Debbie made the best macaroni salad. She called it a "BLT" salad. She used the finest seasonal ingredients the summer offered, mixing bits of fresh bacon and chunks of succulent Jersey tomatoes in with the pasta. For desert, we had homemade cherry vanilla Italian ice.

It had been a long time since we were able to relax, enjoy, and smile at life's simple pleasantries. I had envisioned a moment like this when I was in my darkest period. It was my true self's visualization of who I was and where I wanted to be—made manifest.

Following our late afternoon lunch, we went back to the apartment to relax, watch a couple movies, and later eat a light meal.

During this most enjoyable hiatus, Julian and I discussed how we would like our relationship to change from where it was before his admittance into rehab. We agreed that we'd like to see an open line of communication, honesty, and trust. It was a pleasant conversation which I knew he understood, contrary to our meaningless, combative altercations when he was wasted on drugs. At seven thirty, Angel said good-bye at the apartment, and Brandon and I drove him back to the facility.

* * *

Following his furlough, I continued visiting Julian ever Wednesday over the next few weeks. One day, I got a phone call from his primary counselor. "Julian is going to be promoted to the final level and discharged on the seventeenth of September. His completion ceremony is scheduled for September twenty fourth."

"That's fantastic!"

The counselor chuckled in obvious appreciation of my jubilance.

"But it gets better. He's not only completed the credits he needs for his junior year of high school, but ... you ready for this?"

"Sure, go on ... "

"Well, Dad ... your son made the honor roll."

I almost shit. "Holy shit! I don't even know what to say. I'm so happy and proud of him."

"Don't worry," the counselor said with a hearty guffaw. "Julian is standing right next to me listening to our conversation, and his smile tells me that he understands how you feel."

The week before Julian's discharge, I converted a storage room in our apartment into a bedroom for him. I went to the mall and bought a twin bed, a radio, and some posters. I decorated the room with the new things, as well as what I packed away when he went into rehab. Organizing his pictures, posters, album covers, and awards throughout the room as if it were my own ... I was thrilled. I wanted him to be surprised, happy, and comfortable in our new home together as a family. I also stocked up on the different types of food he fancied as well as toiletry supplies of his liking.

CHAPTER FORTY-FOUR
~REHAB COMPLETION~

I picked up Julian on Wednesday, September seventeenth, and took the next two days off from work to spend quality time with him, getting him settled into his new life at home. In the back of my mind, I wanted to keep an eye on him. While I felt excited he was home, I was also somewhat anxious. Would he be persuaded to go back to his old behavioral patterns, hanging out with the wrong people? Would he slip into his old addictive lifestyle? I didn't want him to make the same mistakes I had made repeatedly during my long and bumpy road to recovery.

Julian and I set up his schedule. The first appointment on our list was registering him into his intensive outpatient program (IOP). After that, I registered him in an alternative high school where he was accepted. We went and applied for his driving permit, filled out job applications at various places, and to the cellular dealership; I was giving him back his phone privileges.

In the middle of running errands and taking care of business, I dropped off Julian at his grandparents' house to do some work for his step-grandfather and earn a little pocket money.

Elated and excited to have my son home, still my anxiety and fear of him relapsing built. I questioned and pressured him on every move he made. Whenever I was away from the house and couldn't reach him by cell phone, I rushed home thinking he was up to no good. I was a prisoner in my own home again, afraid to leave, fearing that something would be destroyed or stolen. I had visions of finding Julian stoned with a bunch of his old derelict chums, freeloading in my house. I was treating him as if he *was* back doing drugs, stealing, and disrespecting my rules.

I was fortunate to be cognitive enough to catch myself. I recognized this errant behavior, and reprogrammed my thinking to acknowledge his hard work and success. I was surprised that he was understanding and patient with my mistrust.

I gained confidence during the week, as he awoke for school on his own and attended his outpatient program each day. It was refreshing to see him motivated to succeed and function as a normal part of society.

The day of his completion ceremony had come. I excused myself from work to be refreshed when I stood up in front of the crowd to say a few words about Julian's recovery. For the event, the families brought in dishes for a meal to be shared. I picked up a family portion of Chicken Lo Mein and a large platter of fried wontons. Julian's grandparents were unable to come because they were out of town, but his Aunt Donna and Uncle Lawrence attended and brought a homemade macaroni salad.

We arrived at the rehab center fifteen minutes early. There was a crowd already assembled in the facility's cafeteria. As a rule, the counselors typically announced that there was a limited amount of food. They'd ask everyone to make sure there was enough for all. That wasn't the case for this ceremony. It was one of the largest turnouts—not only in number of people attending, but also in per capita meal offerings—and they thanked the families for the abundance of food.

There was a wide variety of ethnic delicacies spread out on the row of tables lining the length of the cafeteria. New York Jewish-style deli sandwiches were piled high in the shape of pyramids with all the fixings and side salads. Boxes of pizzas, thin crust and Sicilian, with all the toppings, were stacked on one table alone. There were containers of lasagnas, baked ziti, spaghetti and meatballs, sausage and peppers, and antipastos. Deep trays of Chinese food, fried chicken, buffalo wings, chicken cutlets, hot roast beef, meatloaf, mashed potatoes, and numerous vegetables were lined up in a row, three trays deep per table. A few families even brought four-foot hoagies that were sliced in sections. At the end of the smorgasbord were two tables with pies, cakes, and doughnuts to satisfy the sweetest of teeth. Throughout the buffet line, parents who prepared or bought the meals were saying it was their child's favorite. The youths were saying, "Wait till you taste my mom's cooking." They couldn't wait to dig into real food.

There was a special celebratory sensation in the atmosphere that night. The participants smiled as they devoured the various culinary offerings and laughed as they conversed with other families. The adolescents playfully teased each other, appreciating the first intimate meal with their loved ones in a long time. Mothers and fathers, brothers and sisters, grandparents, aunt and uncles, cousins and close family friends, were all at peace with each other for this joyous occasion.

Following the meal, each patient was called up to the podium by their primary counselor to address the assembly. They told their horror stories with drugs and how the rehab changed their lives for the better. The graduate's parents and counselor followed with a brief speech.

Julian was the fourth patient out of the five graduating to be called up by his counselor. The crowd erupted with applause and screams when he walked to the podium. My body tingled with goose bumps. Julian's smile radiated. I gazed at him in awe. He had transformed from a hopeless child hell-bent to a life of destruction to a promising young man, taking swift and sure strides toward a life of success and happiness. The audience smiled in anticipation of Julian's speech.

Unfolding the papers he pulled from his back pocket, Julian grinned as he looked out at the crowd. His writings reflected on the progress he had made, not only his mental state but also his academic achievement. He stated his love for hallucinogenic drugs, especially LSD. He correlated his drug use, choice of friends, and disobedient behavior to the disturbance of our fragile household, as well as the theft of everything worth anything in our home. He discussed how hard the program was at first. He confessed he had contrived to coast and *fake out* the program. The plan was to grit his mental teeth, play the game, get through it, make everybody *oh-so-happy* as if they were all *so great* for helping him so much, and then ... go right back to using drugs after he got out.

Julian explained that once his head cleared, he could not go through with his insidious scheme. He had by then understood the program, what its true value was, and where the destructive life, if returned to, would lead. He said at that point things started to click: he began enjoying his sobriety and the rehabilitation program. He concluded his speech by saying how grateful he was for everyone's help in getting him to where he was now. He thanked each individual therapist. He spoke with confidence. I was proud.

Julian's counselor was up next. "His hair was down to here," he said with a laugh, pointing to the middle of his back. "But then his dad came along and took him home on furlough a few weeks ago and had most of it cut off. I won't even begin to explain how awful his scruffy beard was!" There was a pause as the crowd roared with laughter. "But he put hard work into the program. In the end, Julian opened up and relieved a great deal of the issues on his mind."

My bottom lip quivered. I became flush, trying to hold back tears.

The counselor looked into Julian's eyes. His voice cracked as he said, "I'm going to miss you. I know you're going to make it." As they closed in for a bear hug, I noticed tears in their eyes.

I was called to the podium. All month I had been thinking about what I would say. I thought about taking an excerpt from my manuscript—this memoir—reading the passage about first dropping off my son and the first visitation. I had written that part as it was happening.

I hoped to give the families a perspective from someone who had dealt with addiction from both sides. I wanted them to have an understanding that the issue at hand was something deeper than using drugs for recreational fun. There was distress or pain lurking in their child's psyche that was pleading for relief. My intention was to give the families a brief informative and psychological point of view of my own experiences with the developmental programming of my son's mind and that I had a responsible role in that development. I wanted to be careful, because I knew there were a few families who raised their children the best they could and their kids may have been led astray from some other external variable.

For the adolescents in rehab, I wanted to tell them that I understood why they were medicating themselves from the tedious and torturous pain life can dish out. It was well worth the constant struggle to fight the urges of addiction. I wanted to tell them that life has much to offer without having to be high to revel in it. I desired for them to recognize that you can overcome any obstacle no matter how high or deep, if you keep moving forward, striving to do the right things. But most of all, I intended to let everyone know how proud I was of my son. This was his moment, and I wanted the spotlight to be shown on him.

So much for fastidious preparation and lofty intentions. When I stood in front of everyone, my mind promptly went bye bye. I became flushed, tight, and adrenaline accelerated my heartbeat. I paused for a moment, gained my composure, picked my head up, and stared out toward the silent crowd.

"Hello. I'm Julian's father, Marco. It is unfortunate, but ... I must say that I'm an addict."

A wonderful thing happened at that moment. Following my admission of being an addict, the students in one unified, loud, and excited reply said, "Hi, Marco."

I was astonished with the enthusiasm the teens had toward my acknowledgment that I was like them. I looked out at the parents and counselors. I had their undivided attention. They waited to hear what I had to say next.

I took a deep breath. In a stern and powerful tone, I said, "Drugs have devastated my family. They contributed in tearing apart and destroying our family unit. I was both the predator and the prey when it came to my experience with drugs."

Looking out toward the children, I poked the podium with my finger several times and said, "Get it now while you're young! You don't want to be my age and in my position to get it. You don't want to wake up at forty years old in a psychiatric hospital, with four kids, six figures of debt, and a multitude of adult problems and responsibilities when you finally understand the horrors of the lifestyle you are leading."

I noticed the look of amazement on the counselors' faces as they admired the intensity and sincerity in my speech. At that point, I stopped and switched the recognition to my son.

"Even though I forced Julian to enter rehab, he was the one who did the hard work and was successful in its completion. I'm proud of him. Even though our relationship was rough when he was using, I missed him when he was away. I am very grateful to the rehab facility for all that they do, and in particular, to my son's counselor. Thank you everyone!"

The crowd erupted in applause. I turned to Julian and we embraced, patting each other on the back. As we went back to our seats, I cringed. My speech was dreadful. I forgot what I wanted to say. Surely they all must've thought I was a babbling idiot, not making any sense.

My ex-brother-in-law, Laurence, walked up and patted me on the back. He gripped my arm sharply and said, "Good job." His acknowledgement suppressed my shame from feeling like I ruined an extraordinary moment.

Other parents came up to me later, telling me what a wonderful job I did speaking to the kids. They said it was a great message. They thanked me for being forthright and honest.

After the ceremony, Julian hung out with his friends and counselors. Angel soon wanted to leave, saying several times, things like, "Dad, tell him we have to go," and, "Please make him leave," but I ignored her. This was Julian's special evening. I wanted him to take pleasure in his moment and socialize in a healthy manner.

He wrapped up his conversations in a half hour. We drove home, hopeful that he would not have to return as a patient, but as an alumni coming back to share his success.

CHAPTER FORTY-FIVE
~THE BLESSING OF TRUE LOVE AND COMPANIONSHIP~

She caught my eye as soon as I saw her. Her flowing blond hair caressing her shoulders and unique multi-colored eyes that sparkled when she smiled made me shaky when she'd get close. She and I worked out at the local gym with our children. She had an athletic build, perfect to my liking. Her daughter, I'd learned, worked at the front desk.

I'd glance around the gym to catch a glimpse of her between workout sets, and at times I'd catch her sneaking looks at me. During my lowest moments in therapy when I'd dream about the perfect wife, she was it.

Every weekday on my way to the gym, I'd get butterflies in my stomach in anticipation of seeing her again. But with the excitement came depression. I assumed that someone that perfect must have a good man already.

One day, I took Angel to the tanning salon next door to the gym. My *dream* woman was hanging out there when we came in, talking to her daughter—who also had a part-time job at this establishment. They got a kick out of a miniature credit card I had attached to my key chain to pay for the tanning.

When this goddess smiled and looked into my eyes, my knees would unhinge. My heart raced. I noticed for the first time that she not only didn't wear a wedding band, there was no 'white ring' on her finger where one would be worn. I wanted to talk with her, but ... didn't know what to say. I convinced myself she had to be in a relationship and walked out.

I had been frequenting a popular local sports grill once a week to watch a ball game and order takeout for the kids. It depressed me to watch with envy the singles crowd drinking and playing head games with each other.

One Friday night, before my takeout was ready, I felt a tap on my back.

"I see you go to other places than the gym," a woman behind me said.

When I turned around, I almost fell from my chair. There she was, her gorgeous, big bright eyes staring directly into mine.

"Uh ... yeah. I go out on occasion to pick up dinner for the kids."

"How are your kids doing?"

"They're good. And how about yours?" I said, hoping something brilliant would come to mind to add to the conversation.

"Oh, they're doing great. My daughter is doing well, working at both the gym and the tanning salon. My younger daughter babysits to make a few extra bucks, and she enjoys working out with me in the gym. My son is doing okay in school and loves basketball." She finished her report with a firm nod and a smile, put her hands on her curvaceous, sexy hips. The delicious nuances of her every expression and motion turned me into a hopeless blob of Play Dough. I wished I could mouth some lustrous literary lines, perhaps recite an astounding refrain from a poem, but ...

"Do you wanna get a drink?" I sighed internally. *That's all you got?*

She turned to the girlfriend she was with and raised her eyebrows, but the friend shook her head, seemingly annoyed and anxious to leave. My lovely lady turned back to me and rolled her eyes. "We're going up the street to Red Stone. Do you want to come?"

My mind screamed, Yes! But no, damn it, I couldn't. I sighed outwardly this time, smiled. "I'd love to. But I have to get dinner home to the kids. I'm kind of tired from the long work week, and I probably wouldn't be good company."

"Are you sure?" she said, leaning a little closer my way, tilting her head.

"Yeah, I better get home." It was unthinkably absurd. Everything inside was saying 'yes,' but the words were coming out as 'no'.

Her voice was pouty. "You're really sure?" She lowered her eyebrows, looking genuinely disappointed.

"My kids are waiting for dinner. But believe me, there would be nothing better than to have some adult company for once ... especially with you."

Her alluring lips turned upward and her eyes twinkled. "Well, I hope to see you around," she said, then turned and strutted out the door with swishing hips and a wave. I hated to see her go, but oh my God ... I sure did love the view.

When I got home, I told Angel what happened.

"Are you an idiot?" She huffed, threw both hands in the air, then thumped her head twice with her forefinger while grimacing at me—as if to say, *you numbskull, is there anyone home in there?* "I can't believe you didn't know what was going on, Dad. She's one of the most attractive women I've ever seen."

"I was clueless. And speechless." I knocked my head with the palm of my hand. "She showed interest in me, and I ... well, I guess I wasn't sure what was happening."

Angel shook her head and rolled her eyes. I sighed, thinking I may well have lost the woman I'd been waiting for. I resolved to ask her if she was single and if she'd be interested in going out with me some night. I repeated the words over and over so I wouldn't mess it up if I had another opportunity to talk with her.

She was nowhere to be seen over the next month. I went to the gym every night after work. I shopped around the plaza in the area. Every Friday night, I stopped at the sports grill around the same time that I'd seen her before.

As I was about to give up on ever seeing her again, she walked close by, not noticing me at the sports grill. My spine stiffened like a petrified arctic tree limb. I went mentally comatose. My heart was a ferocious palpitating pound of plasma. My breathing increased to where I thought I would go into cardiac arrest. Surely, this was my one and only chance to make an impression on her. But how, in such a state of panic? I was afraid I'd not be able to say the line I had been practicing for the past month.

I gathered my composure. If I walked to the bathroom, I could scan the room looking for her. When I slid my chair back and turned to walk to the restroom, she was sitting right behind me. We caught each other's eyes, and I was terror-stricken. My brain jumped ship, after ordering all the words I planned on saying to walk the plank. She was with the same girlfriend as before, and the two were staring at me.

"Hello, there," she said. "By the way, I'm Ellie."

"Hi, Ellie. I'm Marco." I reached out to her, relishing the opportunity to touch her soft hands. "Sorry I didn't introduce myself before. I was a little nervous."

Ellie giggled. "Nothing to be nervous about."

I shifted my weight from side to side, hoping my hand wasn't too clammy. "Um ... so how are you doing?" *Idiot. You've got to do better than that, Marco.*

"Great. We got here a couple of minutes ago. We're ordering some food."

Stricken with fear, I struggled to think of the words I had practiced over and over. Blood was rushing to my head ... I felt dizzy. I had to say something before I passed out. "Um ... I, uh ... I was wondering?" Looking at the floor, I hoped to release the words. "Um ... are you single?" I dared a sideways peek up at her.

"Yes, I am," she said with the sort of grin an amused parent has at a child's bashful behavior.

I placed my hand on their table to stable myself. The wooziness. My knees. My heart. I steadied myself in preparation for my next question. Do it, Marco. *Say it.* "Would you ... ah ... like to ... ah ... go out some night?"

"Yeah, I'd like that."

I was shocked. I always get the worst. Wonderful things don't happen to me. And now I'm going on a date with this dazzling beauty? *Hurry up and close the deal*—before you wake up and it's all a pernicious dream. *"Fantastic.* Can I get your number?"

She wrote it on a napkin, and I ran out the door without the takeout.

The following Sunday, I drove to her house and knocked on the door. She opened the door wearing an over-sized burnt-orange sweater and a pair of jeans. Her smile made me swoon.

"Come on in and meet my children," Ellie said, standing to the side, welcoming me in. Her kids were watching TV in the living room. "This is my youngest daughter, Elisha, and you know my older daughter, Lilly, from the gym. And ... this big guy is my son, Allen."

"Hi guys. Nice to meet you," I said, shaking hands with each of them.

"You, too," they said, grinning at me.

I turned toward Ellie. "Are you ready to go?"

"Yeah, I'm all set. See ya later kids!"

We walked down the brick walkway. "Where would you like to go?" I said, as we reached the car.

"Anywhere is fine with me. There's this nice little place in Medford that has great appetizers if that's something you'd be interested in."

"I'm pretty easy. I can go for anything."

"Oh, does that include me?" Ellie said with a chuckle.

"Uh ... um ... I didn't mean it that way. I was talking about the food."

"I know. I was joking with you," Ellie said, rubbing my neck, and massaging my aching heart in the process.

I opened the car door for her and she slid into her seat. Her eyes followed me as I walked in front of the car. A feeling of warmth rested in my stomach. It had been a long time since I had a feeling like this.

We began driving to the restaurant Ellie had suggested. "What a perfectly splendid night. And excellent company," Ellie said with a smirk, patting my knee.

"Did I tell you how beautiful you look tonight?" I put my right blinker on, cast a quick glance her way.

"Why, no ... you haven't."

I made a right turn while saying, "You're a dazzling sight, and I'm happy that you agreed to go out with me."

"You're not so bad yourself, handsome," Ellie said as she giggled.

"My daughter thinks you're the most amazing woman she's ever seen."

"How sweet of her to say. By the way, how did you get custody of your kids?"

Ouch. "Uh, oh ... um. Their, uh ... mother ran into a little trouble. I took custody a couple years ago." It was lucky that we arrived at the restaurant just then and the subject was dropped. I wasn't quite ready to explain my roguish past.

After parking the car, I trotted around to open her door. I felt proud walking into the restaurant with her and felt all eyes were on us. When we were seated, we agreed on crab spring rolls and humus dip with pita bread. I ordered a Coors Light, and she ordered a Miller Light. I switched to Miller Light soon after.

We shared stories about our love of the outdoors. She had competed as a bodybuilder in her younger days. I told her about my lifting days. Conversation came easily. The evening sped into night, and all too soon it was time to *call* it a night. We both had to get home to our kids and make school lunches for the next day. When I dropped her off at home, I walked her to the door.

"Can I call you again?"

"Yes, I'd like that."

I wanted to kiss her. My gut told me she wanted it, too. But something told me to take it slow. I smiled and waved, walking backward toward my car, tripping over a planter. I caught myself before falling. Ellie was laughing from the doorway. I waved again and hurried to my car, thankful she couldn't see my reddened face. I took a deep breath before starting the car. Glancing one more time at the silhouette of the gorgeous figure still standing at the door, I slowly pulled away, already missing her.

From that point on, things clicked with us. We got together every other weekend when I didn't have my two younger children with me.

With the little money left from the settlement, Ellie and I took train rides to Philadelphia and walked around Old City, South Street, and Ritten House Square. We saw movies, plays, and ballets.

During the Christmas season, we spent the night at a luxury hotel where we saw the Old Wanamaker's Nutcracker Light Show. Later, we saw the Pennsylvania Ballet's version of the Nutcracker, followed with dinner at the Palm Restaurant.

For the first time in my life, I rejoiced in pleasant events with a female companion and with a healthy mind. I wasn't thinking about only the sex. I had a beautiful friend, partner, and lover to experience life with.

We worked out together, took bike trips, went rafting, hiking, and took frequent walks. We loved any form of athletic activity. Golfing ranges, miniature golf, bowling, tennis, and pool were some of our favorites. She could even play baseball. We'd hit fly balls with her son in the local park.

She was a great cook. One night out of the week, we'd prepare a hearty meal together, followed by a desert, which was usually some form of pound cake, symbolizing the peace and tranquility I had with Poppy and Nanny. We would play board games at night. We were happy relaxing on the couch, watching a rented movie and snacking on candy treats.

As Ellie and I grew closer, we realized we were in love. She was more than I had ever hoped for in a partner. Before I could ask her for a long-time commitment, I had to explain my past issues with her. I called her on the phone, nervous, but committed. "Could you come over? I need to talk to you about some important issues."

"Sure, Marco. I can be right over." She paused; I could hear her woman's intuition sensing possible problems. "Is everything okay?"

"Yeah. Oh, yeah. Everything is great."

"Okay. See you in a few minutes."

Ellie drove to my apartment, and I greeted her at the door with a warm embrace and soft kiss on her lips. "Let's sit outside," I said. My hands felt clammy. I was biting my lip, searching for a way to start the conversation. We walked onto the porch overlooking the landscaped tree line. The stars were bright, and the moon was beginning to rise. We sat on the lounge chairs and breathed in the cool breeze passing by.

"Um. I ... ah ... have something really important to tell you before we commit to each other any further." I stood up and paced back and forth in front of Ellie—searching for the nerve to tell her.

"What's the matter, hon?" Ellie said. "Whatever you have to tell me, that's so important, will not change anything that we share together."

"I hope it doesn't, Ellie. I've made huge mistakes in my past. Mistakes that may change the way you look at me." There was a look of concern on Ellie's face.

She stood up and walked over to me. Putting her hands on my shoulders, she sat me back down. Taking my hands in hers, she endearingly looked into my eyes and said, "What is it Marco? You're making me nervous. Please tell me ... *now*."

"Okay. Please hear me with an open mind. It's so hard to talk about."

"You don't have to be afraid to tell me anything, Marco. You know that I love you. Please ... just say it."

I inhaled slowly through my nose. I looked at my knees. Ellie's gentle touch lifted my chin. She looked directly into my eyes. "It's okay," she whispered.

"Oh, man. My childhood was kind of rough. Things got out of control. I know it's not my fault but, I ... ah, was ... um ... abused by a Catholic priest when I was ten. It screwed my head up for a while."

"Oh, my God!" She paled and clutched at her heart. "That's *horrible*. But," she tilted her head to the side with a quizzical look, "why would you think that would matter to me?"

"Well, to be truthful, I've done some deplorable things. I've hurt a lot of people. I ... uh ... self-medicated myself with drugs. I've been in numerous hospitals because of it."

Ellie sat on my lap, wrapping her arms around my shoulders. She kissed me on top of my head. "How long has it been since your last hospitalization?"

"It's been three years."

"Marco, I know you. I know what's inside your heart. And I love you," she said, holding my face in her hands. Even though this is serious, I've done things in my life I'm not proud of. This doesn't change a thing between us." She rested her head on my shoulder. "But I hope I can trust you to not go back to your drug use."

I stroked her hair, pulling her close. Resting my head on hers, I said, "You can trust me, Ellie. I don't want to lose you or my children." I tipped her chin up and gently kissed her. "I love you for accepting me for who I am. Thank you for being so understanding."

After our discussion, I knew she was the one love that I wanted to spend the rest of my life with. The following week I purchased an engagement ring and took her to our favorite restaurant. I got down on one knee ... and proposed to her. She accepted.

* * *

Ellie and I spent as much time outdoors as we could. Camping out was the best. We'd set up our tent and decorate the picnic table according to the season. In the fall, we'd place fancy miniature gourds on top of a tablecloth printed with fall foliage.

We'd hike or bike, coming back to prepare our dinner over hot coals produced by a roaring fire. We would bask in the glow surrounding us, coming from candles we'd positioned throughout our campsite. She'd push miniature dark chocolate hearts into the marshmallows we roasted on sticks. We would feed them to each other before playing a game of cards or checkers.

The night ended with us huddled together in our cozy nylon tent. Our arms and bodies melded together when we held each other like two matching pieces to a puzzle. Her shapely curves were God's masterpiece. Every bit of her was perfect in my mind.

Ellie brought out the best of my senses. I noticed the harmony and artistry in the world whenever we were together. She helped me realize my accomplishments. The demanding work of rectifying the damage of my past was now rewarded. Sights, sounds, tastes and smells were more magnificent than ever. Our relationship was meant to be.

She was strong and structured, giving me additional strength and inspiration to solve the remaining issues with my disastrous past. She provided guidance and advice with my single-parenting questions with her first-hand knowledge of being a single mother for eight years. Ellie was raising three children, ages seventeen, sixteen, and fourteen, with no help from her ex-husband other than child support. She was tough minded and taught me how to say *no* to my children.

With a simple smile from her angelic face, she put to rest the beast that paced within me. Her caressing strokes on the back of my neck radiated an intense energy of love that eased the raciness of my compulsions. The comfort that she provided me, from her mere presence, was as sedating as any narcotic I had ever consumed.

I felt a closeness that could not be explained. I wanted to experience everything that life had to offer with this woman. I wanted to be in her arms when the last breath left my lungs, the last vision left my eyes, the last touch was felt, and the last beat of my heart pounded in my chest.

CHAPTER FORTY-SIX
~SAVING MY EX-WIFE AGAIN~

Living in bliss, I no longer held resentment toward Louise. What remained was sorrow and compassion for her situation. She, too, was paying the price for my abuse. She couldn't conquer the demons of shame and guilt from a life of sexual perversions and addictions. People close to me convinced me that I was enabling Louise if I didn't enforce the child support order by the court. I wanted to help her get back on track, but my own financial struggles prevented me from doing so.

Angel barged into my bedroom late one night and screamed, "Mom was arrested for not paying child support. It's *your* fault. I can't even look at you." She ran from my room sobbing.

I jumped out of bed and ran to Angel's bedroom. "Can I come in? Can we talk?"

Through sniffles, she said, "I ... I ... guess so."

I took a deep breath and opened the door. Angel was face down on the bed, her body trembling. I walked over and sat on the edge of her mattress. "Don't cry," I said, rubbing her back and stroking her long hair. "It's not my fault that your mom's in jail. She went to court and claimed that I had used her credit cards without her knowledge and put her in thousands of dollars of debt. Which wasn't true. There was a time that I was in the same situation, and your mother didn't have sympathy for me. I paid every penny of my back child support. I even tried to help your mother by moving into her apartment for eleven months to take care of you guys and pay all her bills. Over the last two years that you and your brother have been living with me, she's never helped with any support at all."

"I don't want to hear this," Angel said, sitting up. "Mom was getting her act together. She had a job. Now she's going to lose it because of *you*. Because someone does something wrong to you, doesn't mean you should do the same."

"Your mom may be trying to get her act together. I'll see what I can do to help her tomorrow. I don't want you to cry over this. I'll make some phone calls and see what I can do."

The following day, I called the probation department. I thought I could approve Louise's release under her own recognizance as long as she would start making payments toward the child support and arrears.

The only way she could be released was if I rescinded the warrant for her arrest as well as the child support order. I'd have to testify in court or submit a notarized statement prior to her hearing in order to do this.

I was furious that she'd get off the hook once again. She always found people to bail her out. Angel's words, which softened my heart the night before, meant nothing to me as extensive thoughts of Louise's reprehensible and damaging actions replayed in my mind.

As I knocked around my resentment and debated within my mind what to do, Angel and her grandmother were pleading with me to help. If something wasn't done the next day, Louise would spend the Christmas holiday in a jail cell.

I couldn't live with that. That my past sins played a role in shaping Louise into the addict she was today affected my compassion toward her situation. I wrote the letter rescinding the order and gave it to Debbie to submit to the courts. She was released the next afternoon. My daughter was ecstatic, and Debbie expressed tremendous gratitude. That night I slept well.

CHAPTER FORTY-SEVEN
~DAUGHTER'S SEARCH FOR JUSTICE~

In the midst of resolving the complications in my life, Angel and I were cooperating with the prosecutor's office, attempting to bring her abuser to justice. The lead detective in the case thought it would be in my daughter's best interest to strengthen her mental state through her current therapy. He was hoping she'd be strong enough to solicit a recorded confession from Rich over the phone.

Angel spent a month of intense therapy before making the phone call. When we arrived at the prosecutor's office, the investigating team escorted us into an office and described the game plan on how best to bait her abuser into apologizing for what he had done. The lead detective and one of the sergeants explained how the equipment operated.

They instructed Angel on how she should conduct the conversation if Rich answered the phone and what they would be doing as the conversation progressed. The detective would be taking notes and producing cue cards to flash at Angel, advising her of what to say. The team assured her that she was in a safe place and everything was going to be fine. Following a half hour of instructions, the prosecuting team asked Angel, "Are you ready." She nodded her head.

I was escorted from the room to a reception area. Pacing the room, I made an effort to center myself. The literature they gave me about sexual abuse didn't help. Twenty minutes later, the detective came out with Angel. The numbers they had on file weren't good. More investigative work was needed. They'd get back to us as soon as they located the guy.

Over the next two weeks, I researched and contacted anyone who might have known Rich's whereabouts or how to get in contact with him. By chance, I spoke with a certain friend who had access to the database for a utilities authority. They looked up the name I supplied, and a message popped up on the screen. It said that the meter couldn't be read at the house because the resident of the property was naked in his yard and had recently flashed a female reader.

Memories zipped across my mind. I had asked Louise about Rich having a restraining order against him. She had blown me off, claiming that his ex-wife was a whacko. How could I have not seen the flags? I had been angry at the world for not recognizing the signs when I was abused. I had allowed this predator to feed on my daughter. My stomach felt sick. This animal had gotten away with this for years, and he was still out there victimizing people.

When I was able to get four legitimate phone numbers, I called the detective and scheduled another appointment. The investigating team tried to call the numbers I gave them with Angel in the room. Three were disconnected.

A man answered the fourth number. "Is Rich there?" Angel said.

"No Rich lives here, hon."

He hung up. "I think it was him. He used to call me 'hon' like that."

The lead detective sensed that it was him, too. He said the team would collaborate with the prosecutor, and then get back to us on how they were going to proceed with the case.

The next day, it was decided that the investigators would try to get Rich into the prosecutor's office for an interview to elicit a confession or some type of verbal incrimination to build a case.

After several weeks of staking out his residence, the detective in charge decided to contact Rich. Because his rap sheet showed he was familiar with the justice system, it was a long shot—they had little faith in his agreeing to come in. The abuser wasn't obligated to come in without a warrant against him. But it was the best shot they had, so the detective attempted the ploy anyway. It was the only hope for the case. The detective made the call, connected with Rich, and asked if he would come in for questioning and cooperate with an investigation his office was conducting. We were all surprised when he agreed to come in for an interview.

The detective called me after the interview. "In talking with the guy, he first thought he was brought in for questioning about lighting fireworks on his property. Once I told him I wanted to ask him about accusations he molested your daughter, he panicked and denied everything. He cooperated for a while and answered a majority of the questions before he ended the interview."

"Did he take a polygraph test?"

"He first agreed, but then retracted and declined."

The next step was to interview Louise. The investigative team asked if I could reach out to her since there was no contact number. I talked it over with Angel, and she agreed to tell her mother and ask her to contact the detective in charge.

By fortuitous coincidence, Louise called me the next day while I was in the grocery store. I had to be vague because of the other shoppers around me. "We've been in touch with a detective. He needs to speak with you about inappropriate behavior Rich had with Angel."

"What happened?"

"Figure it out."

"I knew something happened, but she never confided in me. Why didn't you tell me sooner? It could've made a world of difference in convicting him."

"You've got a lot going on right now and it's not the best time for you to get too involved yet."

"You should've said something sooner. Who are you to say what I should do?"

"How do you figure I can think you can help when you've been out robbing homes and smoking crack?"

There was silence for a moment, and then sniffles.

"I'm sorry. Look—the detective wants to talk to you about Angel's case. He's not concerned with the current warrants on you. Can I give you his phone number? Will you call him?"

"Oh, okay. I'll call him right away."

Didn't happen. Over the next few weeks, the detective called several times asking if Louise was going to contact him. There was no way to get in touch with her. Her cell phone—I had taken the number from my incoming call registry and given it to him—was disconnected, apparently soon after she called me. I figured she was again moving from house to house, wearing out her welcome and searching for somewhere else to live.

At three in the morning one Sunday, Louise left a voice mail message asking me to bail her out at the Cherry Hill, New Jersey police station. I didn't hear the message until I woke up a few hours later.

I called the detective immediately and gave him her whereabouts. By the time he got there, she was gone. The detective, looking in the system at the type of warrants that were out on her, couldn't understand how she had been released. He thought there must have been a mistake on the precinct's part, or else the higher warrant must not have posted until after her release.

I later found out she was bailed out by an old friend of ours. He had worked with us at the racetrack. We used to party heavily with him, doing coke and crack. He was now letting her stay with him.

Over the next week, Angel and I were able to convince Louise to call the detective and discuss the case. But she didn't offer much. The lead detective said he would gather what evidence he had and consult with the prosecutor.

Two weeks later, the detective called me at work. "We're not going to be able to pursue prosecuting your daughter's abuser."

"You what? I can't believe you're not going after this animal. Where's the justice in this?"

"I'm very sorry, sir. But we don't have enough evidence to pursue the case."

"What do you mean you don't have enough evidence to pursue the case? The guy has a criminal past, a restraining order against seeing his own daughter, and there's documented evidence he's a flashing pervert. He won't agree to take a polygraph test, and you're telling me there is nothing in support for our case?"

"Unfortunately, sir, our hands are tied. That's the prosecuting department's stance. I'm sorry."

I slammed the phone down. A numbing sensation came over me. I left work right away. Once again, life hadn't gone my way. It was like swimming against a strong current to get anything accomplished. It felt like God had put a curse on me and my children, setting me off in a rage of resentment at every living thing.

It was a restless night, but I made it into work the next day. I called the prosecutor's office to see if there was anything I could do to obtain justice. They said the only recourse at this juncture was to sue the abuser on behalf of my daughter through a civil lawsuit.

I called my attorney who represented me during the settlement with the Catholic Diocese, asking if he'd take the case. He declined at first. But I was persistent and asked him to reconsider, explaining the oddities of her abuser. He agreed to look over the documents if I sent him a consent letter to review the prosecutor's files. He'd get back to me if there was enough corroborating evidence.

A month later, he declined again. There wasn't enough physical evidence to prosecute. The chance of collecting on a settlement was too risky for his law firm to take on the case.

How do I tell Angel? This isn't fair. She's going to be crushed. I had my therapy session with Keith that night to help me deal with the issue.

"Why the fuck did God curse my children and me? Not one fucking thing in my life has gone smoothly. I've worked myself into a state of exhaustion, trying to accomplish anything in my fucking life. From the smallest of issues to major occurrences, my expectations are always let down. Yes, I know my perfectionist and striver parts, along with my ego, play a big part in my disappointments. It's not right the way life is going for us. It's not even a battle. It's an all-out war from the moment we wake until we go to sleep in order to maintain our sanity. I have worked hard to survive and make ends meet."

Keith agreed and did his best to try to get a word in between my repetitive gloom and doom rampages. When he was able to jump in, he said, "The first time you sat in my office a few years ago, Marco, you were at one of the most vulnerable points in your life. You now have everything you said you wanted at the time. You have your career back. Your children are living with you. You have a beautiful fiancée. A great deal of debt has been erased."

"Hmm," I said, sitting back in the chair.

"Even after receiving these valuable blessings on the top of your priorities, you felt a disheartening loneliness of being without who you thought was the most wonderful woman in the world. You were then brightened by an incredible relationship of friendship, companionship and love with an even more magnificent woman."

"You're right," I said with a sigh. "I no longer view the female species as a meaningless vessel to satisfy my sexual mental disorders. I found love in the true sense. My love for Ellie makes me want to spend every moment with her until the last breath of air is exhaled from my lungs. But it's tough for us to be in a relationship. It's difficult to be there for each other in times of need when we're so engulfed in our own children's problems when we're apart."

With each blessing that Keith pointed out, my faith increased in restoration. My clouded vision cleared as I realized there was still hope for my family. I wasn't the least bit grateful for having a job during the current economic times; instead, I was angry as hell for having to live from paycheck to paycheck. I had a high-ranking responsible position and was producing a quality work product.

The following day, I restarted the search for justice. My therapy session rejuvenated me. I was going to continue fighting for my family. I emailed my attorney, explaining my disappointments and struggles. I asked for advice on how to proceed. He responded that the Division of Youth and Family Services (DYFS) might be able to assist me in requesting a meeting with the prosecuting team to discuss revisiting the case.

I first called DYFS and explained our situation to a caseworker. She explained that due to the lapse of time, and the fact my daughter wasn't in danger, there wasn't anything they could do. She said the support and therapy I was providing for her was the most important thing I could do.

I called the prosecutor's office to see if the case could be reopened. They wouldn't listen to my request and transferred me to the Child Advocacy Center. I spoke to a child advocate, and she said she could arrange a meeting with the investigating team, but it wasn't going to change their position on pursuing the case.

It wasn't what I wanted to hear, but I requested they schedule a meeting anyway. I wanted to hear their reasoning and plead with them to change their minds on the matter.

About a week later, I was ecstatic to receive a phone call at work from the assistant prosecutor who was involved with the investigation. I was hoping to receive some sympathy and reconsideration in my daughter's abuse matter. I could never have been more wrong.

"What exactly didn't you understand when we first told you that there was nothing we could do?" she said.

A tremendous lump leaped into my throat. Tears formed in my eyes. I had trouble responding because my lips were quivering. I could tell she was trying to rush me off the phone, so I desperately attempted to gather my composure in order to say something to keep her on the line.

Before I could utter anything, the cold witch reiterated, "You've already been told this case isn't prosecutable."

"Your rude response is disappointing and unfeeling," I said, and hung up.

I pushed my chair away from my desk and closed my office door. Sitting back down, I put my head in my hands and cried. The world seemed so cold and heartless. I wondered if there was anyone who understood what my family was going through.

I went home after work and gave my daughter the news.

Tears formed in her eyes. "I hate my life. I want to die."

"So do I."

CHAPTER FORTY-EIGHT
~SLIGHT RELAPSE IN THERAPY~

The flame of hope my therapist persuaded me to believe existed was extinguished. I dragged myself to my next session. "I don't know what to say anymore. I'm tired of fighting. The battle is exhausting, and I don't know if I'll be able to keep my sanity and continue working to straighten out everyone's life I've affected. It's hard to act like I'm grateful for what I have. I've had to work my ass off for every single thing I have. I deserve to get a break," I said, turning into a puddle of tears.

Keith was quiet.

"I gained my sanity and reprogrammed my mind to think, feel, and act like a normal person," I said. "I fought the Church for the little money they gave me by organizing, gathering, and debating every piece of evidence to prove they were in large part responsible for my immoral behaviors. My actions led to my family's endless depressing abyss of mental torture. I struggled to get back on my feet and get custody of my children. I brawled with life's unfair punches, one after the other, taking it on the chin while still standing.

"I'm tired of being told to be grateful for your health and the health of your children. Yes, I do have two arms and two legs. But, I want to detonate whenever I hear those phrases. The mental grievances my kids and I are experiencing are intense. In our minds, the pain and exhausting disorders are comparable to any physical ailment. I'm tired of wading through the rough waters of life. I want to stop struggling and sink to the depths of the murky seas and fill my lungs with the waters of death."

For the first time in my three years of therapy, I witnessed Keith removing his glasses to wipe a tear from his eye. It was as if he had been there before.

"I can't address any of your questions," he said. "You're too overwhelmed with despair. I don't believe you could take a step back and answer the questions from the true self."

As I walked out his door that night, he hung his head and patted me on the back. The gesture told me that he understood and cared.

I let my attorney know that I had no success with his suggestion to contact the DYFS. He sent me an email telling me about a certain attorney who was speaking to the senate in Washington, D.C. the following month on victims of crimes who were not compensated fairly. It was obvious my attorney was moved by my email. I could tell he was researching my issues on the Internet by the links and articles he forwarded to me.

When his email arrived, I was at work. I got a rush. There may still be hope for my daughter. I dropped everything I was doing. I searched the Internet for the attorney's name my lawyer had given me and located the firm where he was a partner. Through his firm's web page, I drafted and emailed a brief account of the atrocities my family had and still endured, highlighting my daughter's injustice. I followed up with a phone call to his office to confirm whether he received the message. His secretary said it would be best if I contacted him directly, and she gave me his email address.

Shortly after resending my message he answered me by email, sympathetic for my family's miseries. He asked me to call him on his cell phone.

I replied the next morning that I would call him after I got through my meetings that day. I got tied up and wasn't able to call him until the evening. He answered the phone and sounded thrilled that I called. But he was with a group of people. He wanted to talk to me and asked if he could call me later that night. I rescheduled to the next day instead. I would've been too tired after working all day, and then dealing with my single parenting duties, to describe the issues in a coherent manner.

When I called the attorney the next day, he once again sounded supportive regarding my family's predicament. It was comforting to talk with someone who appeared attentive to my situation. I filled him in on my daughter's case not being able to be prosecuted. I told him of my own abuse at the hands of my parish priest when I was ten, and that I'd written a manuscript documenting the story.

"What would you like from me?" he said.

"First and foremost, I want to see my daughter's abuser put behind bars and for him to pay for the crimes he committed."

"What are the details in the case?"

After I told him the details, he said, "I can see where there'd be a problem with the length of time that's passed from when the abuse occurred. But you might be able to file for a grant from the Victim's

Compensation Board to help with costs associated with therapy for your daughter. Can you send me by email the names of the officials involved with the case, along with your attorney's name and phone number? I'll follow up to find out the details on their decision to not pursue the criminal investigation and see if there is anything further I can do in regard to the matter."

"Of course," I said, enthused with his interest. "I'll get the information right out to you. I also wondered if you would be able to assist me in getting my family's story out to the public through contacts you might have through the victims group you're involved with. I want to tell my story about how the sexual abuse not only affects the person being violated, but also everyone that person comes in contact with."

"I know some editors and writers that might be interested in assisting you in ghost writing or co-authoring your memoir. I'm the executive director of a magazine called *The Victim's Voice* that has anywhere from ten to fifteen thousand copies distributed per issue. If you're interested, maybe the magazine would be willing to print your family's story."

"I would indeed be interested in telling our story to the magazine."

"Send me an email with your information, and I'll get back to you."

I emailed him the names and phone numbers he requested along with the query letter and book proposal for my story. I waited for his reply.

CHAPTER FIFTY
~DAUGHTER'S DOWNTURN~

While all I could do now was wait to hear back from the attorney, my primary focus had to return to Angel—who wasn't doing well. She feared her abuser would come after her now that he knew she'd made his crime public. She was stressed out because of the ineffectiveness of the system to protect her and prosecute the pervert. She was also dealing with the shame of having been abused.

With her mother absent in her life, and me having my own issues and other children to deal with, Angel became unstable and moody.

She had become jealous of the relationship I had with Ellie. I was spending two to four nights at her house over a two-week period. Ellie didn't like to stay at my apartment and leave her kids alone. My daughter would call with a list of unnecessary complaints, demanding I come home right away. She'd want me to buy her cigarettes. I knew it was wrong when she was only sixteen years old, but I wanted to keep peace with her. Ellie was getting impatient with the situation.

Angel became very standoffish. She'd swear at me, causing me to feel like a failure. I wasn't able to come through with the promise to take care of her and not let the injustice that happened to me happen to her.

My pessimistic outlook on life consumed my mind. I was afraid the disappointment of not being able to prosecute Rich would dominate this chapter in her life, leading her to conclude there was no bright future possible for her.

I never heard back from the attorney who said he'd see what he could do to help with my daughter's case. He must've been only concerned with the possible monetary dividend. He wasn't the concerned and compassionate human being he masqueraded to be. Once again, my children had to pay the price for the curse that seemed to encompass my life.

I felt alone; there was no one out there to help my family or me. All I could do was wait out the storm with my daughter's emotions. I hoped she'd overcome her abuse through the support and therapy I was providing for her.

My financial situation stabilized as I persevered through painful negotiations with the remaining collection agencies I owed. The Internal Revenue Service didn't accept my offer of compromise because I still had some settlement money in my bank account. They didn't take into consideration the money was for pain and suffering from the abuse. They wanted their money, and I had to pay the amount I owed in full. It took close to the entire balance of my savings. I requested leniency on the penalties and interest, which were almost ten thousand dollars, but I had to pay the balance in full before they would consider my request.

When I sent them the payment, I prepared the medical documentation package with meticulous precision. I supported my claim for clemency, proving the irrational spending behaviors and poor financial management were caused by my post-traumatic stress disorder. They were more than fair, refunding nearly six thousand dollars shortly after receiving my payment and packet.

I thought once my issues were calmed and the missing pieces of my life were fulfilled, the stress would dissipate. My achievements over the past few years were great, as my therapist pointed out. Debts were paid and my divorce was finalized. I had custody of my two older kids, giving them structure in their lives. I had found Ellie. There was satisfaction in taking responsibility for my past actions. I had much to be thankful for.

Mary was a wonderful mother to Jennifer and Brandon. They lived in a loving household. Mary accepted a fair child support payment, and I covered the kids on my health insurance policy. She understood my accomplishments. She considered Julian and Angel her stepchildren and was proud of me stepping up to be responsible for them. Why couldn't I be happy?

As before, when I received my settlement and custody of my kids, the abuse's defender parts had tried their best to persuade me to regress back to my shameful ways. These traits were striving, with fearsome progress, to take over running my life once again. I worked hard in my therapy sessions to identify and unburden myself from their negative self-perceptions and ill-conceived manner of conducting my life.

The conductor, the true self, was supposed to be administrating my life. But it had become distracted from solving my problems and caring for my devastated family. With the multitude of issues to resolve, I became preoccupied by the constant restlessness of the defender parts I had worked hard at taming in the past. I had let my guard down and was unconsciously allowing the restless emotional components pilot my life. Like a tiger pacing in its cage eager to be free, these elements of my psyche were in continuous motion. These parts never wanted me to have peace, keeping me on edge and vigilant.

Julian was slipping. He was making it to school and his outpatient therapy program, but needed his hand held to get there. I had to get on his case to find a job. It was difficult maintaining my strength to keep him in line. It was a full-time job coordinating with his grandparents and other family members to get him where he needed to be.

There was no doubt he was better than before his rehabilitation treatment, but it drained energy from me to stay on top of him to do chores, make it to school and do his homework. I worried where he was and what he was doing when I wasn't home. He had returned to hanging out with his old friends. No words worked in convincing him how dangerous that was. His attitude converted from that of a grateful child, eager to build on our relationship, to a know-it-all, thinking everything would fall into his lap without having to work for it.

As he became more comfortable at home, he grew more outspoken. There was a knock on my bedroom door one day. "Dad, can I speak with you?"

"Sure Julian. I'll be right there." I got up from my desk where I was working on my laptop. Opening the door, I said, "What's up?"

"It's been bothering me for a while. You never let me do *anything*." He stomped his foot for emphasis, looking me right in the eye.

"I love you and don't want you to fall again," I said. "I have to be strict with you." I pointed my finger in his face. "And you *know* that."

"You let Angel get away with everything. You're not that strict with her."

"This has nothing to do with Angel. She didn't get herself into the trouble that you have. You're not only on probation with the law, but you're on probation at home."

"It's not fair," Julian said, storming down the hallway.

I followed him to the living room. "Can't you have sympathy for what Angel's going through?"

"I do everything right and you don't trust me. It's you that are psychotic, not me."

"You've worked hard to make improvements in your life. I'm proud of you for that."

Julian grabbed the door knob, and threw open the front door. "You don't act it," he shouted, walking out.

I was hurt. I was overburdened. Now I had, to go along with everything else, to once again deal with the physical and mental demands of trying to keep my son straight.

CHAPTER FIFTY-THREE
~LIFE'S STRESSES: DAUGHTER~

Angel eventually came to a place of acceptance that we couldn't prosecute her abuser. She dealt with her exploitation and depression in therapy. After this breakthrough it wasn't *as* much work to keep her in line, but there still were several challenges dealing with her. I tried my best and, in her own handicapped way, she did too. In some respects progress was evident. I taxied her to all the places she wanted to go. We were getting closer as we became more comfortable with each other. We shared in simple conversations, as well as attending occasional joint therapy sessions together.

It was demanding to work with Angel and her therapist. The focus was on the depression she suffered because of the absence of her mother, abuse, and injustice from her abuser getting away with the crime he committed.

Despondency would creep up from time to time, paralyzing her to where she couldn't get out of bed and function. When I would try to communicate with her during these episodes, she would either be in a state of confusion, crying out of control, and not knowing what was wrong, or she would lash out at me with a disrespectful rampage of spiteful and obscene words.

When she was in this frame of mind, she would disregard my orders. I didn't know what to do. She wouldn't keep up with her chores. She'd smoke in her bedroom. At times she'd extinguish cigarettes on the bedroom furniture, in a drinking glass, or on a plate of food she'd bring into her room. I'd seek help through her therapist or my own.

I cried to her, pleading for cooperation, complaining I had enough on my plate to deal with. I needed her to respect me. She'd give me a deadened stare, as if I didn't exist. I was frustrated with her lack of respect, but proud of her conquering the demons of sexual abuse and overcoming the pain of losing the physical presence of her mother in her everyday life.

The stresses from parenting and solving my family's problems were one predicament, but also there was anxiety at work. I needed to take time off to care for my children's problems and my own. My workload had increased as my talents and skills with numbers and leadership were recognized. I became knowledgeable and comfortable with the State Authority's operations and, as a result, was given considerable autonomy on what needed to be done and how to do it.

Various departmental directors and officers assigned specialty tasks to me as challenges arose during the course of business. The Chief Executive Officer acknowledged my work product by asking me to design and implement a workshop on purchasing policies and project management oversight.

The personnel director and I became a team, tackling any problem that arose. We expedited and improved on existing operations. My talents had freed up some of my director's time, and he was able to concentrate on his executive duties, being recognized by our industry's local magazine as the "go-to guy".

My perfectionist trait had contributed to my acceleration at work. But it was wearing me down, as I tried to put out an error-free work product every time. The high performance standards I set for myself added to the stressors that I allowed to take over my thoughts.

So, in addition to this tension at work, as I said earlier, I needed to take *off* or *leave early* at times to solve the conundrum of my family's well being. Paranoia sunk in, worrying I'd be terminated for absenteeism. There were times I was too depressed or exhausted from anxiety to come into the office.

Added to the work stress, I was confronted with an incident that sent me deeper into anguish, creating an uncomfortable work environment for me. I was carrying out a project for the Authority's Public Relations Director when my personnel director, a couple of project officers, and our secretary, Doreen, came into my office. They started a casual conversation that led to the topic of church.

"Who was an altar boy?" This innocent query floated out. Innocent to all but me, to whom the abuse issues were ignited. Another senior officer, Mike, who held the same position as I did, talked about one of his uncles who was a priest. He assured us that his uncle was straight and told him that the monastery school was, "Floating with flamers."

It started as a joke. Everyone laughed, making innuendos about their parish's priests. Doreen said, "There's nothing wrong with gay priests, but they should leave the innocent children alone."

It was like she sensed something, looking right at me. The room went silent for a moment.

Mike asked, "Why are you so quiet."

Heat raced to my face. My sweat glands reeked. I pulled a napkin from my desk drawer and pretended to blow my nose. "I'm not feeling well," I said.

Not feeling well—I was *devastated*. I wanted to resign at that moment. I wanted to holler, *Everyone out!* None of you know what it's like to live life after being preyed upon as you prayed. I wanted to let them know why I'm in my office working and not hanging around having casual conversations. I have to keep my mind occupied to keep my emotional disorders under control, caused by what they think is a big fucking joke. The rest of the day at work was torturous.

Throughout that night, my subconscious recognized that my psyche was disturbed. I was in a state of alertness with disrupting nightmares, which crippled me to where it was a struggle to go into work the next day.

While I was in an exhausted and vulnerable state, Mike called the director, Chris, Doreen, and me into his office, which was next to mine. We talked about a project in which we had granted an award to fund construction of a facility for the same Catholic Diocese that was responsible for my abuse. In order to receive state funds, the diocese had had to agree the facility would not to be used for religious purposes. Doing so would violate the First Amendment of the United States Constitution, which guarantees separation of church and state. It was later exposed that they were using fifteen percent of the facility for religious ceremonies, a direct violation of the terms of the contract, and a constitutionally criminal act. I was asked to analyze a reasonable amount of the funds already contributed to the Church to be reimbursed back to us.

True to the egregious and self-serving form of the Church I had come to know, upon being presented with our demands, they had the audacity to request leniency. They asked for a reduction on the amount they would be required to repay. They requested we deduct a depreciated formulated rate off the balance they owed. I pointed out to Chris they would be receiving twice the benefit. The Church already benefited on the depreciation of the capital given to them when they received their certificate of occupancy, almost five and a half years ago.

During this discussion, a local parish priest's name came up, who happened to be Father Nelson. Mike asked us, "Have you heard the joke about Father Nelson?"

I freaked. "Yes, I've heard it many times."

"They didn't," he said. "Let's show them."

Sweat formed at my temples. "Come on, guys. You *must've* heard that old joke."

"No, I've never heard it," Chris said.

"Me neither," Doreen said, shaking her head.

My cohort proceeded to perform the joke, culminating with his humping me from behind. I was put back in time, feeling the physical and mental pain from the abuse as if it was occurring. The shock annihilated me. I couldn't function for the rest of the day. I had to take the next day off, using another sick day to recuperate from the after effects of the trauma. Once again, here was another sign of the world not understanding the demolishing impact of clergy abuse.

CHAPTER FIFTY-FIVE
~LIFE'S STRESSES: YOUNGER CHILDREN~

On days leading up to every other Friday afternoon when I would pick up Jennifer and Brandon for a weekend filled with anticipated fun, I'd race around the house, keeping up with the household chores. I would shop throughout the week, wanting to have all provisions in place so I could provide them with my undivided attention.

Brandon would poke Jennifer at some point in their visit. She'd smack his butt. He'd overreact that he was severely injured to get his sister in trouble. Jennifer would deny any wrongdoing. Brandon would disagree with, "Uh *huh.*"

Most of the time, I loved to watch their playfulness and how they tried to manipulate me. But this weekend? I had no patience. I was exhausted trying to keep them in line. The perfectionist trait kicked in, preventing me from doing what I intended to do with my two little ones. I found myself not only continuing to keep the house and my life in perfect order, but also my younger children.

I dropped them off at their mother's home on Sunday, paralyzed with pessimism and hopelessness. I hadn't shown them the love I had for them. We'd spent no quality time together. I was worn down striving for excellence and control. The harder I worked at possessing the perfect environment, the more imperfect life was.

I found myself in survival mode again, trying to straighten out everyone in the family. My hope at the time was to be able to recognize the symptoms of my mental disorder and provide my soul with peace of mind. Looking back I understand I was stuck in the same cyclical pattern of concentrating only on the present issues. Disregarding—consciously unaware of—the inner parts that tormented me, I was teetering on the precarious precipice of crash and burn.

Blinded, I was unable to acknowledge my various and significant accomplishments. I couldn't see that I had more than most people in life. There was a roof over our heads with plenty of food in the fridge, cable TV, Internet, cell phones, clothes for my children, and a car to drive. Despite everything I had to be grateful for, I was as pessimistic as ever, equal to being at my lowest mental state. Nothing would ever be enough to satisfy my desires.

CHAPTER FIFTY-SIX
~LIFE'S STRESSES: FINANCIAL FAILURE~

Oh, my God! I smacked my forehead in disbelief, a blank stare of stark futility fixed on my personal financial statements. I had depleted the money that was saved from my settlement with the Church. With all the distractions going on, I was living above my means, unable to support the life style I was living with the money I made from the state.

I could budget multimillion-dollar projects to the penny and let nothing in the contract slip by me, but I was unable to budget my own personal finances. The vast majority of my settlement went to past debts and establishing a life for my family. I should have been more prudent in my spending. Even though I was aware my current spending behavior would eventually deplete my funds, I had had a grandiose idea that I would be successful before I exhausted them.

At the time, while spending, I didn't care. I wanted to give my children and fiancée everything I could. I wanted to delight in life for the first time, thinking the best way to do that was to give items and do things of monetary value.

I bought my children the best in name-brand clothes to wear and toys to play with. I purchased the latest technology; iPods, cell phones, video games, and computers. We had nice furniture in our apartment with flat-screen plasma and LCD televisions and the entire package of premium cable channels and high-speed Internet. Our home was filled with food and snacks. We lived it up with takeout Chinese and pizza twice a week. Ellie and I had good times eating dinners at the best restaurants on the weekends we were together, in addition to the occasional camping trips and adventures to either the shore or the mountains.

It was foolish and risky of me to waste the money as recompense for the tormenting anguish suffered over three decades. The compensation was gone in two short years. When the realization hit me, I resolved to get a grip on what was the truth of my situation. I needed to face the cold, hard facts.

I designed a spreadsheet to analyze my expenses versus my income. I created a banking register program that identified all that I spent. I made sure at least ninety-five percent of my purchases were through my debit card, so I could reconcile and identify my purchases daily. I had the data at my fingertips and could ascertain the information for the analysis.

When I had finished the budget, my heart palpitated at great speed. I had begun to sweat, unable to catch my breath, entering into a full-blown panic attack. The preliminary analysis showed I was living at a rate of negative one thousand dollars a month.

I eliminated all the unnecessary items and expenses to see how far I could improve on the monthly deficit. I was able to cut it by a few hundred, but I was still in the red by $700 a month. I had to do more. I cut corners on *everything* in my life.

I had to borrow money from my daughter, a friend at work, and my children's grandparents for a few months so I could stabilize the damage. I was living paycheck to paycheck. I paid bills right before the shutoff notice expired, the eviction notice went out, or I ran out of gas and food.

I budgeted to have at least a dollar in my account the day before I got paid, so I could fill my empty gas tank to get to work. From my financial experience, I knew when you used a credit/debit card at a service station, the vendor would only verify that you had at least a dollar in the account before approving the sale. The actual financial transaction for the full amount would not occur until two days from the point of sale, after the direct deposit for my pay would hit the checking account. My deficit was snowballing. I was snowballing down the slopes of destitution once again.

I had reached my three-year employment anniversary with the state. I found out I could take a loan of up to fifty percent of my pension contributions. With contributions over nine thousand dollars, I thought taking advantage of this option would enable me to catch up on my past-due household bills, the balance owed for my divorce, and the apartment damage from the vandalism and theft. If I could borrow from the pension account, I'd be able to budget and survive without the stress of barely surviving from one payday to the next.

I felt a tremendous relief knowing I had this prerogative. But when I logged onto the state's website to apply for the loan, my personal information was five months behind. I had started my position with the state on October 30, 2005. It only posted to June 30, 2008. The state pension department posts quarterly, sixty days subsequent to the quarter. At this rate, I wouldn't be eligible for the loan for three more months. I'd incur four thousand dollars more debt and back bills by then.

Life did not want to cooperate with me. The disappointing curse I felt vanquished my will and sent me into another deep depression. The defender parts once again took advantage of a negative situation and blew it out of proportion. Fear, anxiety, and despondency smothered me.

Nightmares started. They weren't about frightening things, but woke me through the night. I'd wake up exhausted from negative, haunting thoughts and worries of financial burdens. It wasn't worth getting up and going to work. I wasn't making enough money to live and provide a comfortable life for my family and Ellie.

CHAPTER FIFTY-SEVEN
~SUBJUGATING DEPRESSION~

The gloom and desolation carried over to my relationship with Ellie. Our every other weekend together had always been delightful. This time, on the last day of our weekend, I moped around, complaining. "I hate our time apart. I want to spend every moment with you."

"You know that we're still raising our children," Ellie said. "We'd need to get a much bigger place."

"With my financial situation, it's going to take forever."

"You have to be happy with what we have."

"I can't be happy unless I'm with you all the time."

I not only ruined the weekend, I continued to complain even during our time apart. Ellie was affected by my constant bemoaning, becoming depressed and pessimistic about everyday events. I was ruining our special relationship.

My attitude at work also changed. I was quiet and stayed to myself. On Thursdays, the development department would go out to lunch together. I stopped going—couldn't afford it.

The others in the office knew I was underpaid for my position. The two other senior project officers made at least twenty thousand dollars more than I made per year. My director debated the disparity of my salary versus my work product with the Authority more than once, but they rejected his request every time. The Authority used the recession and slim job market as their reasoning.

My therapy appointments turned into bitching sessions over the next two months.

I leaned back in my chair, shaking my head. "All the positive work on my mental state was an illusion. I had the settlement money—a free ride that lifted my spirits. It wasn't because of the hard work and therapy." Standing, I began to pace, flailing my arms about. "My motivation was like a farmer riding on a donkey, leading it with a carrot dangling on a stick. This keeps the donkey moving forward, trying to get the carrot. The settlement money in my account was the carrot that kept me moving forward. I'm exhausted from the pain and fighting. What's the use? I give up." I plopped back into my seat.

"You're circumstances are difficult and more extreme than most people have to deal with," Keith said, folding his arms on his desk. "I understand if you want to give up. But your past positive work was not an illusion. You have accomplished some amazing things using the Law of Attraction, but may not be able to see it right now. In the spiritual world, the good things that happened in your life, including the settlement, was not a free ride. You willed the settlement into your life, along with the other blessings you received."

"Yeah, maybe." I wasn't paying much attention to him, but I was showing up every week and listening. In the back of my mind I clung to small, but still there, semblance of confidence that things would turn around again, as they had done in the past.

CHAPTER FIFTY-EIGHT
~RELAPSE~

At the gym, I was doing heavy lifts with one thousand pounds of weight on the leg press machine. I pushed the weights up with my legs and gripped the sidebars. On the second repetition, I heard a pop in my upper right chest area. I struggled to rack the weight, while concentrating on exhaling to take the pressure off the injury. When I attempted to stand up from the equipment, I started to blackout from pain. I'd had plenty of minor injuries in the past, but I knew this was something serious.

I tried to bear through the pain for a few days. It was so forceful that I had to leave work one afternoon and head to a sports doctor. The physician thought the pain was coming from my neck, but I tried to convince her that it felt and sounded like it was coming from my upper chest area. She explained the neck has finger-like nerves called the brachial plexus that run from there into the upper chest and shoulder regions. She prescribed an anti-inflammatory, a muscle relaxer, Percocet for the pain, referred me for a magnetic resonance imaging (MRI) test, and set up a follow-up visit to discuss the MRI results.

When I returned two weeks later, she showed me the test results which confirmed her original diagnosis that the injury was in my neck. The MRI revealed multilevel cervical spondylosis with focal right lateral disc protrusions at C4/5 and focal right paracentral disc protrusion at C6/7 with cord impingement. In laymen's terms, I had a couple bulging discs which were pinching the nerves in my spinal cord beginning at the neck.

I continued to be in excruciating discomfort over the next month. It felt like a spear was thrust into my chest and pushed straight through my back. I couldn't take deep breaths without wincing in agony. If I coughed or sneezed, I would almost faint.

I went to physical therapy twice a week, but there was little relief. During the first month, I told the physical therapist I thought there was more to my injury than the neck issue. From what I felt, the majority of the pain was coming from deep in the shoulder joint of my upper chest area. I didn't think it was coming from the neck. The physical therapist agreed that I had shoulder damage and called the doctor to request more tests.

I was first given a local anesthesia in the affected area. Then a needle was advanced into the lower third of the shoulder joint space. As soon as the needle touched the injured area, I passed out from the massive agony. I recall waking to the nurses patting my forehead with a cold compress and calling out my name for me to acknowledge consciousness. After I regained my bearings, a diluted gadolinium solution was injected into my shoulder joint capsule and an MRI was performed. The results revealed I had partial tears in my rotator cuff, a superior labrum tear, which is a tendon that holds the shoulder socket in place, and damage to both the anterior and posterior bicep tendon anchor.

With the additional test results, my doctor thought it best to maintain pain management. The physical therapy would begin to treat both the neck and the shoulder injuries. Surgery wasn't an option. I didn't have enough sick time accrued to take the time off from work. I maintained physical therapy and pain management as an alternative for another month.

The doctor was concerned with the dosage of painkillers I was taking and started to wean me off the medication. An epidural of the cervical spine area was necessary, but the doctor couldn't schedule me in for another month. I began getting agitated and anxious from the withdrawal symptoms of the Percocet, preventing me from handling the minute and mundane issues of each day. I was even worse at trying to take care of the unresolved problems with my dysfunctional family.

Unable to get more prescriptions from the physician, I came across a neighbor who sympathized with me. She knew of a doctor who would have no problem helping me maintain my prescription until the procedure took place.

I put off the epidural shot for four months, abusing the ten-milligram Percocet tablets at a hundred and twenty a month. The doctor prescribing the medication had no concern over the damages he had to have known they incurred to my health.

The use of painkillers was a sensitive subject for Ellie. Her older sister became addicted to opiates at a young age while recovering from a broken neck injury following an automobile accident. She escalated from Percocet to heroine, which led to her being incapable of taking care of herself.

So I hid the pills in the trunk of my car, as if they had come off the streets from a drug dealer. Ellie noticed me regularly sauntering out to my vehicle and ... became suspicious. When I wasn't paying attention, she wandered outside, using her spare key to open the trunk. When she found out what the pills were ... she went ballistic.

Storming back into the house, she shouted, shaking the evidence in my face. "I can't *believe* you're taking these pills behind my back. I can't stand the sight of you. Get out."

I struggled to get up from the couch. "Let me explain ... I have prescriptions."

She got right in my face. "This is your drug-addicted past kicking in.

226

You like feeling good and getting high."

I backed up, with palms up, exasperated. "I need the pills for agony relief. It started as a medical issue, and I still need them. Please try and understand."

"Go home," she said, pushing me out the door and slamming it behind me.

I tried getting off the pills. Immediately the beast began pacing within, licking its sardonic chops, craving release. The withdrawal symptoms intensified the anxiety of the animal and kept me in constant turmoil.

I tried to get help before she left me for good. I was first subscribed Xanax to alleviate the anxiety, but she didn't want that in her life either. I was then informed of a drug that helped patients wean themselves off of opiates called Suboxone. I went to a psychiatric specialist who treated addiction disorders to get the prescription.

Soon after starting the medication, I could feel the benefits from the drug. It allowed me to concentrate on the good things in life, distracting my anxious thoughts from worrying about problems. I was able to keep my thoughts in order to solve the issues without them escalating.

At first, Ellie was happy about my intention to get professional help for my problems. When she learned that I was continuing to use medication for depression and anxiety under my therapist's and doctor's suggestions, she started to rethink our relationship.

She called me on the phone just as I came home from work. "Marco, I know you're not going to like what I have to say. But ... I want peace in my life. I've raised three kids on my own, and I'm now ready to take it easy. I'm not so sure anymore about this relationship—what with all your problems. Your kids have problems, too. I need to take a step back and end our relationship. Sorry, Marco."

It was like a bomb imploded my heart. I pleaded, "Ellie, please don't do this. You're everything to me. Please let me come over to talk about this. I've worked so hard to improve my life—and the life of my kids. I can fix this. Please ... just give me a chance."

"I'm sorry, Marco. I've already made my decision. It's final. Good-bye."

My head drooped as I hung up the phone. Tears welled up in my eyes. I started sniffling ... and then I was in an all-out sob. I had to sit down on the nearest chair before my knees buckled. I covered my face with my hands and wailed. I could not swallow this; I gagged emotionally thinking it possible she'd leave me. It was agonizing to lose my best friend, the woman I'd hoped to be with forever. We had a special love. We had a lot in common, something I wasn't used to in relationships. It had been wonderful to experience the affection we shared.

The vision I had dreamed of during my unhappiest hour, which we *had* for one precious year experienced in joy and gratitude, was now ... gone. I was devastated when she left. I was alone once again. I had to stay strong for my kids. For me to have a chance at survival, the true self would have to keep up the fight for life and continue to persevere.

"Why did God have to disappoint me in every aspect of my life, Keith? How could this woman give up on me? Why didn't she recognize the ninety-nine out of a hundred positive attributes that our relationship had? Every moment we spent together was fun and games. We displayed our feelings of tenderness. I loved her more than any other woman I've known. And I know she loved me. Unless I was sending bad vibes and she picked up on that. We had things in common that shouldn't have been destroyed."

He listened. It was yet another bitch session. My sessions over the whole month following Ellie's leaving me were spent pining over my financial devastation and the loss of the woman I wanted to marry.

On Wednesday, December 17, 2008, I was in an especially depressed mood. I took the day off work, lying in bed late that morning. I recalled a conversation Ellie and I had regarding my child abuse.

She had questioned me on personal issues about the abuse. She wanted to know how it made me feel about certain things and relationships. She read from an article written by SNAP, Survivors Network of those Abused by Priests. She questioned me on some of the statistics in the article regarding clergy sexual abuse.

It was one of our most emotional conversations. We were brought closer to each other at the time, easing her mind on certain personal issues. The thoughts were enough to get me out of bed.

I fired up my laptop and searched the web for the organization that wrote the article. When I clicked on the SNAP website, I noticed they were holding a contest, looking for the most inspirational stories of 2008. The deadline was that day. I gave it a try and described the pain and harsh circumstances my family and I had endured. I wanted to say how proud I was of my family. The story read as follows:

As I awoke this morning, the mental depression was too much for me to make it through a day of work. I called out yet another day from the mental depression that I have to experience 24/7 from the crime that was committed against me thirty-four years ago.

I am sure families have experienced and seen first-hand traumatic physical crimes of abuse and murder that negatively impacted their family. My family's traumas might not be of that physical magnitude, but the mental anguish my family and I experience everyday is a full blown-out war to hold our sanity together.

I am all that my children have in this world. Their addictive mother is on the streets from the disorders that she developed throughout our relationship, addictions that you could also argue were developed as an indirect result of my abuse. I have to fight the demons every day since the three years of being raped by a Catholic priest, subjected to massive amounts of inappropriate adult material and alcohol when I was ten years old. I have to fight everyday to hold my spirituality together. I see all the pain that my family has to endure because of my prior actions resulting from the molestation, which I relate as "sins of the abused."

I am a tired man. I fought to get myself out of the depths of hell, with my physical, mental, and financial resources. I fought the Catholic Church to only receive a third of what the damages were (speaking only of monetary debt) caused by one of their priests. I fought from being homeless in a psychiatric hospital to getting custody of my children and getting back on our feet with the shirts on our backs. I fought the creditors and agencies to be responsible and settle my debts, instead of seeking bankruptcy, with the little the Catholic Church gave me. I fought to get my daughter help for her depression from her own molestation when I was absent in her life and in a psychiatric hospital, seeking treatment from my illnesses developed from my abuse. I took her from a manic-depressive, failing student, who couldn't function in society, to a recent honor status. I fought to get my son sober from the addictions he developed from self-medicating himself from the abusiveness that surrounded him in my absence. I supported him and turned him from a stoned high school drop out to an honor student like his sister. I battled to get us a nice place to live, with nice things, only to have it robbed of all of its worthy contents. I struggled to get my career back after my mental breakdown from the decades of holding my abuse in. I am now in a senior-level position, getting there by sweeping sidewalks, breaking up concrete, doing odd jobs, and starting off as a staff accountant with my current employer.

Even though the aforementioned appears to be a blessing, I have trouble appreciating it because of the exhaustion I had to exert to get to where I am today, and the tireless work I have to do to maintain my family's daily sanity. We have worked so hard together, battling the curse that sexual abuse bestows upon a family. However, we have conquered the mental disorders developed from the sins of the abused, and for that, I can hold my head high and be proud of my family.

A phone call came in while I was at work from the woman at SNAP handling the contest. She explained that my story was thirty words too long and asked me to shorten it to meet the guidelines. I told her that I was at work and wouldn't have time to fix it within the deadline.

She paused for a moment. Then she said that she was impressed and moved with my writing. It touched her heart to read that as a family we conquered the mental disorders developed from the abuse and that I can now hold my head high and be proud. She said my story had a purpose. After she thought about it for a couple of seconds, she said that she'd try to get authorization to put the story in as is. She'd get back to me if I needed to edit it.

I was excited with the positive feedback. Being in such a discouraging state of mind, I had started to think about giving up my writing project. Maybe my family's accomplishments are no different than anyone else's. I was thinking that I was a weak crybaby, whining about minute ordinary matters. I was even more excited when I saw my story posted on SNAP's website the next day.

My emotional state of mind was jump started. Every morning, I made it a point to think and concentrate on positive affirmations from the moment I opened my eyes. I'd start my day as soon as I gained consciousness by saying out loud, "It's going to be a great day! Great things are going to happen today!"

I repeated my positive affirmations diurnally. I am strong, stable, successful and confident, yet humble, peaceful, patient, and well mannered. I am loving, kind, caring, compassionate, generous, and gracious. I am mentally, physically, and spiritually healthy. I have a stable, structured family with an abundance of happy and healthy children, family members, and friends. I would finish with affirming that I have a plenitude of financial security and peace. I then meditated on all these things being true.

I noticed that events in my life improved as I radiated a positive attitude and outlook. I appreciated what I had instead of complaining about what I didn't have. I enjoyed going to work again and accomplished a great deal more than when I was gloomy.

During my emotional evolution, my mood was kicked into high gear on Christmas Eve, 2008. I worried about paying my normal household bills, along with having little money for Christmas gifts. But I wasn't going to let it bother me that morning. I woke up and repeated my positive attitude ritual.

A little later in the morning, my kids' Aunt Donna called, telling me she had some of their mother's money from her dad's passing. It was put aside for the kids, and she'd like to give me a couple hundred dollars for each of them to get a gift card.

In addition to that four hundred dollars, I noticed an envelope stuffed in my pocket when I put my jacket on to leave work that day. I pulled it out and opened the flap. There was *another* four hundred dollars inside. Unbelievable. I confronted everyone at work who I thought might be responsible. Every one of them wore the ostensible expression of innocence and denial on their faces. The generosity of my cohorts flooded me with tears of gratification. At one time I had thought I wasn't worthy of receiving a penny from anyone. Now I was blessed with people's impressions of me being deserving of such kindness.

What made that Christmas Eve even more blessed was winning one of the top five spots selected as most inspiring by the SNAP community in their writing contest. I was elated that people who were familiar with sexual abuse and also victimized by representatives of the Church voted for my story. My own peers read my words, understanding the pain and struggle to fight the mental anguish of such heinous, horrifically hypocritical abuse. They knew about the hell we have to live with every breathing moment of our lives. My equals acknowledged the fight we have to overcome to rectify the damage caused from the sins of the abused.

It was a great moment for me, and it was another turning point in changing my thought process from dark to light. I realized an amazing correlation between myself and the success of the organizations I had been involved with, envisioning myself as a link in the chain. This chain-link concept came to fruition when I tried to search for some additional positive affirmations to lift me out of my depressing period.

I thoroughly analyzed my past and brought the concept to my therapist. He reinforced the validity of my theory.

In my six years of Pop Warner football, two years in each weight division, my teams won three tri-state conference championships, each in the latter year of the three weight classes. In baseball, I made the all-star team. Our team won our division and made it to the district finals in our region to play in the Little League World Series.

In high school, I was part of a state championship wrestling team that was undefeated and held the national win-streak record my freshman through junior years. Even when I transferred halfway through my senior year to another school, I relocated to a team that beat my prior team, ruining their national win-streak record and taking over the number-one ranking in the state.

When I moved on to college, I was on the wrestling team that won the southern conference. We were ranked eighteenth my freshman year, and eighth my sophomore year, in the Associated Press national top twenty-five poll.

In my first bodybuilding competition, I placed third out of fifteen competitors in a national qualifier. Hell, even when I played one year of softball in a bar league, my team went undefeated and won its division.

This is not to mention my professional career of being a controller for the largest financial exchange in the Tri-state area and one of the top twenty-five construction management firms in the country. My current senior-level position with the State Authority was also an amazing achievement. Thinking back to the multitude of accomplishments in my life, my eyes were opened and spirits lifted by recognizing that I was a link in the chain of every one of those winning and rewarding affiliations.

The humiliation I had felt melted away as I reflected on my positive traits, attainments, and association with successful organizations. My anger at life dissipated as I started to further understand the difference between when my true self was conducting my life and when I was allowing the different defender parts of the abuse to keep me from living my life with zest.

An important lesson had been learned. I had needed to be put in my place—to experience the anguish again—to appreciate what is most important in life, with nothing to rely on but myself. I had moved too fast in my therapy to recognize the core of its meaning. I had taken the auspicious, facile steps and had become successful by taking shortcuts.

But when a crisis arose, I was unable to step back, recognize the situation, and lead through my true self. Instead, I'd go into survival mode and manage the problem through the controller and striver parts.

I understood that the only way for me to appreciate how to live life and put my abuse behind me was to come out of the murkiness without the carrot on the stick to lead me to the light. The only way for me to appreciate the hard work and obstacles my family and I had overcome was to begin to accept life for what it is and live it.

CHAPTER SIXTY
~FAMILY UNITED~

It was time for me to take care of each of my unresolved quandaries. Although I missed Ellie, I realized the stress and worry of mediating between my daughter and her were gone. I was now able to give undivided attention to my family unit and myself.

First on the agenda was to get my children's birth certificates and social security cards. The friend Louise had lived with and stole from held our children's personal information in hostage. She wouldn't return them until she was paid back for the items taken. She'd changed her number because Louise had been harassing her, so contacting her by phone was not going to be easy.

I had to take a day off from work to drive to the township where the kids were born and get copies of their birth certificates. I stopped at the Social Security Office and submitted the information needed to process new Social Security cards.

After getting my children's personal documentation in order, I took them to get their driving permits validated. Julian had already passed his written test and only needed to get his permit validated to be able to get behind the wheel. Angel had failed her test the previous year and had to take it over. Even though Julian wasn't fully cooperating with my demands, and was not the best behaved young man, my bad conscience prompted me to allow him to get his driver's permit.

I took them to the local motor vehicle office. We got Julian's permit validated, and Angel enrolled in a private driving school to take the test. She'd need six hours of lessons behind the wheel of a car with a personal driving instructor, which cost around four hundred dollars. Her grandparents offered to pay for it. I accepted.

I allowed Julian to drive home from the motor vehicle office. Oh, what a ride. My eyes bulged from my head and I gripped the dashboard, turning my knuckles white. It was a relief to make it home in one piece. A couple weeks later, there was a repeat performance while Angel drove home with her validated permit from the driving school.

I made appointments with the optometrist to get Angel new glasses, the dermatologist for her blemishes, and the gynecologist for her woman issues and to prevent ... you know what. I set up dates for checkups with doctors, and the dentist for cleanings. Like taking a car in for maintenance, I was maintaining and repairing my family's administrative and physical needs.

I started to deal with Angel's mental anxiety. To alleviate some of her stress, I allowed her to decrease the level of difficulty in the school courses she was having trouble with. This made a world of difference in not only her grades, but also in her attendance. I stayed mindful of showing interest in her schoolwork by asking her on a day-to-day basis how she was doing. Most days she would beat me to the question, calling me from her cell phone after receiving her positive grades. She made the honor roll after the first quarter.

Angel found a job as a hostess for a popular Italian restaurant chain. Her attendance in school improved from the previous year, and she stayed motivated at work, never missing a scheduled day. Rescheduling her therapy sessions to night hours allowed me to attend them in the beginning to voice any concerns. This not only strengthened my relationship with Angel, it alleviated the burden on her grandmother to get her there.

I had to take a different approach with Julian. He'd be turning eighteen in a few months. I reinforced my commitment to send him packing on his eighteenth birthday if he didn't find a job and maintain daily attendance at school and work. He was expected to enroll in the local community college as a full-time student the following fall semester. When he put in the effort, it didn't take him long to find a job at a local retirement home in the dietary department, and begin the process to apply for financial aid.

I stayed home and cooked family dinners every night, adding a few extra pounds on all of us. Although the heartache from losing Ellie was still distressing, the displaced time I had been spending with her did make it possible to draw closer to my kids.

Being home on a regular basis enabled me to keep watch on what was going on in the apartment. The parties and shenanigans that occurred when I was away came to a stop. There was no more smoking in the apartment. It was well maintained when I wasn't there, and my children started to show more respect for me. This resulted in more love and laughter than ever before. It was an amazing turnaround of events. We had a deeper appreciation for harmony and love in our family unit.

CHAPTER SIXTY-ONE
~CRASH~

I was accustomed to the ups and downs by now, hardly naïve enough to believe in Hollywood 'and they lived happily ever-after' life scenarios. Still, I hoped that my family and I *would* live an ongoing, relatively happy and serene life. But, that's not how life goes for victims and families of child abuse, or any other types of abuse. We had struggled to conquer our issues but, all of a sudden, things crashed around us.

There was tension building in the household. My son and daughter were up in the early morning hours traipsing around the house. I couldn't quite figure out what was going on.

The following morning, I said, "What was up with you guys last night? I heard you both moving around the house." They shrugged their shoulders, and kept feeding cereal into their mouths.

Between bites, Julian mumbled, "What're you talking about? I got up to go to the bathroom."

I thought he was anxious because he knew he had to respect my residential regimens or be thrown out of the house on his eighteenth birthday. But, I wasn't sure why Angel was up through the early morning hours. Her school attendance and grades were great, but something was different. I had heard through a friend that Angel was smoking pot and drinking on weekends. Her unhealthy choices could be causing her anxiety. Even though I tried to address these potential points of contention with them, all I got in return were empty stares.

It wasn't long before my edicts were once again being ignored. There were strange people in my home when I wasn't there. They were flicking cigarette butts from the patio to the front lawn below. The house was a fright, and no chores were being done.

At two in the morning one day, I woke to Angel's deafening shriek. Jumping out of bed, I ran to her aid. She and her brother were rolling around the living room floor, grappling. I broke up the fight and sent them to their rooms. I screamed at the closed doors, "You're destroying your lives with drugs. It sucks that you treat me like shit. Can anyone tell me what's going on?" I tromped to my bedroom and slammed the door shut. Climbing back into bed, I rolled over and bawled at the chaos that surrounded me.

A week later, I was in my bedroom after coming home from work. There was a small piece of paper slipped under my door. I picked it up and read:

Dad, I can no longer function or face the kids at school. I'm dropping out. Someone from school started a My Space page saying I'm a drug-addicted, pregnant prostitute.

I wept, trembling, the darkness of chaos again encircling me.

Not much later, I heard that Julian had resorted to snorting heroine. I called his school counselor and principal, asking if they'd surprise him with a drug test. The following Sunday, I got an early morning phone call from my son's principal. She said he had dodged the drug check for two days in a row by ignoring her request to stop by her office. He had gotten on the bus and went home instead. She asked me to administer a home version and let her know the results before he was allowed back in school.

I went to the local drug store and purchased the test before driving home. Julian emerged from his bedroom with a blanket around him, stumbling onto the couch and falling back asleep. I shook him awake.

"I got a phone call from your principal," I said, holding the test cup behind my back. "She said you failed two days in a row to show up in her office despite having been ordered to do so. Just so you know, you were, and are, going to be given a drug test." I held the container in front of him. "So, get up and pee in the cup."

Julian rolled his eyes and formed an audacious smirk. "I've already gone. I can't go again."

I got in his face. "Get up and take the test."

"I'm tired." He rolled over in a huff. "I'm going back to sleep."

"No. You're. Not." I pulled the blanket from his shoulders.

"It's cold. Give me that," he said, pulling the blanket back.

We played a brief, pathetic game of tug of war, which I won. When he realized I wasn't going to give up, me standing over him the victorious keeper of the blanket, he grabbed the cup from my hands. Cursing, he stormed into the bathroom. He came out with a half-full cup. I screwed the cap on and set it down until the results were displayed on the lid. The test came up positive for opiates and marijuana. Once more, I went in my bedroom and sobbed.

I felt like a failure as a father. Looking at the loneliness and damage that had forever and still plagued my family, I wondered why life had to be this painful. Is there a purpose for all the suffering?

I met a special man and woman during this time. Reaching out to the only support network I had, I found them through the contact information on the SNAP website.

They had gone to high school together in Michigan. Helen went on to travel from coast to coast, settling in the eastern part of the country. Curt stayed put, raising a family and enjoying his life close to home. He had been the class clown and a school athlete, later working in sales. She was an entrepreneur with her own business and had several artistic talents. Both were strong single parents, who raised their children well.

When she met him again at their thirtieth high school reunion, the burly man whom she remembered had made others laugh was reduced to rubble and tears. A 'man of God' had manipulated and robbed him of his wife. His four daughters were sexually harassed by this pastor, losing their childhood innocence. She had deep sympathy for his plight and an immediate desire to come to his aid. She lifted him up, dusted him off, and imbued him with the resolve to once again achieve, and to *do something* about what had happened to him. Together they wrote his story and began a determined crusade to alert the world of what lurks in the dank shadows of the churches.

The two listened to me as I wept when telling them about my own children slipping in and out of behavioral problems. They took the time to pay attention to my screams, consoling me and giving me hope through the pain and despair. Like two wise and older siblings, my new *big sister* and *big brother* were more caring and concerned than any family member I had. We realized that our communication was destiny and meant to be. They began assisting me in telling my story and took over when I was feeling down.

Curt supported me with inspirational verses, answering my tears with a motivational verse from the Napoleon Hill Foundation: "*When the going is hardest, just keep on keeping on, and you'll get there sooner than someone who finds the going easy. If you think achieving great heights of success will be easy, you either don't understand at all how the process works or you have your sights set too low. Reaching the top of any field is difficult, time-consuming, and often tedious. The reason it isn't crowded at the top is that most people won't do the things that are necessary to achieve success. They are all too willing to give up when the going gets tough. If you need inspiration to persevere, read the biographies of men and women who have achieved greatness in their lives. You will find that they prevailed because they refused to quit. They continued to toil alone long after the masses had given up and gone home.*"

Like having a good night's sleep, my inner soul became rejuvenated, and I began to keep on keeping on.

The following week, I wasn't feeling well and knew I was coming down with something. Julian pushed me to the edge once again, bringing people into the house against house rules, creating a mess and arguing with me about it. Not feeling up to a confrontation at the moment, I let it go—biding my time, conspiring to deal with him once I had the strength to fight back.

I set up a conference call with his principal and guidance counselor from the alternative school he attended.

"What can we do with him?" I said.

"Because of the severity and nature of the drug he tested positive for, your son will not be permitted back in school unless he enrolls in an

Intensive Out-Patient Program," the principal said. "He can stay today, but you'll have to get him in a program right away."

This called for another day out of work. No time to see the doctor for my own matters. I called and described my symptoms over the phone. The doctor told me there were numerous cases of the same thing going around. He prescribed medication for the high fever and upper respiratory infection I had and called it into the pharmacy.

I called the outpatient rehab facility where Julian had attended a couple of months before. They understood my situation and fit me in that same day for an intake to assess Julian to get him back in the program.

When he arrived home from school, I was waiting for him. "Get in the car."

Dropping his books on the table, he said, "What're you talking about?"

Walking to the front door, keys in hand, nodding my head to the side, I said, "We're going to get you back in the out-patient program."

Julian followed me to the car saying, "I don't need this. It's only pot. I don't have a problem."

Climbing into the car, I said, "Then how come you tested positive for opiates?"

"It was only a couple of Percocets," Julian said, sliding into the passenger seat. "It won't happen again."

"How come I heard you snorted heroin and you tested positive for it?"

Snapping his head my way, he snorted, "What? Are you serious? Heroin?"

"The only way you're staying in my home is if you go back into the program and prove you can get clean again."

We pulled into the parking lot of the facility. The intake took an hour. The counselor suggested an intensive program, four days a week. I agreed, and we left the building.

"I'm not going four days a week," Julian said. "And I'm not going to stop smoking pot."

"Then you can start planning now for leaving my home when you turn eighteen," I told him, looking straight ahead. "Your choice."

After arriving home, I picked up Angel and drove to her school for a meeting with her guidance and crisis counselors to talk about her dropping out of school.

"You're doing well in school," she said. "You've made the honor roll. Dropping out now is going to be devastating for you."

Angel sat with her head down, shaking her head.

"We've heard about the My Space incident," the counselor said. "We want you to know that we will deal with the Internet harassment and provide a safe and secure environment for you on school grounds. Dropping out of school in your junior year will affect your whole future."

"I'll get my GED," Angel said. "I want to go to beauty school."

"A high-school diploma would be much better for you. I know you can do it. Maybe we can get you into the alternative school where your brother goes."

"I want to get out of this high school. I can't go back."

I left the office with two contingency plans. The first was to get a doctor to agree that my daughter was unable to interact with the other students on a social basis. She'd be able to receive home schooling through a state-funded tutor. The other plan was for her to prepare for and take the test to attain her general equivalency diploma (GED).

After I thought more about the options, I wasn't satisfied with either of them. I scheduled an appointment with her therapist to try one last time to convince her to go back to school. That session didn't go well.

"Honey, I really wish you'd reconsider going back to school," I said, sitting next to her in the office.

"I'm not going back there. The kids hate me. I can't face them anymore."

"You're doing well in school," the therapist said. "You could get into special classes and finish the year."

"The school will take care of the My Space incident," I said. "Tell them who's responsible."

Angel fidgeted in her seat and took in a deep breath. "You don't know how it is. You want to leave me on my own like you did when I was little. Where were you when I needed you? If Mom had her own place, I'd move in with her. I miss her."

My eyes filled up, and my lips quivered. I glared at Angel. "I'm done," I said. "My daughter thinks she's an adult and can make her own choices in life. She'll have to pay the price for those decisions. I've done all I can to help her."

With that, I took the ten-dollar co-pay out of my pocket, dropped it on the therapist's desk and walked out the door. Outside, I took a couple of deep breaths. My teeth were clenched together. My daughter followed me in silence through the parking lot to the car.

Neither of us spoke a word on the drive home. I stopped in front of the apartment and Angel got out. "I'm going for a ride," I said.

She closed the car door and stood staring at me while I drove off. A couple of minutes later, I received a text message from her.

"Sorry."

A half an hour later, I drove home. Angel greeted me with a hug.

"Sorry, Dad," she said. "I didn't mean those things I said. I was mad."

I gave her a hug. We sat and talked. We decided that she'd get her GED and then go to beauty school.

I had done what I could for my children. It was now up to them to take over and make the proper decisions in life from what they were taught. Whatever choices they made, they'd have to live with them. I was sick and exhausted. My bed was a blessed relief for my aching body that night.

Amazingly, my children seemed to finally get it. A couple of days later, Angel said, "Can we talk?"

"Of course," I said, taking a seat at the kitchen table.

She stood in the kitchen doorway, smiled. I marveled at how pretty she was.

"Dad, I don't want to settle for a GED. I want to get my high school diploma through the alternative high school."

"Oh, honey. This is such good news!"

She walked over to me as I rose to receive and return her embrace. She cried. "I love you, Dad. I don't want to leave here. I trust you and will support any decision you make."

"I can't tell you how wonderful it is to hear you say that," I said, stroking her long black hair.

All week, as I waited for the enrollment paperwork to arrive from the alternative high school, Angel kept up with the house chores and we had satisfying conversations. She expressed how she loved our relationship and all her friends were jealous she had a father like me who could talk about any issue, no matter what it involved.

At the end of the week, my son's guidance counselor called. "Julian has made a complete turnaround in his attitude this week. He's determined to finalize his financial aid application, and he's been in school on time all five days."

That was outstanding news. I had seen a change in him, too. He didn't have his deadbeat friends over all week and was cleaning up his messes when he raided the kitchen. That was a miracle in itself.

I had been here before. But, something was different this time, providing me hope for the moment.

I had worked hard to bring them to this point in their lives. Maybe they'd choose the right path this time. Could they sense, and appreciate, the stability I'd provided? We began to bond together again, gaining strength to break the cycle of the abuse's curse to live a peaceful and content life.

CHAPTER SIXTY-TWO
~WRITING MY STORY~

My intention was to end this chapter of my life rejuvenated, having conquered forever the negative impact of sexual and drug abuse. I had a vision of being healed from the scars. My hope was, and is, to provide guidance to both parties affected by abuse and addiction, having experienced the negative impact from both sides, with a self-help psychological manual to assist in recovery. My writings are an attempt to provide strength to people confronted with life's unpredictable twists and turns. People should know about the burdens of those who have been exploited, having to suffer every moment through their lives, hoping to grasp a few special instances of peace and tranquility. This is the price to pay for a predator's repulsive crime. The rippling effect precipitates consequences for everyone in the victim's life. It is similar to that of a plague or curse, spreading out among the household until everyone is infected with the scourge and adversity of the disorder.

It is important to understand and recognize the signs of abuse. Victims' families and friends who want to help, or be helped, should be educated on how to handle this traumatic event. Children need early intervention in the crucial developmental years. Those inflicted will unconsciously exhibit wrath and inappropriate, destructive behavior if not dealt with early on with a compassionate and understanding professional therapist.

The Catholic Church has been irresponsible in dealing with the clergy sexual abuse crimes and aiding the victims in the scandal. The Church's lawyers search for whatever possible that will start the clock for the statute of limitations. It takes years for most victims to come forward and tell and, for justice to have any chance to prevail, the statute of limitations must be abolished. We go to the Church with trust that we'll be safe and looked after in a spiritual way. But, victims of clergy abuse leave with a loss that never goes away. It can be pushed aside for a while, but it's always there to come back and haunt.

The Church is big business—bottom line. It's about egregious profiteering and squelching expenses. It's not about to disturb any dependable source of income, and will fight any such disturbance at all costs. The Church does not do what is morally appropriate in cases of clergy abuse, but goes to extremes to keep the status quo. They've become accustomed to the decadence. Their reprehensible arrogance must be exposed.

My wish is to provide hope and inspiration for people who are mentally ill. The mind *can* heal from despondency and be reprogrammed from feeling captivated in grief to seeing and appreciating magnificent surroundings and enveloping serenity. Thoughts and behaviors can revert to the innocence that once existed within, even if at one time overwhelmed with decaying thoughts of inappropriate and immoral actions. People can change through perseverance with proper help, education, and support from loved ones.

Abuse not only psychologically destroys a pristine life, it affects all parties involved. I do not make excuses for my inappropriate actions of the past. I am ashamed of my former behavior and regret the pain I inflicted on loved ones in my life. I've taken responsibility for my past and have tried to rectify the damage I've caused, humbled by the people who've helped me along the way. I'm forever grateful for the kind element of humanity that does exist in this world and for those who worked hard to understand the negative role corruption has played.

My life is burdensome, having to be responsible for actions I committed from the abuse's persuasive influence on my behavior. I have to fight a heavyweight battle twenty-four hours a day to maintain stability for my family. I agonize over having to see my family suffer from my past irresponsibility.

But, as tough as it is, it has to be let go. I realized this while watching the ending of the 2007 Academy Award winning best picture, "No Country for Old Men," by Cormac McCarthy. I happened to catch a scene in the movie where a paralyzed man was asked a question about the person who shot him and left him in a wheelchair for the rest of his life. I recall his brilliant answer, which was along the lines of, "The more you try to fight to get back what was taken from you, the more you miss what's going out the front door right before your eyes." It made me envision everything I was allowing to go out my own front door.

I had hoped for the happy ending with the love of my life becoming my wife. I had it in my grasp. I wanted to share a house and white picket fence with her and all of our children. Coming home from work, I'd plant a big kiss on her soft lips, while holding her close. I could see myself successful in my career, with my wife at home and another baby. She'd care for our structured family with love and understanding. We'd have dinners together and set aside a special night each week to play games or watch a movie.

As I dreamt—this was just recently—of being again united with this perfect-for-me-in-every-way woman, I received a text message from a number I didn't recognize. It said, "How are you?"

Could it be my love? My heart took a pause. I didn't know what to do. I waited and worried for a whole day. I asked Helen, my "big sister" for advice. She told me to respond with, "Who are you?" to first see what the answer would be. She also reminded me that there was a lot going on in my life right now, and it probably wasn't a good time to get back together.

I followed her advice and asked who it was. The reply came back, "Sorry, wrong number."

I was obliterated. If only she was still thinking about me, then maybe there was hope of us someday being together again. I still loved that woman with all my heart. My feelings were strong that we could make it work out.

Helen suggested I call the number and see who answers. I followed her advice, and punched in the numbers. The call went right to voice mail. It was Ellie's sweet voice on the recording. It saddened me to think that she'd gotten cold feet, claiming she called the wrong number.

In keeping with my new outlook on life and trying to find the positive in every situation, I knew she had been thinking of me. She still cared. How I longed to make contact with her again.

* * *

I still do long for her, even as I sit here now working through the final touches of this manuscript. I know it's not right at this moment in time, but maybe someday our relationship will be sparked once again. Anything is possible, and I'm living proof that it—anything—*can* happen.

I don't yet have the picket fence, the perfect, *always* obedient children, or a wife to go home to. Just being honest, real. I still have to work paycheck to paycheck to barely maintain my bills. It's not the fairy tale ending that you would maybe expect from a book intended to provide inspiration to people who have been affected by abuse and addictions.

What I *can* say is ... the fight is worth it. Life is better when struggling and working for *something*, whether the end result is known or not. The brief moments of life's pleasures are worth the days of tortuous work.

The pride I have for my children's efforts in overcoming the obstacles in their lives brings an abundance of jubilance to my life, making it all worthwhile. At the end of the day, we can hold our heads high and be proud of our family's determination to conquer the curse that has been cast by an abuser. The scars still exist, pain remains, and problems keep arising. This is the price that one must pay for the sins of the abused.

And wait ... there's another text message. It's from that *unknown* cell phone number ...

About the Authors

Marco L. Bernardino, Sr., is a survivor of clergy sexual abuse and works to bring hope and help to others in similar situations. He has five children and lives in Marlton, New Jersey, where he works for the state as a Senior Project Development Officer. Mr. Bernardino aspires for *Sins of the Abused* to offer a path to recovery for victims who feel alienated from mainstream society — a direct and insufferable result of the actions of predators lurking in the shadows of our churches. Visit http://sinsoftheabused.webs.com/.

Helen J. Wisocki, who has two grown children, owns a retail business in Newburyport, and resides in Massachusetts. She has published shorts stories in the anthologies, *Forever Friends* and *Forever Travels*. She co-authored *Innocence Betrayed* and helps others put their life stories on paper.
Visit Helen at www.helenwisocki.webs.com and www.innocencebetrayedbyclergy.com.

ALL THINGS THAT MATTER PRESS ™

FOR MORE INFORMATION ON TITLES AVAILABLE FROM
ALL THINGS THAT MATTER PRESS, GO TO
http://allthingsthatmatterpress.com
or contact us at
allthingsthatmatterpress@gmail.com

Made in the USA
Middletown, DE
28 October 2022